Praise for *Black Folk*

"In *Black Folk*, Blair LM Kelley ties the exodus of another six million or so to a moving memoir of Black family migration, as well as to the wider sweep of time from slavery to the present. . . . *Black Folk* also has a bone to pick. When we think of 'the American working class,' we think of whites, she notes. But much of that class is Black, and, compared with white laborers, a higher proportion of all Black people are part of it. . . . Race is again central, and we're having a hard time talking about it. The very human stories in [this book] could be just the thing to break the ice."

—Arlie Russell Hochschild, *New York Times Book Review*

"A groundbreaking account of the Black working class in the generations that have come after Juneteenth. . . . Juneteenth recognizes and honors a struggle that continues. Like Labor Day, it recognizes the past successes and undermining of workers as well as the unfinished work left to secure equity for them. Amid increasing efforts to criminalize and erase Black history, what better day to shine a spotlight on what Black labor has endured, and the overdue compensation their descendants are owed?"

—Jamil Smith, *Los Angeles Times*

"Kelley's book is admirably sweeping in narrative and scope. By reclaiming the stories of black workers in the United States over centuries with richness and care, Kelley's *Black Folk* does justice to the memory and legacy of the countless black men and women who toiled in deplorable conditions to make a life for themselves and their loved ones."

—Keisha N. Blain, *Jacobin*

"One of the greatest books I have read about labor in America. The fascinating, revealing, at times heartbreaking—yet inspiring—319-page

T0372526

volume chronicles the role of the Black working class who contributed mightily to this country's wealth and development as a global super-power."
—Thomasi McDonald, *INDY Week*

"Remember how totally dry your high school history books were? Yeah, this is nothing like those. *Black Folk* lets readers get to actually know people who lived a century ago or more. It's like being carefully handed a living, breathing story to hold."
—Terri Schlichenmeyer, *Washington Informer*

"Kelley's indictment of the systemic barriers that have affected countless Black families in work, housing, and more begins with her own family history of enslaved ancestors. . . . Kelley explores the topic of the Black working class in America by following a clear chronology, adding a necessary subtopic to the field of contemporary labor studies."
—*Booklist*, starred review

"A poignant and celebratory chronicle of Black labor movements in America. Alongside more well-known stories, such as the unioniza-tion of Pullman porters, Kelley also sheds new light on Black women's contributions to labor struggles. . . . Full of persuasive insights into Black working-class life and the legacy of communal care spearheaded by Black women, this is a powerful reimagining of the history of labor in the U.S."
—*Publishers Weekly*

"Award-winning historian Kelley, director of the Center for the Study of the American South and author of *Right to Ride*, provides a powerful counter to the assumption that the term *working class* refers only to Whites. Rather, she argues convincingly, Black workers have been the nation's 'most active, most engaged, most informed, and most impassioned working class.' . . . A well-researched, engaging, corrective American history."   —*Kirkus Reviews*

"Brings a dazzling blend of compassion, storytelling, and deep research to a subject that is vital to anyone aiming to understand the future direction of American politics and the nation itself."

—Martha S. Jones, author of *Vanguard:*
How Black Women Broke Barriers,
Won the Vote, and Insisted on Equality for All

"*Black Folk* is at once a love song, a blues, and an epic account of the Black working class in the United States. In lyrical prose, Blair LM Kelley draws on her own family history to tell the story of how Black laborers built, fed, repaired, served, cleaned, cared for, enriched, and worked to democratize this country. By tracing the roots of the Black working class, Kelley reveals the history of the whole nation. The toils of 'Black folk' made the soul of America."

—Robin D. G. Kelley, author of *Freedom Dreams:*
The Black Radical Imagination

"*Black Folk* is a revelation, indeed one of the most important works of history to come across my desk in a long time. . . . Far from a small nameless and faceless group, the Black working class has been and continues to be the very heart of dignified working America and the animating force behind so much of our unique American culture."

—Michael Eric Dyson, author of *Entertaining Race:*
Performing Blackness in America

ALSO BY BLAIR LM KELLEY

Right to Ride:
Streetcar Boycotts and African American
Citizenship in the Era of Plessy v. Ferguson

"African-American laborer with Lincoln Memorial in the background. Washington D.C." Skilled Black laborers were essential to building the nation.
HARRIS & EWING, *LIBRARY OF CONGRESS*

BLACK

The Roots of the
Black Working Class

FOLK

BLAIR LM KELLEY

LIVERIGHT PUBLISHING CORPORATION

A Division of W. W. Norton & Company

INDEPENDENT PUBLISHERS SINCE 1923

In memory of my ancestors

Copyright © 2023 by Blair LM Kelley

All rights reserved
Printed in the United States of America
First published as a Liveright paperback 2024

For information about permission to reproduce selections from this book, write to
Permissions, Liveright Publishing Corporation, a division of W. W. Norton & Company, Inc.,
500 Fifth Avenue, New York, NY 10110

For information about special discounts for bulk purchases, please contact
W. W. Norton Special Sales atspecialsales@wwnorton.com or 800-233-4830

Manufacturing by Lakeside Book Company
Book design by Daniel Lagin
Production manager: Lauren Abbate

Library of Congress Control Number: 2024936045

ISBN 978-1-324-09557-6 pbk.

Liveright Publishing Corporation, 500 Fifth Avenue, New York, N.Y. 10110
www.wwnorton.com

W. W. Norton & Company Ltd., 15 Carlisle Street, London W1D 3BS

1 2 3 4 5 6 7 8 9 0

If scholars were to emphasize the efforts of the enslaved more than the condition of slavery, we might at least tell richer stories about how the endeavors of the weakest and most abject have at times reshaped the world.

—VINCE BROWN[1]

That is why we black folk laugh and sing when we are alone together. There is nothing—no ownership or lust for power— that stands between us and our kin. And we reckon kin not as others do, but down to the ninth and tenth cousin. And for a reason we cannot explain we are mighty proud when we meet a man, woman or child who, in talking to us, reveals that the blood in our brood has somehow entered his veins. Because our eyes are not blinded by the hunger for possession, we are a tolerant folk. . . . Our scale of values differs from that of the world from which we have been excluded; our shame is not its shame, and our love is not its love.

—RICHARD WRIGHT

CONTENTS

BLACK FOLK

Solicitor

The sound of his father's voice at a whisper startled him out of his sleep. On Sundays, John Dee loved hearing Solicitor's baritone, especially when it reverberated off the walls of the tiny wooden church, his father singing until the spirit moved the congregation to shout even before he began to preach. On weekdays, John Dee was also accustomed to hearing Solicitor bellow across the wide field just outside Cannon, Georgia, warning him to stop playing the dozens with his big brother, Obbie, and get back to work. But that unusual night when he heard Solicitor's voice lowered, he knew things were serious.

Even as a rebellious teen, John Dee was not in the habit of talking back to his father, but that night there was a particular urgency in his father's tone that made it clear that there was no time to ask what was

---

"Negro sharecropper with twenty acres. He receives eight cents a day for hoeing cotton. Brazos riverbottoms, near Bryan, Texas. 'Some of 'em don't get nothin. They just make these niggers chop that cotton. Few leave the bottoms. They ain't got nothin' to go on,' June 1938."

DOROTHEA LANGE, FARM SECURITY ADMINISTRATION,
LIBRARY OF CONGRESS

---

happening. Following directions, John Dee packed without lighting the lantern he usually used to illuminate his steps. Muffling his curiosity, he helped his brothers and sisters load the wagon using the moonlight as their guide.

What my maternal grandfather, then only fourteen years old, did know was that just a few days prior his father had come home empty-handed after settlement with the white man who owned the land Solicitor Duncan sharecropped. Rather than work the acreage himself, the landholder, who had inherited the property, had subdivided it into tracts of between thirty and sixty acres and contracted with sharecroppers to farm it. In exchange for the plot and fertilizer, the white owner would get half of the value of the crop. If he only provided the land, he would get a fourth.[1] However, that year the plantation owner told Solicitor that the harvest—several massive bales of cotton—had produced nothing but a debt. Indeed, he claimed that after one year of hard work in the fields, Solicitor owed *him*. The owner, who had not even turned over his hands to make the land productive, decided to keep all of the shares, knowing that there was nothing a Black man, even a man as esteemed within the Black community as Pastor Solicitor Duncan, could do about it.

Born there in northeast Georgia, Solicitor had done this work all his life. Breaking the hard red clay to plant the rows, pulling weeds, irrigating the young plants, and then carefully harvesting soft lint cotton from the hard bolls until his fingers were numb, Solicitor knew what he deserved. Young John Dee had watched his father go over the math based on the market value of the harvest over and over. The cash settlement was essential for the annual purchases his family needed, and to his ability to care for his sick wife. As furious as Solicitor was, he dared not speak up. Any public hint of anger, even a calm and measured protest, could result in a lynch mob appearing in front of their home. So, when the landowner lied and gave him nothing but a debt against the

"Even small boys are often kept out of school to plow. Macon Country, Georgia."
Boys working in a field, not far from where my maternal great-grandfather fled in the
1920s. ARTHUR FRANKLIN RAPER PAPERS #3966, SOUTHERN HISTORICAL COLLECTION,
THE WILSON LIBRARY, UNIVERSITY OF NORTH CAROLINA AT CHAPEL HILL

next year's crop, Solicitor determined that there would be no next year
in that place. He decided to take his family and run.

John Dee climbed into the wagon in silence, and sat down behind
his mother and father among his four siblings and his family's simple
belongings. As they made their way up the hilly dirt road, John Dee
didn't even look back at the tiny house where they had lived—a converted slave cabin just a few miles away from where generations of his
ancestors had toiled in bondage. He imagined what runaway slaves must
have felt. Emancipation had come decades before my grandfather was
born, but Black sharecroppers still faced circumstances almost as degrading as those of slavery. They were ostensibly free, yet in reality they had

no rights that white men were bound to respect. They labored without fair pay or any recourse when they were cheated. Those who organized against the white supremacists who owned the land faced violence or death. There were no labor laws that could adequately defend them, only lawless rules that tied them in perpetuity to debt. So, they ran.

John Dee looked forward to wherever his family might go. As they left the state of Georgia, Solicitor made sure to tell his children that they had nothing to be ashamed of, that it was injustice that made them flee up the dusty road that night, not their own wrongdoing. They were God's people. You wouldn't have seen it by looking at their scant possessions, but the Duncans carried an inheritance of their own.

They ended up in North Carolina, where the boy grew to be a man in search of an independent life. Soon after his mother died at the young age of fifty-three and his father remarried, John Dee set out on his own. At over six feet two inches tall and broad-shouldered, he looked like a man even though he was not yet twenty years old. Hoboing on train tops with Obbie, he hoped to find a town where he could work as a carpenter or woodworker. His large and powerful hands were skilled. He knew he could build anything; he had worked constructing cabins and even making furniture for others on the Georgia plantation. He heard that they might be hiring in Thomasville, North Carolina, which boasted one of the largest furniture factories in the state and a massive sixteen-foot-tall chair welcoming visitors in the town square.

In Thomasville he met Brunell Raeford. She was the eldest of six surviving children and the last in her family to have been born in rural Newberry, South Carolina, 80 miles due east of the Georgia town, called Cannon, where John Dee was born. The circumstances of their childhoods were also parallel: they were both the children of sharecroppers in rural communities not far from where their ancestors had been held as slaves for generations. Both the Raefords and Duncans came

"Negro family moving, Opelousas, Louisiana." Black families left during the Great Migration, often with few possessions, but carried a vision of what might be possible.

LEE RUSSELL, *FARM SECURITY ADMINISTRATION, LIBRARY OF CONGRESS*

from a long line of people who survived the unthinkable during slavery, and in freedom built a rich network of family, grounded in independent Black churches and schools. In spite of their effort to be truly free people, disenfranchisement backed by lynch law left little room for them to achieve, or even to simply *be*. The Raefords and the Duncans were among the many Black families who, in the first decades of the twentieth century, fled from the rural South to the urban South—an internal migration prior to the Great Migration north—in hope of finding better jobs and safety from physical threat.

John Dee and Brunell thought that the relative anonymity of a larger town might provide them with opportunities to advance. In Cannon and Newberry, there had been no high school for Black students to attend—the one-room schoolhouse in both towns ended at the eighth grade—but in Thomasville there was a high school for Black students. Brunell was bright, an avid reader of newspapers and interested in national politics. Only fourteen, she started attending high school and was early to class every day. But even after she graduated, she found there was little to do in Thomasville other than clean white folks' houses or work as a washerwoman alongside her mother. For both the Raefords and the Duncans, Thomasville was not substantively different than the rural counties they had fled.

By 1938 John Dee and Brunell had a baby on the way, so they married. When he applied at the Thomasville Chair Company to support his young family, he was told that Negroes were never hired as carpenters or machinists. The only jobs Black men could do were sweeping the fine sawdust off the floor and assembling boxes for shipping. John Dee took the job and watched with disgust as young white men with no experience were hired to do the work he had wanted at twice the pay he earned cleaning the factory floor. Like countless skilled Black men of his generation, he discovered that white employers reserved the better-paying, skilled work for white men.

John Dee and Brunell determined that they needed to move again, to leave the South altogether. Brunell had family who had migrated north to Philadelphia. Those relatives had bragged about the pay, the schools, and the absence of legal segregation. Thomasville had offered only disappointments, and they wanted more. The couple and their infant daughter—Frances Geraldine, Jerry for short—left their tiny shotgun house on 300 Church Street bound for Philadelphia, becoming part of the Great Migration: three individuals among the six million Black southerners who would move north between 1910 and 1970.

Adjusting to Philadelphia was hard for the young family. The City of Brotherly Love wasn't welcoming. Housing discrimination, violently enforced by white residents, left thousands of Black migrants crowded into just three areas in the city. The Duncans rented a room, really just a tiny partition of a larger apartment, in North Philadelphia. The white landlord didn't allow children, so Jerry hid silently under the bed whenever he was around.

Even with its shortcomings, John Dee knew that Philadelphia was not as bad as Georgia or North Carolina. Here he'd try again to be a carpenter. He joined the local branch of the United Brotherhood of Carpenters and paid his dues. However, the white union representatives who negotiated decent wages and regular hours for working-class white carpenters actively worked against Black men like John Dee. He was sent to jobs hours outside the city, in towns that were hostile to Black workers. When he complained about the long distances he had to travel or about the slurs hurled at him by his co-workers, union officials laughed, saying that if he couldn't do the work he should quit and leave carpentry to white men.

Brunell faced profound disappointments, too. Though she was a high school graduate at a time when fewer than one in ten Black people could claim as much, she found that in Philadelphia she was still living in a place where white employers would not hire Black women for white-collar jobs. So, as she had done in Thomasville, she found work cleaning for a white family. Brunell's story was the norm; throughout the urban North, Black women were shut out of secretarial work or better-paying factory jobs, consigned to household work. To John Dee, domestic work was the demeaning labor his late mother had been forced to do to make ends meet; it was work he wished his smart and pretty wife could avoid.[2]

Yet John Dee and Brunell Duncan still managed to build a community in the North Philadelphia neighborhood where they lived. The couple found a Black Baptist church where they could worship, shout, and sing like back home, and get help with food when things were tight. They bought city clothes and found places to dance and drink on an evening out. Sitting out on the freshly washed white marble stoop, they communed with family and made friends with other migrants from Georgia and North and South Carolina. They would remember when and strategize out the present, sharing prospects about better jobs and warnings about bad ones. All along, they remained connected to where they came from. Each summer they sent Jerry back to North Carolina to stay with John Dee's sister Lucille, or with Solicitor, so she could spend the summer with her favorite cousins and go on long car rides with her grandfather as he called on his church congregants, who were excited to have a visit from the pastor and to dote on the round-faced girl.

Even as Brunell struggled to find her feet as a mother and a migrant, like many working-class Black women then and now she was buoyed by her passion for politics. Philadelphia was imperfect, but at least here she could register to vote. So, she did, and she encouraged John Dee to do the same. Late every evening when she finally had a moment to sit, she read the newspapers to catch up on the news of the day. Stories in both the Black and white newspapers made her feel more hopeful about possibilities for change—for new opportunities beyond scrubbing floors on her hands and knees. She closely followed President Franklin D. Roosevelt's New Deal as well as the work of his "Black Cabinet." Like most Americans, she closely followed the war, worried as much about the men fighting for democracy abroad as she was about the fight for democracy at home. Distraught at the news of FDR's death in 1945, Brunell took her still-little girl firmly by the hand to see President Roosevelt's funeral train as it passed through 30th Street Station on the way to New York. Even though she did not cry often, tears welled in her eyes when she saw the casket inside the brightly lit car; she worried that no other president would care as much for Black people as she believed FDR had. Tears rolled down six-year-old Jerry's cheeks; she explained that when she saw her mother cry, she couldn't help but cry, too.

Through it all, John Dee worked, just as Brunell did. They both dreamed of a day when they would own their own land away from the city. She wanted to grow a kitchen garden and plant fruit trees. He wanted to build a home for his wife and children with his own hands. They both wanted an education and a future for their little one. So, they continued to take whatever jobs they could find in the hope that Jerry would never have to clean the white folks' toilets.

My great-grandfather, Solicitor Duncan, was the Black working class, men who were the children of former slaves, sharecroppers who made land they did not own productive and yet struggled mightily to be treated fairly in the segregated South. My grandfather, John Dee Duncan, was the Black working class, skilled men who were denied the opportunity to do skilled labor in both the North and the South, not because of a deficit in ability but because of the color line. My grand-

Solicitor Duncan.

mother, Brunell Raeford Duncan, was the Black working class, women who despite their hopes, education, and skills were consigned to household work. Like the majority of Black folk in the first generations after freedom, they were relegated to jobs that provided little pay and did not lead to much except more toil.

SOLICITOR'S, JOHN DEE'S, AND BRUNELL'S ANCESTORS WERE brought to this country not as immigrants, but as slaves. They were forced by the men and women who held them in bondage to labor on land forcibly taken from the Indigenous people who had lived there for centuries. In order to sustain chattel slavery, a unique system of racial hierarchy was created in law and in practice. Black people became inextricably connected to intergenerational bondage. White indentured servants who arrived on the shores of colonial America had their time in bondage limited, if they faced any at all. Their freedom was the reward for their service; their color, as they saw it, became a promise of success.

In reality, in the years after the American Revolution, the profits from slavery made a small white elite extraordinarily wealthy but left most white workers poor and fundamentally unable to compete with the productivity of vast plantations on which the enslaved labored without pay. The Black enslaved were characterized as lazy and inferior workers, and the white poor as pathological. Indigenous people were removed, said to have vanished, part of an unknowable past. Dismissed as "white trash," the working white poor were blamed for their place at the bottom of white society's hierarchy and comforted only by the knowledge that at least Black people were consigned to a status below them. Even in the wake of Emancipation, a century after the nation's founding, the systems of labor that replaced enslavement were rooted in dispossession, exclusion, and exploitation. The white working poor were

Brunell Raeford Duncan.

Frances Geraldine Duncan.

still dismissed, and the Black working class were thought of as useful only for their compliance.

All the while, Black people were keen observers of the world around them, critiquing the wider society and its hierarchies. They understood the profound value of their labor even when they were thought of as just chattel and, later, as an emancipated people. In the first moments of freedom, they took advantage of their mobility, and sought out not only improved working conditions but stronger connections to their families, past and present. They built unions all their own, and, even if they had no choice but to take jobs similar to the ones they had done in bondage, they organized new neighborhoods and communities. They erected schools and churches. They taught their children to see America, as twisted as it was by the legacy of slavery and its aftermath, through their own eyes.

They did not believe that they were trash just because they were poor. They knew their worth, even as the world told them they had very little. They carried their knowledge, of themselves and their pasts and their abilities, to Southern cities, and then to the North and the West. They did their best to pass their legacies down. Though they lived in a nation tilted against them, Black people built and rebuilt vital spaces of resistance, grounded in the secrets that they knew about themselves, about their community, their dignity, and their survival. One of those secrets was joy in spite of sorrow: amid their endless labor, amid the violence, amid the hate, ordinary Black people managed not only to resist but to laugh and to make fun and to love. They insisted on it. Their insistence was political, as was their insistence on collectivity and faith.

My work as a historian has always begun with the stories of my ancestors. *Black Folk* is no different. It is both a personal journey, rooted in the stories of my family and other Black working-class families, and a history of Black labor in the United States from slavery to our

present-day freedom, though with a focus on a critical era, after Southern Emancipation and into the early twentieth century, when the first
generations of Black working people carved out a world for themselves.
Although there had been free working-class Black people in the North
and South before the Civil War, their numbers were relatively small;
they, too, encountered new opportunities and obstacles after the war
ended. *Black Folk* is also a human exploration of Black working people,
one that seeks to recall and re-create the pathways they followed. Given
that the majority of Black people are, or are descendants of, the Black
working class, one book can never capture all of what Black working
people have endured, or all the jobs they have done; the stories are too
numerous, the labor too diverse. Instead, *Black Folk* attempts to capture the character of the lives of Black workers, seeing them not just as
laborers, or members of a class, or activists, but as people whose daily
experiences mattered—to themselves, to their communities, and to the
nation at large, even as it denied their importance. This book introduces
numerous individuals, the kinds of people who, in many prior histories,
have been described only generally or presented as representative cases.
Sometimes they aren't even named. *Black Folk* names them, and tries to
reclaim them in full.

For some readers, "Black folk" will suggest a reference to W. E. B.
Du Bois's classic work *The Souls of Black Folk*. Certainly, that 1903 mas-
terpiece set a standard in African American literature; its intellectual
frameworks still animate the study of the Black past today. But my use
of "Black folk" here is not intended as a parallel to Du Bois's. After all,
Du Bois wrote in part as an outsider, a Northern-born Black man who
grew up in a majority white community isolated from a wider Black existence until he traveled South to attend Fisk University in the 1880s.
Souls' framing of "two-ness," or a double consciousness as "an American, a Negro, two souls, two thoughts, two unreconciled strivings; two

warring ideals in one dark body," speaks to his status as an observer. The Black folk I call on here are not outside of me. I am the descendant of the enslaved people who labored in Georgia, Virginia, South Carolina, and Maryland. I am Northern-born but raised by Southern-born, working-class people. My relationship to these stories is not as a sociologist, or only as a historian, but as a member of the family.

My invocation of Black folk is the feel of the fuzzy string beans in my hand as my grandmother recalled how she learned to pick them without hurting the plants themselves back in Newbury, South Carolina. I learned the folk in the rhythm of the chatter of women gathering in the churchyard for what felt like hours, my grandmother in her deaconess all-white sharing laughs and raised-eyebrow looks under the brim of her hat, as well as insights and ideas, under the shade of the big oak tree. My Black folk is the smell of roasted salt pork stewing in the pot liquor of my grandmother's turnip greens, as I nestled against her round hip as she stood on line to serve mourners in the church basement during the repast. Her lessons of independence, community wisdom, and service are how I first came to know myself. Black folk is what my community calls itself, the joy in our connection, our coming together. My people.

Tracing the roots of the Black working class, I found again and again that Black folks' sense of self was supported not by the jobs they held but by their place within their own communities. From Georgia to Philadelphia, Florida to Chicago, Texas to Oakland, African Americans knew that they were much more than the labor they performed and the unfair conditions they faced. Aware that the outside world would always be arrayed against them, they found their value away from that world— such as in the backyard of a laundress's house, where women of multiple generations would labor all day, talking and laughing in a space free of white supervision and largely beyond white knowledge.

Within such havens, Black people created the collective power that would drive their political engagement with the world. As they organized mutual aid societies, played card games, shot pool, worshipped in Black churches, and went to segregated schools, they maintained their own vision of what it meant to be Black and what they could hope to gain through their labors. They debated politics and formed strategies grounded in who they were and where they came from. It would be in these spaces where they learned to resist and organize, drawing on their knowledge of the past and building visions of the future. They reminded one another that their right to access good and fair employment was inextricable from their fight to be full, free citizens. The descendants of the enslaved knew that their rights as workers were human rights. Their fights against racism and against labor exploitation were always one.

Today in America, the term "working class" usually conjures images of ruddy white men in hard hats or white waitresses in Midwestern diners, increasingly disgruntled and left behind by the epochal transformations that have reshaped this nation and the world in the last decades. Put simply, the words "working class" are synonymous with the white working class. And in our current political culture, the white working class is synonymous with supporters of Donald Trump—never mind that his base is really the non-college-educated upper middle class. Think pieces seeking to better understand the minds of the fabled Trumpian white working class abound, but the notion that the American working class is white is an assumption that long predates Trump's time in office. Indeed, all my adult life, the representative American working man and American working woman have been most often thought to be white.

Our national mythos leaves little room for Black workers, or to glean any lessons from their histories. Rarely do we speak of how the nation's racial hierarchy of segregation and discrimination sought to ensure that Black people would always labor in a stratum below white people. When Black workers are mentioned at all, the very idea of *work* is dropped entirely, and instead they are described as the *poor*, and often implied to be unworthy and unproductive (if it isn't said outright)—an echo of the characterization of the Black enslaved as lazy and unmotivated. Never mind that from slavery to the present, Black workers have been essential to the nation's productivity, and indeed—as was demonstrated during the Covid pandemic—to its basic functioning.

Black Folk does not discount the formidable trials that any working-class people—whether white, or Indigenous, or Latino, or Asian—have faced and still face in America. Working people of all origins have been rendered invisible in a country so fixated on centering the white middle-class suburban family as a stand-in for all Americans. And working-class coalitions across racial lines, including white workers, have been powerful forces in this nation's history. But Black folk, Black workers, have had a distinctive experience—and that experience points to better futures for all workers. When we look back at the lives of these grandmothers, when we see the communal support at play at the cookouts, when we listen to the organizing talk in the hour after church lets out, when we see the beauty in the Thursday-night outfits of household workers reveling on their only night off, we can discern a story about working-class life informed by care for themselves and others, and shaped by a dignity that could not be shaken despite the circumstances. When we see grandfathers, once young men, returning home South during fall homecoming, in their city suits and big shiny cars, with cash to tuck into their mother's apron, we see networks of concern and pride. When we study the Black men who shined shoes and worked for tips organizing into the largest all-Black union in American history, a union that not only improved their working lives but also provided the infrastructure for the modern civil rights movement, we see their bravery in facing down injustice. When we trace the advocacy of Black postal workers and their fight for equal inclusion and fair pay, we can better understand why the postal service was targeted by those who seek to undermine American democracy.

The distinctiveness of the Black working class is manifest today. Black people are not only more likely to be the working class than white Americans, but Black workers are also more likely to be union members than people in any other group—a remarkable statistic, particularly given that most Black workers live in the South, the region where business works harder, and more successfully, to crush labor organizing.[3] Even in the face of a steep decline in the number of union members nationwide over the past twenty years and a concentrated national campaign against labor unions by massive corporate entities like Walmart and Amazon, it is no accident that Black workers are at the forefront of some of today's most important labor movements. From the fight for a $15 minimum wage to unionizing Amazon workers in Bessemer, Alabama, and Long Island, New York, Black people are helping to lead historic calls for change. Even in exploitative conditions, which from the outside appear to leave little space for them to exercise any power, Black workers draw on an unusually strong legacy of collective activism.

The enslaved took church songs and work songs and made them into messages of resistance and escape. Free Black women used their monopoly on laundry to take collective holidays. Rail workers used the segregation of Black men and women into jobs as porters and maids to organize an unbreakable union. Migrants moved community networks with them to new regions of the country to find jobs, and organize in new cities. *Black Folk* demonstrates that those churchyards, factory floors, railcars, and postal sorting facilities were sites of possibility, and that warehouse processing centers, supermarkets, and nursing homes can be the same today. In doing so, it seeks to lay out a vision of a better collective future.

———

EVEN TWO GENERATIONS AFTER THE GREAT EMANCIPATION, my grandparents were still fervently struggling to be free. Free from racial violence, job discrimination, and the insults of segregation. Free to earn enough to establish their independence. Free to educate their children. As the descendants of people who saw enslavement end, they knew change was possible. My grandparents' vision of a home and land of their own, of growing enough to feed themselves and sustain the local community, that modest vision, as hard it was to realize in America, was what was passed down to them. I can trace that fervent vision of freedom back to John Dee's own great-grandfather, Henry, born in bondage in Elbert County, Georgia, in 1822.

CHAPTER ONE

Henry, a Blacksmith

It is impossible for me to know much about him, my earliest traceable ancestor in my maternal grandfather's line, a boy born sometime in 1822 named Henry. He is the first in this branch of my family whose name I can find in the historical records.[1] He was born in bondage in Elbert County, Georgia, in the part of the state closest to the South Carolina border, just west of the Savannah River. Its acres of fertile clay and gently rolling hills were stolen from the Creek and Cherokee and distributed in land lotteries to white residents, who didn't have to pay a cent. Slaveholding sons migrating from Virginia and the Carolinas settled in Elbert County, exploiting their holdings of people in bondage to make these stolen lands productive. They broke long-held treaties to violently displace many of the remaining settlements of native people in

---

"Photograph of baptismal service, Wilkes Country, Georgia, 1913." The community of faith, gathered at the river. This congregation is the New Salem Baptist Church, Washington, Georgia, one county south of where Henry was born.

J. W. STEPHENSON, COURTESY *GEORGIA ARCHIVES,*
VANISHING GEORGIA COLLECTION, WLK122

order to clear the land, even as they broke up enslaved families by bringing Black men and women to labor in Georgia.[2]

To add to the number of the enslaved they transported in the migration, white settlers established a slave market right there on the banks of the Savannah River in "a big open field on the Georgia side." Elbert County became one of the many hubs of the domestic slave trade in the state of Georgia; thousands of enslaved people, including both those born in West Africa and those born in the Upper South, were sold to the highest bidders at auction. Such trade was not unique to Georgia; just short of one million Black people were dislocated, moved with, or sold by their slaveholders.[3] Charles Ball, an enslaved man born in Maryland who was violently separated from his family, was one of the many "sold South" to Georgia. He recounted that a slave trader let his master know that "slaves were much in demand . . . that purchasers were numerous and prices good." One Elbert County descendant recalled, "They would go down there and the big shots order so many, and pay for 'em. They auctioned 'em off. . . . They pay so much for a head." The toil of the enslaved changed the landscape; they did the arduous work of sculpting the clay-packed soil, extracting ancient trees to clear the land first for tobacco plantations, and later, for cotton.[4]

After the end of the War of 1812 brought stability to trading markets on both sides of the Atlantic, rural counties like Elbert became the pulse of the cotton boom in the Piedmont, "the most productive cotton-growing section of the entire country," while Georgia would grow to be the world's leading cotton producer.[5] Plucking the cotton from its thorny blooms without damaging the still productive plants required skill and dexterity. The ambitions of landholders who hoped to reap giant profits meant that the crop also required quick hands and tremendous physical endurance.

Charles Ball detailed the labor the crop required. The cotton was "planted in hills, in straight rows, from four to five feet apart." Each person, called a "hand or picker," was "provided with a bag" that was "hung round the neck" and designed to hold at least a bushel of cotton. The hand would work their way down the row, reaching from side to side, quickly clearing "all the cotton from the open burs, on the right and left." When the bag was full it was set aside in a storage space and replaced with another, until nightfall, when the overseer weighed the cotton gathered by each hand, measuring their productivity by the pound rather than by the number of rows cleared. Ball reported:

> In a good field of cotton, fully ripe, a day's work is sixty pounds; but where the cotton is of inferior quality, or the burs are not in full blow, fifty pounds is the day's work; and where the cotton is poor, or in bad order, forty, or even thirty pounds, is as much as one hand can get in a day.

"Picking cotton." Enslaved laborers and Black workers after Emancipation utilized their skill and knowledge to harvest cotton, the crop that made the nation wealthy.
WILLIAM HENRY JACKSON,
DETROIT PUBLISHING COMPANY, LIBRARY OF CONGRESS

Picking continued for months on end "from August until December, or January; and in some fields, they pick from the old plants, until they are ploughed up in February or March, to make room for the planting of the seeds of another crop." Ball recalled that "the picking of cotton may almost be reckoned among the arts."[6]

There was rabid demand for "prime hands." The population of the enslaved in Georgia grew exponentially to meet the expectations of the men and women who sought to make their fortunes from the boom. Young boys and men were in the highest demand. One slave trader explained that "young niggers, who would soon learn to pick cotton, were prime articles in the market." Landholders seeking to exploit this labor-intensive crop purchased more and more enslaved people, fueling the domestic slave trade and the exponential growth of the enslaved population well into mid-century.[7]

On the eve of the Civil War, in 1860, there were almost 500,000 chattel slaves in Georgia, counted by the census at over 44 percent of the population. Given the incentives created by the three-fifths clause in the US Constitution, white settlers and their descendants grew stronger politically as the numbers of people they held in bondage increased, amplifying the power of slaveholders in Congress. The expulsion of native people and the large-scale displacement and migration of thousands of enslaved enabled a small cadre of extremely wealthy white men to hold the power to shape local and state government to suit their purposes.[8]

Henry, my ancestor, and the many thousands of other enslaved people were subject to a particularly brutal system of labor. Some men and women who called themselves masters or mistresses weren't extraordinarily cruel; others were.[9] More important than the cruelty of any individual is the underlying truth that there were no consequences either way. The right of the men and women who held people in bondage to extract their labor was complete; no law balanced their power. Brutality was simply an easy way to gain control and keep the enslaved fearful of what might happen if they fought back.[10] The results of that lawless brutality were horrific.

The slave code of the state of Georgia required slaveholders to assert physical control over the enslaved, compelling plantation owners to hire overseers to monitor the fields and obliging municipalities to employ patrollers to watch for runaways. The general belief was that the enslaved, who were forced to work from dawn to dusk, were naturally lazy. There was also a tremendous fear of insurrection, so overseers were often aggressive, both to tamp down resistance and to keep fieldwork at a quick, and tiring, pace, with the goal of making the enslaved exhausted, compliant, and reluctant to resist. Patrollers, too, were known to be vicious, as a deterrent to those considering escape.

The employment of overseers and patrollers also kept working-class whites invested in the system of slavery. Few working-class white people would ever be able to afford the high cost of purchasing an enslaved person. However, their work controlling other men and women's chattel undercut their ability to be critical of the very system that devalued their free labor. For payment, overseers and patrollers were given not just cash, but also access to the privileges of white supremacy. As free white men, they could demand respect and punish enslaved people who challenged their authority. White privilege and the doctrine of Black inferiority would keep them from building alliances with the enslaved. If the white workers of the American South had allied with the Black enslaved, their collective power would have easily overshadowed that of wealthy planters. Instead, the white working class enjoyed the "wages of whiteness"—the reality that they were not at the very bottom of Southern society.[11] Evidently, these perceived wages paid so well that many landholders could afford to be distant from the everyday business of slavery; many slaveholders lived in cities miles away from their plantations, with little fear that their authority would be challenged in their absence.

Overseers built their reputations based on exacting, brutal discipline. With no financial stake in the health of the enslaved, they were known to be particularly cruel in keeping bondsmen and women working at a rapid and inhumane clip. Charles Ball noted that on the Georgia plantation where he was held, there were "two hundred and sixty slaves," but that "the number was seldom stationary for a single week. Births were numerous and frequent, and deaths were not uncommon."[12] Summoned at dawn by the overseer's horn, Black men, women, and children labored under the keen eye of white overseers who exacted painful punishments for minor transgressions. William H. Heard, who was also born in bondage in Elbert County, knew of overseers who regularly beat those who were judged to be too slow or recalcitrant until "blood would run from their heads to their heels." Their lacerated flesh would be rubbed with salt to continue the torture.[13]

Even away from the fields, there was tight control over the enslaved. Patrollers watched the roads to ensure that the enslaved did not travel without permission, enforcing the regulation with physical punishment. As Ball reported, "no slave dare leave the plantation to which he belongs, a single mile, without a written pass from the overseer, or master; but by exposing himself to the danger of being taken up and flogged." A Georgia woman recalled that once when her father was caught slipping away from the plantation quarters to visit a woman at night, patrollers "beat him so bad you couldn't lay your hand on him nowhar' dat it warn't sore." Ball described the sick calculus of their torture: everyday punishments were designed to be extremely painful, and yet not so harsh that muscles were permanently injured or bones irreparably broken. The high market value for slaves—particularly young men and women in their childbearing years—made it illogical for slaveholders to kill those they held in bondage. In spite of their attempts at painful but preservative punishments, it was still not uncommon for slaveholders and overseers to torture people to death. Heard recalled one master who in a fit of anger beat a pregnant woman so severely that she miscarried and she and her child died. No charges of murder were brought against him.[14]

Such vicious and random punishments led many to run, which became the most effective means of denying cruel masters the value of their labor as slaves. Heard knew that some "would go to the woods and stay there for months, yes, some of them years." Such "marronage" or "laying out" was not uncommon in Georgia; one man held in bondage, Isaiah Green, knew of a runaway named Jesse who "dug a cave in the ground and made fairly comfortable living quarters" in a place in close proximity to the plantation he had escaped. He returned to the plantation at night for provisions and to visit his wife and family, and stayed successfully hidden for seven years.[15] Over time, his cave served as a respite for other escapees. These acts of resistance and (partial) escape should not be thought of as simply running away, but as nascent labor negotiations, strikes that demonstrated to the community of the enslaved the value of their labor and their power to withdraw it, even if that withdrawal might cost them their lives.

In Elbert County, even those who could not run to the woods around the Savannah River could take revenge by diminishing their own effectiveness as workers, and therefore the price their bodies would fetch at auction. When her mistress threatened to remove her from her family and auction her to the highest bidder at the New Orleans slave market, one woman "took her right hand, laid it down on a meat block and cut off three fingers, and thus made . . . sale impossible." In her mind, that profound violence to her body was less than the violence of being separated from her family for the rest of her life. Countless numbers of the enslaved mutilated themselves or took their own lives, a reminder that enslaved people were well aware of the monetary value of their bodies.[16] They knew the only way to upend their status as chattel was to destroy themselves when escape was not possible.[17]

I cannot know what Henry endured as a child, but I do know that despite what he suffered he was part of a community.[18] Community, for enslaved people, was not an unchanging thing—not least because they were regularly sold away or murdered—but rather a process, and one made and remade in the intimacy of the quarters or slave settlements, and working shoulder to shoulder in the fields. They sought opportunities to commune, to provide one another with space—space to breathe, space for their minds, space for their spirits. Every moment, every inch was a treasure.

They learned to speak to one another in song—work songs, worship songs, and bawdy songs—that only they understood completely. They met in secret, to teach one another, to share what information they knew about goings on in the plantation house or in town, about who had run away to the east in hope of escape. And they worshipped in secret in the quiet places in the woods, building churches with no walls. Others kept the traditions they remembered from before their bondage, bowing to the east or praying to an angry god, waiting to fly away to their ancestral home when they passed away. But they didn't just pray and mourn; they danced in the woods, too. They fellowshipped by sharing the animals they had trapped and the fruit they had gleaned. They gained sustenance from the forbidden foods they had cooked for the families of their slaveholders and then slipped into their aprons and skirts. They ate meat clandestinely to get enough filling food to stay alive and feed growing children. They cooked food that reminded them of where they had come from: pots of richly flavored rice, stews of the vegetables they grew in hidden gardens. They courted in these secret moments too, made new marriages, dissolved old relationships, and created families. They named their children after their ancestors.

They took in the motherless. They cried. They argued. They fought with one another. They disagreed with one another about the best ways to survive. They came together to mourn their dead. They did not forget the wrongs they suffered. Out of the fragments of their past and present, they wrote their own songs and made a new way, one grounded in the idea that justice would one day come for those who held them in bondage, and that jubilee would one day come for them, just as it had for the Hebrew slaves.[19]

Together, in this community, they could imagine other possibilities. They steeled themselves to survive by crafting their own vision and collectively building a faith that was balm for the crippling realities they faced. It was a way of seeing the world, a faith way and moral code, a sense of justice about what was owed for their labor, a belief in their collective strength, a way out of no way that they made together. They knew their value as skilled farmers; after all, it was their knowledge and acumen that built the wealth of others. They imagined that the sweat of their brow might one day provide a way for their own families on their own land. This outlook, developed in the overlooked communities of the Black enslaved, would one day come to serve as the cornerstone of America's Black working class. Their work, the independence of their outlook, their uniquely African and uniquely American modes of expression born in these spaces would carry them forward.

THE ENSLAVED MEN WHO WORKED TO BUILD THOMAS JEFFERSON's Academical Village, the University of Virginia, were skilled. Most of their names will never be known. A few names were recorded in the ledgers maintained by Jefferson or the members of his faculty: Willis, Warner, Gilbert, Sam, Caesar, Nelson, Lewis, and Ben. Others were not listed by name but simply as "hands," "laborers," "boy," or "negros."

Although it was illegal for them to learn to read, they could follow intricate plans to perfection. We can see the evidence of their handiwork today, in the curves of the serpentine walls and the sturdy little homes that line the wide green Lawn framing the Rotunda. This space, now venerated as a World Heritage Site, was constructed by enslaved men who fired the bricks, forged the nails, smoothed the plaster, and carved the stone. While we can hardly know what happened to them, we can imagine that while their skilled labor was valued, their lives were not.

Despite all their work, as if to mock their condition, America mythologized enslaved workers as lazy and ignorant. In his treatise written to a French colleague, later published in 1784 as his *Notes on the State of Virginia*, Thomas Jefferson described the people he enslaved—I suppose this would eventually even extend to his own children with Sally Hemings—as if they were a different species altogether.

They seem to require less sleep. A black, after hard labour through the day, will be induced by the slightest amusements to sit up till midnight, or later, though knowing he must be out with the first dawn of the morning. . . . They are more ardent after their female; but love seems with them to be more an eager desire, than a tender delicate mixture of sentiment and sensation. Their griefs are transient. Those numberless afflictions, which render it doubtful whether heaven has given life to us in mercy or in wrath, are less felt, and sooner forgotten with them. In general, their existence appears to participate more of sensation than reflection. To this must be ascribed their disposition to sleep when abstracted from their diversions, and unemployed in labour. An animal whose body is at rest, and who does not reflect, must be disposed to sleep of course.

Jefferson framed the men, women, and children who toiled from dawn to dusk in the shadow of his home and the university he founded as sleepy due to laziness and a lack of deep intellect. When he glanced out the window of his study while working on his intellectual pursuits, he saw backs bent tending crops in the fields and thought of the labor of these enslaved workers as rightfully his own. In his notebooks he imagined away their full humanity, their skill, their knowledge of the land. By the nineteenth century, Jefferson's assumptions about the propensity of the enslaved to sleep would become commonly held beliefs about Black people. The enslaved were viewed, by many white Americans, as terrible workers who shuffled their feet and only wanted to nap. Defenders of slavery argued that the violent controls of enslavement—the whips, bits, brutal punishments, patrols—were necessary to keep the enslaved productive.

Although Jefferson asserted that their sleep was empty of thought, we know that the enslaved did dream. Indeed, much of what they envisioned centered on what laboring as free men and women might truly mean. We see shadows of what might have been their fates if they had sought to ply their trades as free men. Stephen Byars was an enslaved man who worked as a groom and a stableman in service to the residents of the university for two decades, but when he purchased his freedom, he was required by law to leave the state. As a slave his work was valuable, but as a freeman his skills were a threat.[20]

For African Americans, work was first defined in the binds of slavery. Coming to the country not as immigrants but in bondage, their labor became a commodity that was traded globally and enriched the world. Just as they constructed universities, they helped build countless sites throughout the country. Enslaved men blasted through mountains and graded the land to lay railroad tracks. Their embodied knowledge of crop science turned tiny seeds of rice into wealth for the planters who owned them. Their careful, constant tending of growing plants and their quick hands harvested so much cotton that the young nation became a leader in the global economy. Their toil over pots on open fires created Southern cuisine. The enslaved were ironworkers, seamstresses, masons, housemaids, carpenters, wet nurses. They were the midwives who delivered Black and white children. They built the walls that curve around Thomas Jefferson's university gardens. They quarried the stone for the White House.

Well before Henry was born in Elbert County, there were emancipations as well as opportunities for Black workers to challenge the assumptions about what freedom might mean. Indeed, thousands of free Black people lived in the new nation; some were formerly enslaved people who had been manumitted by their owners; others had escaped bondage by purchase or by running away; still others were freed by gradual emancipation plans adopted by Northern states. The first enslaved Americans to be freed knew that their labor had had value for the men and women who owned them; and in freedom they were determined to work together to labor for their own benefit and the benefit of their children. However, they soon found that the justifications that helped to maintain enslavement shifted to become the limitations that would prevent them from enjoying equal opportunities for jobs and education. Their enslavement had ended, but its assumptions lived on.

In every sector of society, the choices of free Black people in the North were limited by white prejudices. Even as they sought out education and tried to apply the skills they had been trained in, they were constrained at every turn. The 1819 valedictorian of the New York African Free School asked the attendees at his graduation, "What are my prospects? To what shall I turn my hand? Shall I be a mechanic? No one will employ me; white boys won't work with me. Shall I be a merchant? No one will have me in his office; white clerks won't associate with me. Drudgery and servitude, then, are my prospective portion." Indeed, the 1820 census listing the employment of the over 220,000 free Black people living in the North shows that they worked almost exclusively as domestic servants, barbers, laundresses, day laborers, porters, coachmen, seamstresses, mariners, and cooks. Any middle class among this free Black population was notable for how small it was. Almost 90 percent of New York City's free Black laborers were listed as working in what were designated "unskilled" professions.

Even as this stunted freedom began in the North, misshapen by caricature and custom and law, the slave states grew more reflexively oppressive as fear about the possibilities of Black freedom grew. Black northerners led calls for equality in the North and abolition for their brothers and sisters in the South. Southern slaveholders did all they could to silence those voices, banning abolitionist literature and passing laws preventing Black workers from even handling mail unsupervised.

However, enslavement did not limit the minds of those in bondage, or their ability to account for what they had built: the plowed rows of cotton as far as the eye could see, the majestically tall tangles of sugarcane, the flooded fields of rice. They knew that it was their skill that grew the crops that made the land prosperous, no one else's. They were the ones who tended the children, who fed white women's newborns from their breasts, and cooked delicious meals over hot flame. They scrubbed the floors, polished the woodwork, sewed and laundered the clothes, pressed the fine linens with coal-stoked irons, to make homes for others. With their strength they helped erect counties and towns, cities and states. Their work was the pulse of the economy. Surely, they took note of all of that.

———

TODAY, WHEN PEOPLE TALK ABOUT REPARATIONS FOR SLAVERY, most often they talk of numbers. What would be a fair payment to the descendants of the enslaved? How should payment be given? Should it be funding for education? Should we receive land? Should we get a check? These are fair questions. After all, my family tree can be traced all the way back before the founding of the nation, and it includes on its branches some of the millions of enslaved Africans whose labor became the foundation of the United States. Should we trace their suffering back to the slave ship that made the long voyage from the coast of West Africa? What price should we put on the grief of African families whose young sons and daughters were stolen and shipped away, never to be seen again? What value should be returned to their descendants as the victims of a market that made Europe wealthy and left Africa in political chaos?

I've found it hard to contemplate the matter in such broad strokes. Instead, I think of Henry. Henry as a child who probably began working— carrying water, gathering wood, working with child-sized tools—soon after he could walk well on his own. Henry as a teen who toiled in cotton fields from "'kin to can't," stopping only at midday for the dinner bell. Henry as a man who worked as a skilled blacksmith most of his adult life to enrich others. Henry whose labor multiplied made the cotton boom. Yet I do know that Henry had the opportunity to stand apart from those who went before him in an important way: he would live to see slavery perish, taking with it the man who held him in bondage.

That man, Joseph Rucker, was the largest and wealthiest slaveholder in Elbert County. Called Squire because of the vast lands he held, he maintained twelve separate plantations and the majority of the cultivable land in the county. With the immense wealth created by the more than two hundred enslaved people he owned, and the additional fifty owned by his son Tinsley, Rucker founded the Bank of Ruckersville, noted as one of the first financial institutions in Georgia. Joseph Rucker's estate, now on the National Register of Historic Places, was reached via a long, tree-lined walkway up to the white, clapboard-sided mansion, which featured an oversized chimney built of bricks laid in an intricate diamond pattern by skilled, enslaved masons.[21] It was said to be one of the most beautiful plantation homes in the county.

On the eve of the Civil War, Joseph Rucker's land was valued at more than $75,000 and his personal estate value—that is, the market value of the enslaved he held in bondage, along with his livestock and furniture—was $257,100, figures that today equate to over $2.3 million and over $7 million, respectively.[22] His family would be wealthy and influential for generations. Squire's grandson Joseph Rucker Lamar, who attended the University of Georgia and then Washington and Lee for law school, would be elected to the Georgia House of Representatives and the Supreme Court of Georgia, and go on to be appointed to the US Supreme Court. Another grandson, Tinsley White Rucker, Jr., attended Princeton University and became a US congressman and a US attorney. The Rucker family was not unique among their slaveholding peers. Georgia planters were some of the "richest people not only in the nation but in the world" due to their vast holdings in human property.[23]

When Henry was finally freed in 1865, he legally adopted the surname Rucker. This practice, of adopting the surname of the family who had held a person in bondage, was done not to honor the slaveholding family but as a way to mark their home place and the community of formerly enslaved people of whom they were a part. The hundreds of Black Ruckers in postwar Elbert County weren't all related by blood but were members of a home community, what they would have thought of as "home folks." That community of family beyond blood ties still held meaning after freedom.[24]

It is impossible to find the name "Henry," or the names of any of the men, women, girls, and boys Rucker owned, in the records of slave schedules created as part of the US Census.[25] Most of the enslaved, much like the livestock that was assigned value alongside them, were not recorded as individuals by name, but rather only by age—which could be imprecise—along with gender and color, which could be either "black" or "mulatto" and coded "B" or "M" in the rolls. According to the 1860 census, Joseph Rucker held thirteen men in bondage between the ages of thirty-three and thirty-six who were described as black, and three more described as mulatto. His son Tinsley held four more men all listed as thirty-five years old and black. Another Rucker who lived in Elbert County, a woman named Frances Rucker, held four slaves, two of whom were described as thirty-seven-year-old black males. The 1870 census is the first one in which Henry Rucker appears by name, along with his wife, Phoebe, and seven of their eight living children. Henry and some of his children were listed as mulatto. Henry would be listed with that descriptor in every census that included it as a category, so it is most likely that Henry was one of the three mulatto slaves listed on Joseph Rucker's slave schedule.[26]

In Rucker family lore, it was said that Joseph "violently opposed" secession, not because he favored the Union but because knew in advance that the Southern states would fail and that he would lose the wealth derived from the men, women, and children he held captive. He was said to have pointed to an enslaved young man standing nearby when he explained his sentiments to his son-in-law, exclaiming, "See that fellow? A year ago, he was worth $1,500, today, he isn't worth a thrip." I wonder if this story is apocryphal, intended to demonstrate that Rucker was a Confederate but one who was savvy enough to know the difficulty the "Lost Cause" faced. Indeed, if the story is true, Rucker was correct. The system of chattel slavery would end, along with a society that depended on the theft of labor from a captive people. If the story is true, I'm also left wondering what the young man standing in earshot of Rucker's pronouncement thought about his own value.[27]

Joseph "Squire" Rucker would not live to see his prophecy fulfilled. He died in August of 1864. While conditions in Elbert County weren't recorded in Rucker's papers, at the time the state of Georgia was at war from within and without. The state's Confederate soldiers faced bad odds on the battlefields, while the enslaved on plantations quietly refused to continue to work for the Confederacy.[28] Rucker's wife died soon after he did.

Just a handful of the 170 enslaved men, women, and children whom Rucker held at the time of his death were mentioned by name in his last will and testament. Remarkably, Henry's name was there. "My negro man Henry a Blacksmith" was to be given as property to Elbert Marion Rucker, along with a house and its adjoining five acres of land. Although this is a small mention, these few words hold so much meaning. They reveal that Henry was considered a skilled worker and of particular value within the population of enslaved whom Rucker held in bondage. Willing my ancestor to his youngest son was a sign that Joseph Rucker thought Henry's labor would be of benefit to a young planter, particularly one just starting out. A blacksmith was a maker of the hardware necessary for a plantation and the surrounding community. Blacksmiths would have been participants in local commerce for the plantation, and perhaps, with some negotiation between the enslaved and the slaveholder, for themselves. Henry would most likely have been known as a leading figure because of his interactions with both Black and white people and his mobility. He would have been a foundational, "essential" worker among the hundred-plus people held as chattel, and, more importantly, an asset to the community of people held in bondage, given his knowledge of the comings and goings in town and his ability to earn money of his own.

Indeed, like my ancestor, many of the enslaved learned the basics of what it would be like to be part of a working class by earning at the margins of enslavement. Charles Ball recalled that on the Georgia cotton plantation where he was held, the enslaved were incentivized to work more quickly in the field by the promise of a bit of cash if they outperformed their daily quota. Ball also remembered that the men and women on his plantation were permitted to work on their overseers' land for pay on Sundays. The enslaved found myriad ways to trade or even earn small amounts of money on the side, making baskets, carving bowls, selling cooked food or the extra produce from their garden plots, or performing skilled labor as hired slaves. This additional work gave them crucial opportunities to participate in the wage-based economy, and enabled them not only to purchase personal indulgences like tobacco or rum, but also to make collective plans as part of extended families about the best ways to support one another as a community of workers. The informal rules governing such side work differed from place to place and over time, but should be thought of as rather common to plantation economies across the South. Perhaps more impactful than the funds enslaved people earned were the ethics that governed their lives as wage-earning or bartering workers, beliefs that were centered around the need to support a wider circle of kith and kin, or, as one historian described it, "placing the imprint of kinship on the organization of labor."[29]

Although we can't be sure if Henry's skill and his value as a worker allowed him to earn an income as a hired slave, we do know that his position as blacksmith made him a valuable asset in Joseph Rucker's will. Henry was not freed when his slaveholder died, though some of the wealthiest plantation owners did choose to manumit some of their slaves in their wills. Notable also is that Rucker's will made no mention of Henry's family; it made no allowance for keeping Henry with his wife or any of his then four living children, aged twenty-three, seventeen, eleven, and seven. Instead, his family was counted among the unnamed, to be divided up among Rucker's heirs as they chose. Henry was passed down, not as a man with a family, but like a trust fund or antique furniture. The documentation of this horror did not erase his skill, nor did it sever his connection to his family or the larger community. Joseph Rucker's will would not be the last surviving archival record to chronicle Henry's life, but it was the last that would denote him as property.

Given the upheaval of the Civil War, it is hard to know if Joseph Rucker's documented wishes were carried out. It is clear that when the war ended, Henry and the other men, women, and children owned by Joseph's sons and daughter were given nothing but the clothes on their backs and the opportunity to keep working the same land that they worked as slaves. Of the fortune in land and money that Rucker left when he died in 1864, not one dollar of it went to those he once held in bondage, those whose bodies were broken to build his wealth. There would be no just accounting for the liberated. All they carried into their lives as free people was the community they built.

AT THE HEART OF THAT COMMUNITY WAS THE CHURCH. IT IS well understood today that the church is an essential institution of Black life in America, working class and otherwise. It is somewhat less understood that this reality can be traced back to the enslaved. The Black Christianity they built would come to serve as the core of Black community life. Working-class fights for education, mutual aid, and political movements—ranging from calls for fair treatment under the law to the fight for reparations—began in Black sacred spaces. African American churches provided not only sanctuaries for the expression of faith, but a launching pad for working-class organization.

Black people became Christians by following their own path. The

West Africans who arrived in bondage on American shores came with many different faiths of their own. Although Charles Ball grew up observing Christianity, he reported that many of the enslaved Africans he knew "believed there were several gods; some of whom were good, and others evil, and they prayed as much to the latter as to the former." He also noted that "natives of Africa, or descendants of those who have always, from generation to generation, lived in the [South] uniformly believe in witchcraft, conjuration, and the agency of evil spirits in the affairs of human life." Ball also met Muslim Africans, whom he called "Mohamedans." He noted that even in bondage one Muslim man who was held on the same plantation as him "prayed five times every day, always turning his face to the east, when in the performance of his devotion."[30] Africans or their descendants who converted to Christianity experienced their new faith filtered through their prior beliefs and understandings about the world.

Indeed, Black Christians should not be understood as simply subscribing to a Black version of white faith. Those who were regularly exposed to what Frederick Douglass called the "slaveholding religion" of their masters did not uncritically adopt it.[31] As one survivor of enslavement, Peter Randolph, explained, slaveholding ministers delivered a tainted faith: "the Gospel was so mixed with slavery, that the people could see no beauty in it, and feel no reverence for it."[32] The enslaved knew their masters did not pray for their freedom, so they remained justifiably critical of such a limited faith and sought to know God for themselves. So little was there to glean from the twisted legacy of the religion slaveholders tried to inculcate Sunday after Sunday that, as the Black theologian Howard Thurman described, "by some amazing but vastly creative spiritual insight the slave undertook the redemption of a religion that the master had profaned in his midst."[33] They took the profane faith handed down to them and built their own churches. Their way of knowing God would blend a diversity of African faith ways with a critical reading of the Bible from their own subjectivity as laborers held in intergenerational bondage. Together, the enslaved maintained an "invisible institution" behind brittle broken branches in the woods, a faith that would buttress a Black working class.[34]

Among the papers of Joseph Rucker's descendants are a handful of historic documents, including a letter from Alexander Hamilton, a bill of sale for enslaved people in the 1820s, and a series of land deeds. There is also a collection of religious tracts dating to 1813 from a British Anglican missionary organization, the Society for Promoting Christian Knowledge. The Society was one of the many faith organizations that called for the Christian conversion of the enslaved without substantively questioning the morality of slaveholding as an institution.[35] Perhaps the Rucker family used these tracts to structure worship for the people held in bondage on their plantations. Slaveholders knew that a community of slaves left to think for themselves could be formidable, and if organized against them, dangerous. In response, they developed a Christian mission that was intended to project their own moral code onto the enslaved. The faith communicated by slaveholders would be a Christianity focused almost exclusively on the role of the slaves as obedient and pliant servants of their earthly masters.

The Society that produced the tracts held in the Rucker papers had a foreign missionary wing called the Society for the Propagation of the Gospel in Foreign Parts (SPG). The SPG believed that its proselytizing could work hand in hand with the project of slavery, arguing that bondage was biblical and in line with Christian principles, and provided an opportunity to teach Africans and their descendants about Christ, an opportunity they would not have had if they had not come under the control of Europeans. The notion that Christianity was compatible with slavery was tested when the SPG was bequeathed a Barbadian sugarcane plantation by one Christopher Codrington, in 1710. Codrington believed in the maintenance of slavery as an institution and wanted to fund efforts to convert the enslaved to Christianity, so he left his 710-acre plantation—including three windmills for pressing the sugarcane, the boiling house (the island's largest) for processing the cane into sugar and molasses, a rum distillery, and 109 men, 115 women, 59 boys, and 28 girls in bondage—to the Society.[36] The SPG would govern the lands and profit from afar for well over one hundred years, under the leadership of a board of trustees that included the Archbishop of Canterbury, the Regius Professors of Divinity at Cambridge and Oxford, and bishops of the Church of England.

Although SPG theologian Richard Baxter's 1673 *Christian Directory* suggested that those who held slaves should "make it your chief end in buying and using slaves to win them to Christ and save their souls" and to "let their salvation be far more valued by you than their service," it is hard to imagine that conditions on Codrington Plantation won over many souls for Christ or that conversion was the driving interest even on a plantation owned in effect by the Church of England.[37] Like all other sugar plantations, it involved an exquisitely brutal form of slavery. Every aspect of enslaved workers' lives—from cutting cane, to processing it in the mills, to working in scalding distilleries—was dangerous. Working long hour upon hour left them vulnerable to catastrophic injuries and death.[38] The dangerous work, combined with the threat of tropical diseases and violent treatment meted out by overseers, resulted in four out of ten of those held in bondage on Codrington Plantation dying within three years of their arrival. The newly purchased were branded with the mark of their owner, leaving a scar that said "Society" on their chests so that if they ran away, they could be easily identified by slave hunters.[39]

The value of the sugar the slaves produced paid for the construction of Codrington College, an institution dedicated to theological education, on land adjacent to the plantation. Although Codrington's will had directed that the college might also be used to educate, though not free, the enslaved people on the island, the local landowners opposed the proposition as too dangerous and the Society honored their directives. Barbadian planters whose wealth was established through tight control over the enslaved so thoroughly opposed proselytizing and educating them that efforts at both were scarce.[40]

In 1833, when British abolitionists finally succeeded in their argument for the end of slavery with the passage of the Slavery Abolition Act, recompense became a focus—not for the formerly enslaved, who suffered to make tea sweet, but for slaveholders. Under the Slave Compensation Act of 1837, the British government paid owners for their newly freed property. The Society received over eight thousand pounds, money that was added to the treasury of Codrington College.[41] The SPG may have been unique as a church institution that held people in bondage, but it was far from alone in efforts to inculcate the enslaved with a version of Christianity that claimed chattel slavery was in tune with God's plan.

The same missionary spirit that sought to tamp down Black independence and emphasize slaves' duties to their masters also existed in Elbert County, Georgia, when Henry came of age. Christianity, stripped of its liberatory message, was promoted by Georgia's earliest colonizers. Slaveholder Daniel Tucker was one of Elbert County's earliest recorded white migrants, and was said to have "felt a deep responsibility toward the Negro slaves" and "spent much of his time praying with the slaves and . . . instructing them in religious matters." Both a Methodist minister and a slaveholder, Tucker did not believe that his Christian faith interfered with slavery; his status as a fellow large slaveholder meant that he would be "warmly welcomed" at other plantations to preach to the slaves. One Rucker family descendant insisted that the "Negroes adored him" and loved to hear him minister, so much so that they memorialized him in song. Tracing the roots of the slave folk song turned minstrel tune "Old Dan Tucker," an Elbert County historian and folklorist asserted that the song was "intended ... to be complimentary" about Reverend Tucker when it was first sung by his slave congregants. However, the lyrics depict Old Dan Tucker as a drunkard who showed up too late for supper, and had such a propensity for putting his foot in his mouth that he "died with the toothache in his heel."[42]

Tucker may have been one of the first slaveholders to travel the county preaching to the enslaved, but he wasn't the last. As a young man, the enslaved William Heard recalled attending "Sunday School [at] ten years of age, in Elberton, Georgia, at the Methodist Episcopal Church South." Heard learned "the Bible and Catechism, and committed much to memory." Lessons were then repeated by "some member of the white family ... during the week; so that there were those of us who could repeat whole Psalms and chapter after chapter in the Shorter Catechism. This was the education that came to a slave."[43]

These catechisms may have been those published by Charles Colcock Jones, a slaveholder and Presbyterian minister who sought to missionize among the people he held in bondage and those of his slaveholding peers. Raised on the wealth of Georgia coastal rice plantations and the prodigious knowledge of the Gullah people his family held, Jones was well educated and well traveled. Called to evangelical ministry at an early age, Jones grappled with the question of slaveholding as a young man exploring the world beyond the South. However, after returning to Georgia, Jones sought to thread the impossible needle of moral slaveholding, writing *The Religious Instruction of the Negroes in the United States*, which promoted a modified gospel to enslaved congregants, one that emphasized obedience to their masters and the importance of morality, marriage, and family. He also tried to foster benevolent paternalism among other slaveholding families, arguing that beneficence would lead to stability, productivity, and greater profits for the slave-holder. His approach, controversial at first, drew converts among slave-holders throughout the region.[44]

Jones endeavored to live up to the code he had constructed, which advised slaveholders to respect the sanctity of slave marriages and keep enslaved families together, while stressing that the enslaved should avoid sex, relationships, and children outside marriage. Yet in no state were marriages between enslaved people legal; their status as chattel was their primary relationship with the law. Nor did Jones adhere to his own dictates. When faced with debt and a slave family's history of resistance against his authority, he sold its members off. In fact, in each generation, the families owned by the Joneses experienced major upheavals and disruptions, as various members of the Jones family died or married and rearranged their property to suit their wants and perceived needs. Charles Colcock Jones's religion was governed by white supremacy and unilateral control by slaveholders.[45]

The enslaved were not empty vessels waiting to accept the lessons, asserted over and over, that "servants should obey your masters" and that it was "the devil . . . who tells you to try and be free."[46] Frederick Douglass was "filled with unutterable loathing when [he] contemplated" the man who "wields the blood-clotted cowskin during the week" and then "claims to be a minister of the meek and lowly Jesus." He had no tolerance for slaveholders who robbed him of his "earnings at the end of each week" and then on Sunday pretended to show him "the way of life, and the path of salvation." When white theologians attempted to convert them to a faith that did not address their subjugation, enslaved people recognized the lie.[47]

For Black believers, education was a key component of their distinct belief system. Heard recalled that his Sunday school instruction did not include learning "to read nor to write, as it was against the law."

Enslaved people were regularly reminded that the passages chosen by white slaveholders represented all they could know and that the punishment "for ... any slave caught writing" was "having his forefinger cut from his right hand." Such severe threats around literacy implicitly signaled the power of reading and writing. While enslaved, Douglass ran a secret Sunday school for those "who were trying to learn how to read the will of God" for themselves. One Georgia woman, Alice Green, noted that her mother learned to read by gleaning what she could from the white children whom she cared for daily, and had even taken one of their old schoolbooks and kept it "hid in her bosom." She remembered that she was "proud of every little scrap of book [learning]" she could clandestinely discern. After freedom, her mother became a teacher. Within the Black community there were always some who could read and write. The literate used their skills to expand what the enslaved knew about the broader text of the Bible and the events of the wider world.[48]

White attempts to monitor the conversion of Black souls failed miserably. Independent of white control, enslaved Black people built new churches that put them, the downtrodden, at the center of the story. As Charles Ball characterized it, "the idea of a revolution in the conditions of the whites and the blacks, is the corner-stone of the [Black] religion." Theirs was a faith that insisted that "those who have possessed an inordinate portion of the good things of this world, and have lived in ease and luxury, at the expense of their fellow men will surely have to render an account of their stewardship, and be punished, for having withheld from others the participation of those blessings, which they themselves enjoyed." The revolutionary Christianity created by Black people was not a faith of submission, but a call for justice in the hereafter for what they had been stripped of in this world.[49]

Given its critical stance, this faith had to be built in secret; one worshipper recounted that when they would gather to sing and pray, they would "take pots and put them right in the middle of the floor to keep the sound in the room . . . [to] keep the white folks from meddling . . . the sound will stay right in the room after you do that." The overturned pot was a remnant of an African faith, perhaps a symbol of a forgotten deity or part of a holy ritual; the details were lost but a sense of its power for the faithful remained. The overturned pot helped to make the hush harbor both quiet and holy, imbued with the authority of their old faith even as they worshipped in a new way.

One Elbert County resident and descendant of enslaved people, Samuel Calhoun, recalled his grandparents telling him about their worship in the woods "formed with a frame of cut pine trees" that blended in with the trees and was hard to discover. Some meeting places were even more simple; descendant Phoebe Turman heard her once-enslaved forebears say that "they would have a place to go to serve the Lord . . . sing and pray. . . . It was a big, old oak tree. Big, old, nice, shady oak tree, and that was their church." Rachel Adams remembered Black worshippers meeting in the slave quarters and then moving from house to house singing songs, reciting the Bible passages they had memorized, and preaching to one another.[50] One former slave minister, Peter Randolph, recounted that "the slaves [would] assemble in the swamps out of reach of the patrols." Guiding each other by "breaking boughs from the trees, and bending them in the direction of the selected spot," they would meet at an appointed time. These spaces were part of what historian Stephanie Camp called a "rival geography"—moving and movable spaces marked by the enslaved.[51] Randolph described their worship:

> They first ask each other how they feel, the state of their minds. . . . Preaching in order . . . then praying and singing all round, until they generally feel quite happy. The speaker usually commences by calling himself unworthy, and talks very

slowly, until, feeling the spirit, he grows excited, and in a short time, there fall to the ground twenty or thirty men and women under [the spirit's] influence. Enlightened people call it excitement; but I wish the same was felt by everybody, so far as they are sincere. The slave forgets all his sufferings, except to remind others of the trials during the past week, exclaiming: "Thank God, I shall not live here always!"

As this congregation finished their worship, they recognized the inherent fragility of their earthly bonds. Randolph described them "pass[ing] from one to another, shaking hands, and bidding each other farewell, promising should they meet no more on earth, to strive and meet in heaven."[52]

Even as new laws designed to stifle Black church meetings were put in place, the desire of the enslaved for congregation grew. In their secret gatherings, new leaders were born: those who could minister, those who could sing, those who could lead others to faith or to freedom. Here the enslaved came to know that they, not Pharaoh in the plantation big house, more closely mirrored God's chosen people. They maintained the faith that they would soon find freedom, a Jubilee and just recompense for their labor. When freedom did finally come, these congregations became the first free Black collective spaces. The churches that started without walls formed the basis of their working-class freedom. The lessons of those hushed conversations were passed down, becoming a guide for the first generations of Black people post-Emancipation.

THE WOOD FLOORS CREAKED UNDER THE WEIGHT OF THE LONG line of men waiting to register. Henry Rucker was unbothered by the heat that July day; he'd felt worse many times before. That day he was determined to be counted. He had been counted many times. Counted by overseers confirming that no one on the plantation had run. Counted by census-takers who did not report his name but ascertained his value as if he were for sale on the auction block. But that day, he would be counted as a citizen.

During the forty-three years he lived as a slave, the law had systematically blocked him from accessing a formal education. So, when he leaned over the table, he did not know how to write his own name. Instead, he marked a confident "X" on the middle of the line, certifying that he was a citizen of the state of Georgia and a resident of Elbert County, the place where he had been born a slave and where he would now be a voter. Even without formal education, he knew that citizenship should mean that he would have a say in what his country would be from that moment forward. Signing that registration book on July 19, 1867, the registrar wrote above the "X" the phrase "his mark." Indeed, even in the face of the violence Henry and his family faced on every side from those angry about the idea of Black freedom and citizenship, Henry made his mark. That day, his X provided rich testimony to his belief in his equality as a man, and his assertion that he should be a citizen. This registration is the only document I have found that was marked by his hand.[53]

For Henry, it must have been a long journey from Emancipation to becoming a voter and citizen. He had hoped that freedom would bring about an immediate change. Perhaps that change meant a bit of land for his family, perhaps it meant a small business, blacksmithing for the town as a free person. Like millions of others, he was seeking a tangible shift. After all, what had the men and women who had held them in bondage done to earn that land? What, beyond an inheritance of trickery and brute force, made them the rightful owners of acres upon acres of Georgia soil? What sweat had they poured into the land? Had the large landholders felled the ancient trees, hewed those mighty logs to build homes, sculpted the clay soil into irrigation ditches to water the crops, dried and fired that clay into bricks to construct plantation houses, forged the nails that held timbers together? Had they planted the vast fields of cotton, hoed row after row to keep weeds and grass from growing around the plants and stealing the nutrients? Did their hands move like lightning down the rows of white cotton? Did they bend low for hours on end in the blazing sun, with an overseer's whip cracking overhead? Had they endured the separation of their families in order to maximize someone else's profits? No. Black people had done that work. Black folk had suffered those losses. Surely, they were owed something. Their sweat and blood had seeped into the soil, it was only right to say that a portion of it should be theirs.[54]

After the four million enslaved people in the South were freed at the end of the Civil War, many hoped to own land or build their own prosperity, applying the skills that had once made them valuable as chattel. Yet while slavery had ended, the dynamics of the institution had not. In the flux of the postwar South, white landowners moved quickly to retain the productive capacity of the land they owned by putting the freed people back to work in ways that looked just like slavery. Free men and women fought back, because they wanted their working lives to be different. They wanted to work like yeoman farmers, in family units whose fortunes would rise and fall with their effort. Women wanted to care for their own children and tend to their own households, or labor under terms of their own choosing, not work exclusively in the fields or labor in white households to the detriment of their own.

Word had spread throughout the South that there was a Union general who had given out forty acres and a mule to the enslaved whom the army had freed. That experiment was being carried out more than two hundred miles away on the Sea Islands and coastal counties of South Carolina and Georgia, but the rumor reached Elbert County.[55] I have no

clear way of knowing for sure but I can imagine, given my own grandfather's abiding desire to own his own land, that his forebear, Henry,
was waiting, like many millions of others, for the opportunity to hold
just enough land to work with his wife and children. Given the size and
health of his family, surely together they could make a good living. Starting out with nothing was hard, but they would take on jobs and tasks
to try and create a strong household.[56] The little ones could help with
the work, but perhaps they would have the opportunity for school. The
family could raise some livestock, keep a kitchen garden, sell the extra
produce at the market. Perhaps they might earn enough to open a blacksmith's shop. His wife, Phoebe, could teach the little ones how to mind
their small home. I imagine that it was a simple vision—indeed, much
less than what they were owed.

But across the South, the white men who survived the bloody and
prolonged war were angry about the failure of the Confederacy, angry
about the ravaged landscape, and angry at the very idea that slaves might
now be counted as their equals. Elbert County was certainly no different. Its white residents did not offer a hand to the people who had once
labored to build the community's wealth; instead, they offered only the
butts, or muzzles, of their guns.

The Bureau of Refugees, Freedmen, and Abandoned Lands, popu-
larly known as the Freedmen's Bureau, was the federal agency established
to broker a peace between Black and white southerners and to help protect the labor rights of the formerly enslaved. Initially, the Bureau had
installed a "two-pronged labor policy in which some blacks farmed independently, while others worked as hired laborers for white employers."
Unfortunately, by 1866, the Bureau gave in to pressure from former
slaveholders and began to push Black laborers to work under contract
to the families that had once held them in bondage, squandering the
possibility for real change. Those freed people who asserted themselves

beyond the prescribed bounds were often murdered in their homes or tortured by white mobs. So, when Henry stood in line with other men, both Black and white, in the temporary shadow of safety provided by the Union troops outside, he was certainly risking his life. But at the same time, he must have felt, at least in this one way, that they might be moving forward to something a bit more like freedom.[57]

Many people in the nation were not nearly as brave as Henry when it came to making freedom for former slaves substantive. President Andrew Johnson, who came into office after Abraham Lincoln's assassination, did not have the stomach to punish the Confederate rebels and cared little about the plight of the emancipated. Johnson was a Tennessee Democrat who had been only nominally anti-slavery prior to the war. As president, he seemed interested in a return to the prewar status quo. Even after meeting with Frederick Douglass, who argued for the full and quick enfranchisement of Black men, Johnson refused to consider the measure; instead, he moved to pardon ex-Confederates and turned a blind eye as Southern states restricted the rights of the freed people. When state legislatures instituted Black Codes, undercutting the rights of Black workers and attempting to return them to servitude, Johnson did nothing. The president didn't even respond when Georgia state legislators elected Alexander Stevens, the former vice president of the Confederate States, and Herschel Johnson, a Confederate senator, to be US senators. Most notably, Johnson was silent when the Georgia state legislature put into place a new constitution that mirrored the old one, limiting the franchise to "free white male citizens," and instituting harsh penalties for vagrancy to limit Black mobility and laws that bound Black agricultural laborers to a form of ongoing peonage.[58]

In response to Johnson's betrayal of the freed people, the US Congress, controlled by "Radical Republicans"—a faction of the party insistent on immediate freedom and equality for African Americans—

sought to establish civil rights and provide protection for former slaves. They passed the Military Reconstruction Acts, requiring the former Confederate states to extend the franchise to Black men on an equal basis with white men and pass new state constitutions that enshrined those rights in state law. The Congress's call for the registration of qualified male voters over twenty-one, regardless of race, became the first mass registration of freed Black men. Henry Rucker's mark signified that he was one of the more than 93,000 Black men who registered in Georgia, doing his part in a historic effort to upend the logic of slavery.[59]

Black enfranchisement was met with white violence throughout the South. In Elbert County, mobs of white men terrorized the Black populace, marauding throughout northeast Georgia and across the Savannah River into South Carolina. According to the accounts of the local agent of the Freedmen's Bureau, throughout 1867 there was a pitched battle between the newly freed and the former slaveholders and overseers for control of the Piedmont. One Georgia Bureau agent begged for additional troop support, writing that "in this section of the state" the former slaves are "not freedmen and women . . . they are nominally such, but their condition indeed is worse than bondage itself and ever will be unless this subdistrict is flooded with . . . cavalry. . . . The US soldiers and the freedmen are alike threatened and despised, and very little respected."[60]

Still facing white violence, the community forged in enslavement now organized in freedom. Even in hard circumstances, this work was meaningful. William Heard recalled the moment that he thought of as the "dawn of political awakening for the Negro" in Elbert County, when "the Rev. William J. White, a Baptist preacher from Augusta, Georgia," and a native of Ruckersville, returned home "as an agent of the Freedmen's Bureau, and made a political speech." Hundreds of Black men and women gathered to hear him. White "was the first colored man [Heard] had ever seen who was well educated, and who could use the King's English readily, accurately and convincingly." His boldness had a big impact on young William, who from that moment forward was "determined . . . to be a MAN, and to fill an important place in life's arena."[61]

Although the moment of freedom provided new inspiration, Black working people already had a sense of the importance of coupling their lives as workers with political engagement and a deep investment in one another. Emboldened by the presence of Union troops, Black organizers began meeting to envision their future. They gathered, constantly and regularly, in order to spearhead the creation of a new world for themselves and their kin. They met in grand conferences and in rural churches, in open fields, migrant campgrounds, homes, and, of course, in the woodsy hush harbors, to discuss the possibility of land ownership, political organizing, and the establishment of labor organizations and mutual aid societies. Black men and women created new organizations formed out of their old beliefs. They founded Union Leagues, electing leaders and practicing the work of citizenship. Laundresses, maids, and cooks met to join forces so that, rather than compete with one another, they could collectively set fair prices for their labor. Black people met to organize schools for their children and one another. And importantly, they met to share news of their place in local, state, and national politics. They cared deeply about what would happen next, in their lives and in the life of their nation. And probably more often than anything else, they met to talk about land. From the beginning, their interests as workers and their rights as citizens were intertwined.

In Elbert County, the presence of Reverend White in his home county as an agent of the Freedmen's Bureau and a voting rights advocate was transformational for Black organizers, but for local white politicians and landholders, he was far from welcome. In response to his organizing, white Democrats attacked Reverend White's horse, plastering the animal with hot tar, no doubt not only to stop his movement but also to foreshadow further attacks on the minister. Undeterred, White had someone treat the horse's burns, and then hitched the injured animal to his buggy, which was now pulled by a new horse, so that he could continue to spread the gospel of collective political self-determination to former slaves.[62]

The threat leveled on Reverend White was just one instance of the terror that became a regular occurrence in Elbert County. The Ku Klux Klan, a South-wide organization of former Confederate soldiers organized in 1866 to assert white power and intimidate the former slaves, was soon dominant throughout the county and the wider region. Klan night riders, disguising their identity under white hoods and robes in the cover of darkness, did their best to intimidate, beat, burn, and kill their Black neighbors in order to silence them as voters and organizers.

Just across the Savannah River in nearby Abbeville County, South Carolina, the Klan undertook a devastating campaign to attack Black voters during the national elections of 1868. Klan terrorists broke into one Black candidate's home and destroyed the Republican ballots the party had prepared. They went on to threaten another man, Frank Talbert, at gunpoint, making him swear that he would vote for the Democratic ticket. The mob rampaged night after night, forcing hundreds of free families to flee to the woods, much like resistant slaves had done during slavery. The Klan murdered one resident, seventy-five-year-old Jake Jones, who in his old age was not fast enough to escape his home as the Klan attacked. The local Freedmen's Bureau agent reported that "innumerable persons have been lying out in the woods since sometime before the election to save being murdered in their beds, their houses having in the meantime been frequently visited at night for that purpose." Publicly declaring "that death would be visited on any one who attempted to vote the Republican ticket," the Klan was successful in keeping hundreds of Black voters away from the polls.[63] White Georgians terrorized Black voters throughout the state.

When Henry Rucker registered and voted, he risked his life. Those risks taken by Henry and thousands of other Black voters allowed the nation to move definitively toward enshrining birthright citizenship and equal protection under the law when the state legislature, under Republican control, ratified the Fourteenth Amendment to the US Constitution. Violence dogged Black voters in 1868 and 1869, yet fleeting victories were achieved during the state constitutional convention and after the general election in 1868, when Georgia elected a Republican governor, Rufus Bullock, and sent thirty-two Black elected officials to the state legislature. Among those elected was Reverend Henry McNeal Turner, a Black minister from Newberry, South Carolina, who was born free and had organized a Union regiment of Black troops and served as their chaplain during the war. Assigned to troops in Georgia by the Freedmen's Bureau, he became interested in running for political office to advance the freedmen's cause. After the war, Turner was tremendously hopeful that the promise of citizenship and equality would become a reality. At an Emancipation Day celebration in 1866, he encouraged the audience to "let by-gones be by-gones" and work to not "insult [white people] for past grievances, respect them; honor them; work for them; but still let us be men." He was optimistic that by demonstrating their willingness to work in a "respectable, virtuous, honest, and industrious" manner, "prejudice will melt away."[64]

Despite Reverend Turner's hopes for peace, white racism in Georgia hardened. White Democrats pushed to reject Black officeholders, arguing that Black elected officials were not explicitly condoned by the state constitution. As a result, only four of the thirty-two Black elected officials were allowed to stay in office, because they were said to be light-skinned enough to be declared "honorary whites." Turner spoke out against the ejection of Black legislators in a fiery response, reminding the legislators:

> Why, sir, though we are not white, we have accomplished much. We have pioneered civilization here; we have built up your country; we have worked in your fields and garnered your harvests for two hundred and fifty years! And what do we ask of you in return? Do we ask you for compensation for the sweat our fathers bore for you for the tears you have caused, and the hearts you have broken, and the lives you have curtailed, and the blood you have spilled? Do we ask retaliation? We ask it not. We are willing to let the dead past bury its dead; but we ask you, now for our rights. . . . We, who number hundreds of thousands in Georgia, including our wives and families, with not a foot of land to call our own strangers in the land of our birth; without money, without education, without aid, without a roof to cover us while we live, nor sufficient clay to cover us when we die! It is extraordinary that a race such as yours, professing gallantry and chivalry and education and superiority, living in a land where ringing chimes call child and sire to the church of God a land where Bibles are read and Gospel truths are spoken, and where courts of justice are presumed to exist; it is extraordinary that, with all these advantages on your side, you can make war upon the poor defenseless black man.[65]

That September white residents in South Georgia mobbed a gathering of Black voters who had marched from Albany to rally in the town of Camilla, ambushing and then mowing them down by gunfire in the town square.[66] Outraged by the egregious violence and blatant voter suppression, the Republican-controlled US Congress placed Georgia under Military Reconstruction for a second time. This brief window of enforced equality allowed the Georgia legislature to ratify the Fifteenth Amendment, which specifically enfranchised Black men.[67]

By 1871, the experiment in interracial governance had collapsed. The Republican governor of Georgia was run out of office. The remaining white Republicans tried to negotiate with white Democrats and only succeeded in undoing many of the gains that had been made. The wide-scale disfranchisement that would characterize the rest of the South in the early twentieth century had already taken hold in Georgia in the 1870s, with the passage of high poll taxes that effectively prevented Black voters from exercising the franchise. The close of Reconstruction and the withdrawal of federal troops in the spring of 1877 opened the way for extreme violence in Georgia. Violence became the norm for any Black person attempting to assert their rights as citizens. Yet Black communities, those hush harbors that began in bondage, would continue their work. Their "memory of the political" would be passed down to future generations.[68]

———

IF YOU SAW THEM FROM A DISTANCE, GLIMPSING THEM THROUGH the trees, you would wonder why those lights were swaying at a steady pace, tracking slowly up the dirt road. Through the low light of the dusk, you'd see a caravan of wagons leaving the small community of Moss, Georgia, wheels creaking in singsong patterns. They were cautious still, but they were finally free. The young fathers were in front, encouraging old mules and mares to go up the road guided by the light of their lanterns. The weighed-down wagons filled with family and friends, young and old, came next. Others came on foot, women with the simple patterns on their Sunday best dresses rustling in the breeze. Men with their hats low and a little to the side walking cautiously behind or guiding

the way out front. Then you would hear them: the young ones chatter-
ing in excitement after not seeing one another for a few days. Traveling
a few miles, as they finally came close to the white clapboard building,
you'd hear the old folks start to sing. They'd feel it deep in their chests,
a resonant call and response in long-meter singing, one of the very, very
old songs that suddenly felt quite new. As they gathered in the neatly
swept churchyard, they shared warm greetings with their church family, and as they walked into the building together they ushered in the
spirit, moving as one. Inside the wooden sanctuary, they would give what
they called testimony, words sung or shouted out about what the speaker
had survived since the congregation had last met, and about the abiding goodness of the Lord that had carried them through. After collective
acknowledgment of what they worked to overcome, and the mighty and

"Sunday in Little Rock, Arkansas, 1935." Fellowship after Sunday service.

BEN SHAHN, *SCHOMBURG CENTER FOR RESEARCH IN BLACK CULTURE,*
NEW YORK PUBLIC LIBRARY DIGITAL COLLECTIONS

matchless work of the Lord, they would sing songs filled with the tones and rhythms of their forebears, then finally listen to a sermon that ended with shouts in cadence from preacher and congregation, transfixed and transformed, praising as one. Those nights of worship, started in secret under slavery, continued on in freedom, in churches that finally had walls.

In the years following Reconstruction, the founding of new churches became a central activity of the Black community. It is said that the Reverend Henry McNeal Turner helped to found at least one hundred African Methodist Episcopal (AME) congregations in Georgia. Many of these churches—AME, Baptist, Colored Methodist Episcopal (CME)—represented the formalization of existing informal congregations. In churches, big and small, informal congregations became formal congregations. Elbert County would have several churches that grew out of the early gatherings.

William Heard was one of the thousands who now formalized his faith. He was inspired by the Reverend Aaron Harris, presiding elder of the CME Church in Elberton. Even before he considered himself a Christian, Heard became active in this congregation, serving as "secretary of the Official Board and Quarterly Conference in the C. M. E. Church."[69] The church at Elberton was part of a network of CME congregations, still considered today a Black working-class denomination. Heard recalled that Elberton was visited by one of the leaders of the church, Bishop Richard Vanderhorst. Listening to Vanderhorst deliver his sermon, Heard felt transformed and newly "determined to be a Christian, and fill important places in the Church and in social life." That night he stood to make the confession of his faith and he was so overcome that his "mouth flew open and [he] shouted for joy."

Many white observers dismissed Black churches as sites of a primitive, ecstatic faith, spaces where Black people could shout and stomp away their troubles. One white woman missionary who came South to teach the free children, Laura Towne, characterized Black worship as "the remains of some old idol worship," and dismissed it as "savage" and "heathenish."[70] Black congregations were thought of as a relatively safe means of occupying the attention of Black workers, to distract them from demanding more. But church houses were more than just places to worship; they retained their subversive power. Churches would be the spaces that nurtured the political vision Black people had for themselves. Small church houses became a training ground to prepare for the next fight. Churches drew less attention than political organizations did, but they could serve similar purposes.

Many of Elbert County's black congregations that are still in existence today were founded during Reconstruction: Mount Calvary Missionary Baptist Church, Tate's Grove, Beulah Baptist, and Hunter's Chapel all grew out of hush harbors. Coming out of the woods, these once secret congregations grew large, baptizing new converts in the river once used to aid escapes from bondage. These churches became what one Elbert County resident, Rufus Bullard, described as "the center of . . . community" born in slavery, still communicating in codes only they fully understood. Like Beulah in the Bible, they would be the fulfillment of God's promise, in a land where they, too, might be favored and blessed by the Lord.[71]

So, freedom fell well short of what Henry and thousands of others had fought for at the ballot box. That his family was alive and with him was a blessing not every free person had. His wife, Phoebe, his children, and now his grandchildren did not live under the constant threat of sale and separation; that must have meant something. He was still part of the community, born in slavery, now surviving in freedom. I imagine him dreaming of what a fully realized freedom could eventually mean for his children. Although he would not live to fulfill it, he had a vision of what freedom should be.

Within that still-striving community, the formerly enslaved kept the story before them. They knew what they were owed even as white people were bent on vengeance for any expression of Black citizenship. There would be no just repayment for the years of labor put in for the enrichment of others, but freedpeople would pass down the knowledge of the injustice to their children and grandchildren. Henry would bequeath his uniquely Black faith. He would teach his progeny about the value of owning your own labor and your own land. That would be his legacy and the continuing ethic of his community. Black people salvaged one crucial thing from the fires all around them. That gift, the idea and the habit and the insistence of working together to build congregation and community, they passed down. This would be the story that would make it, over the generations, to me.

CHAPTER TWO

Sarah at Home,
Working on Her Own Account

Sadie's unforgiving eyes darted from place to place, trying to take in every detail as she walked through the front yard. She saw the mud hole so large she had to jump over it to avoid getting wet, the thin Bermuda grass that was crushed down, and the gluey red clay that threatened to swallow her shoes whole.[1] When the young widow finally made it around the shotgun house and caught her first glimpse of the backyard—and its zinc washtubs, metal rub boards, and four clothes-lines bowed by the weight of a rainbow of undergarments, dresses, skirts, shirts, and sheets—she knew she had found what she was looking for. There were two young women, their black arms deep in white suds, scrubbing away at dirty garments, and an older woman with her head wrapped in a white bandana chatting with a neighbor.

Sadie paused at the corner of the house, just out of sight, listening to the way they spoke. Her breath quickening to the rhythm of their

"Black and white, an informal portrait of a young Negro woman surrounded by laundry in Newport, Rhode Island, 1903." A washerwoman at the turn of the twentieth century.   GERTRUDE KÄSEBIER, *LIBRARY OF CONGRESS*

speech, she gasped when she heard one of them mention jail.[2] Finally, she stepped out and cleared her throat to announce her presence; the women turned quickly and saw her. Immediately, the neighbor retreated and the women in the yard stopped what they were doing. The three of them tried their best to be courteous, offering a rickety chair and a rag for Sadie to clean the mud from her shoes.[3] Her lead had panned out. That cold February morning in 1939 Sadie Hornsby, a white researcher employed during the New Deal by the Federal Writers' Project, had arrived in the yard of an authentic Negro washerwoman.[4]

Later that same afternoon, perhaps with the tune "A Bundle of Rags" from her childhood buzzing in her head,[5] Sadie recalled the washerwomen she had seen growing up. Not just the tall and straight-backed Black women carrying baskets of bundles on their heads like Africans she had seen in real life; she thought also of the distorted images of minstrelized washerwomen, perpetually bent over washtubs with their misshapen, monstrously large buttocks in the air, their heavy black faces accented by artificially distended, smiling lips hovering just inches above the deep white suds in front of them. Used to sell everything from bath soap and detergent to washing machines, such imagery was everywhere. When Sadie was little, her mother may have bought Higgins German Laundry Soap to wash her own delicates in the sink. She could still picture the box bearing an illustration of a washerwoman declaring: "Dar's no use talking Missus. Higgins Soap am de soap."[6] She remembered that, when she was a girl, kids laughed at the calendar cards that came in each box of Higgins Soap, each featuring a washerwoman cartoon representing a day of the week and one of seven uses of their product. The Monday card had a laundress declaring that "Monday is de wash day, an I neber sulk or mope, becase de close am nice and clean by using Higgins Soap."[7]

So when she saw the washerwoman's daughters—the three women

"Beware of Imitations." Washerwomen's black skin being "washed white" was a regular feature of advertisements, as if Black people's skin was brown from dirt rather than melanin. Note that the cartoon woman's right hand is white, in contrast to the rest of her body.   *WARSHAW COLLECTION OF BUSINESS AMERICANA, ARCHIVES CENTER, NATIONAL MUSEUM OF AMERICAN HISTORY, SMITHSONIAN INSTITUTION*

in the backyard were a mother and her two daughters—she may have chuckled and thought back to the Gold Dust Twins, two identical black boys, "Goldie" and "Dustie," used to market Gold Dust washing powder. Depicted as naked or wearing emasculating tutus, the two were often pictured taking a bath in a laundry washtub. The image of the washerwoman was so popular, in fact, that some white women were fêted with a washerwoman-themed bridal shower when they got married. Such events were all the rage when Sadie was a young bride.

Family and friends would don elaborate blackface drag, wearing "big red handkerchiefs on their heads" and "costumes to match" as a fun way to present the young bride with white linens for her marital bed.

In Sadie's childhood, too, she was told spooky tales of Soap Sally, said to be a laundress who lived all alone deep in the woods. The story stood as a warning against exploring wooded areas too deeply or traveling alone for long distances, for fear that Soap Sally would capture young kids and then boil down their bodies in a wash pot, using their fat to make soap and then the same soap to wash their family's clothes. When Sadie recalled looking at Black women in the yard that day in February 1939, sheets billowing in the wind, she may have imagined that that kind of uncontrolled Black womanhood could be deadly.[8]

Drawing on the images bubbling up in her mind, Sadie went home to type up her account of her experiences with Sarah and her daughters, recording their speech in a way that rendered their English almost unreadable, turning the name "Caroline" into "Ca'Line" and the word "sent" into "sont." Meanwhile, she transcribed her own Southern speech—she was a North Carolinian living in Athens, Georgia—as though her words had been spoken in the King's English.[9] After all, without such a discrepancy how could she possibly capture the feeling of being with a real live washerwoman? As she punched down on the heavy keys, she was sure to record the things that caught her eye in the yard that day—the bandanas framing their shining faces, the bubbling of the wash pot, the deep unknowable blackness of the women's skin. It was her job to capture what few white southerners of her generation had seen for themselves: Black washerwomen at work in their own yard. She knew that what she saw that day could have been the scene behind slave quarters more than one hundred years prior, or depicted on a minstrel stage, unchanged by history.[10]

ON THE DAY SADIE ARRIVED IN HER BACKYARD, SARAH HILL had been sick for almost a week, suffering from a flu that brought on a nasty fever and body aches much more debilitating than the usual aches in her back and shoulders caused by years of repetitive wringing and scrubbing. As she had on so many days, she pushed past how she felt, to get up with the rising sun. It was her wash day. Her younger daughter, Caroline, and her oldest, Mary—the one she called Sister—had promised to not seek day work cleaning so that they could help her get all the laundry washed and up on the line. Although her chest was still tight and congested her fever had broken, so she put on her stockings and a clean housedress, wrapped her head, put on her coat, and made her way to her chilly backyard, warmed only by the fires under heavy wash pots full of boiling water.

She sat in her chair to watch her girls do the work she'd taught them when they were little. Now they were young women, but Sarah was still making sure they took meticulous care of each garment in their quick, strong hands, just as her sisters had once taught her.[11] They had to be excellent nowadays, because there was so much competition; some white people used fancy new machines, while others gave their clothes to commercial laundries. When Sarah had started, the overwhelming majority of laundry was done by Black women, often gathering in one yard and sharing the duties of collecting wood and making soap and starch. Together they kept a watchful eye on one another's children. The little folks helped, too, gathering wood to keep the pots roiling. Together, under a few tall trees, they were not only stoking the fires under each other's pots, but also talking and planning. That collective was successful in training younger women; Sarah acquired such a good reputation and had so much work that she had to turn down additional customers and refer them to her neighbors. Yet now, in 1939, she was on the lookout for new ones. Still experiencing the after-effects of the Depression, some customers had asked her to wash less frequently, and most were much more exacting about each and every garment, as if they were searching for excuses to pay less.[12] One week Sarah even had to buy a shirt to replace one that her customer accused her of losing in the wash, costing her everything she had made doing that family's laundry for the week.[13] Even though it was hard to stand for long, she paced in the yard that cold winter morning, determined to make sure that they could get as much laundry done as possible. They needed to make enough money to replenish their cornmeal and perhaps buy a little meat to flavor her beans that week.

Midway through the morning, she was chatting with her neighbor when she heard a knock on her front door. Assuming it was a friend or someone from church checking in on her because illness had kept her away the previous Sunday, she called for them to come around the back. To her surprise, the visitor was a primly dressed white woman walking awkwardly across the rain-soaked yard, staring in horror at the Georgia clay collecting on her shoes.[14] Sarah greeted the stranger, asking her daughters to get her a chair and a rag to wipe her feet, as she tried to figure out what she was doing there. The woman explained that she worked for the government and wanted to know about Sarah's work washing clothes.

This uninvited guest made the congestion in Sarah's chest grip even tighter. She struggled to figure out the best way to get this white stranger out of her yard, wondering aloud why she wanted to know about her. When she heard the stranger's request for an interview, as if she, Sarah, was some head of state, she laughed and suggested that she could probably "find somebody else . . . who had a better story . . . to tell." Sarah was tired and had work to do making sure her daughters got everything just right that day, so she told the woman that she was sure that her work wouldn't be impressive or meaningful to white folks.[15] But the woman didn't leave, so Sarah was compelled to share some of what she could.

Sarah had to open not only her yard and its wash pots and clotheslines for review, but also the interior of her home for anthropological observation. She had no choice; after all, there was no good way to refuse the request of a white woman. The racial etiquette of segregation that governed Black behavior in 1939 in Athens, Georgia, and in most small Southern towns put no real limits on where white residents could go, but enmeshed Black southerners in an elaborate, often unspoken set of customs, enforced by violence, that constrained their every move. These customs dictated that Sarah could never walk through the front door of Sadie's home. Laws prevented Sarah's daughters from eating at a white restaurant in Athens, or staying at a white hotel downtown, or entering the town's esteemed "public" university as anything other than a servant. That day, Sarah wished there was some parallel rule that could have prevented this white woman from plunking down in her backyard on wash day.[16] But there was no real truth to "separate but equal." Segregation was not really about separation; it was a system designed to constantly stigmatize Black citizens.

So, Sarah was pleasant and syrupy. She smiled. She made a fuss about wiping off Sadie Hornsby's shoes, she shared reports of her daughter loving a white employer's children as much as she did the children in her own family, and even suggested that she was not frustrated by that one client who demanded that a whole week's pay be dedicated to purchasing a new shirt.[17] She even offered to share slices of their country ham as soon as it was done curing. She put on her very best "whitefolks manner," a mask of submissiveness that she hoped would maintain a distance and keep her family safe.[18] She showed Hornsby some of the details of the backyard work—the gathering of the water, the boiling of dirty clothes, making starch on the stovetop, the science of keeping close account of each article of clothing, sorted properly by the client who owned it, and the hot and dangerous process of smoothing out the wrinkles with cast-iron instruments.[19]

Halfway through their conversation, Sarah started to hope that perhaps this woman's government connections might help her get her husband a carpentry job or a Social Security pension or assist her daughters in finding steady work with the government. Sarah knew that white women were sent to folks' homes to judge whether they might be worthy of relief. She and the family hinted at those ideas to Sadie, but in doing so they did not reveal much about themselves.[20] Sarah laughed, smiled, extended courtesies, and did what she had to do, while not coming close to giving a full account of her life. She did not share the most crucial details. She talked about the work, but most of her emotions, and her thoughts about her emotions, she kept to herself.[21]

The document Hornsby drew up after their conversation, inexplicably titled "Bea, The Washerwoman," reads like so many of the other Federal Writers' Project interviews conducted by white southerners. The misnaming in the title hints that her accounts were not a strict record of what was said and heard, but rather a set of impressionistic renderings of Black life by a white observer at the height of segregation—full of judgment, disdain, and incomprehension. Sadie Hornsby presented her idea of a primitive washerwoman—her report notes Sarah's "cheap" furnishings, a leak in her kitchen, the mud in her yard. Describing her as "about five feet tall and . . . very black" with a "white cloth wound turban fashion around her head,"[22] Hornsby could only see in Hill the stereotype of a washerwoman that would have been recognizable to white readers: black, ignorant, and profoundly unknowable.[23]

Invisible to Hornsby were the skills Sarah possessed. Sarah knew how to put the wind to work. How to make soap rise from ashes and

"Photograph of African American woman washing clothes, Augusta, Richmond County, Georgia." With a washpot and the wind, Black women could work in their own yards.   COURTESY *GEORGIA ARCHIVES, VANISHING GEORGIA COLLECTION*, RIC195

grease. How to make industrial refuse into wash pots and fire. How to take hold of hot iron to smooth and not to burn. How to make the white people's filthy things bright and white like new. This knowledge wasn't innate; these skills were her inheritance from her sisters, both in blood and in community, passed down from woman to woman working shoulder to shoulder in concert with one another. Taking in laundry gave Sarah the power to choose who she worked for and when, and the pace of her labor was set by no man. Her time was set by her own hand. This work that her ancestors first learned in slavery but then later used to establish their own households after Emancipation formed the foundation of her freedom.

Today, many Americans tend to correlate the idea of freedom with financial success in a capitalist system. Freedom, in this sense, includes freedom from debt, and the ownership of property and wealth that you can pass down to your children. Sarah and other Black working women saw the world differently. They had little in the way of property, but they possessed their own guiding principles that could be traced to their slave past. They came together to build a way of life, a working-class ethic that valued the few things that the Emancipation did give them: mobility, independence, and solidarity. They took the skills that had made them prized property as women in bondage, and put them to work for themselves. Recognizing the monopoly they had on the arduous business of washing clothes, and well before they had the right to vote, generations of Black washerwomen stood together. They took leading roles in organizing movements to set the terms of their labor, improve their pay, care for the vulnerable members of their communities, and determine their political futures. As white politicians increasingly sought to segregate, disenfranchise, and police the Black working class, the women who worked as laundresses were the heart of a community determined to resist and survive. They were essential to that fight.

As enslaved women, they had imagined what freedom might be. Though reality fell far short of their expectations, as they faced the violence and degradation of a post-slavery world still ruled by the white men and women who had held them in bondage, they did not fail their families or one another. Like the generations before them, they drew on the resources of community that they had built and made what they needed to survive. Just as urban assembly lines would lead to union organizing, the yards or urban alleyways behind washerwomen's houses fostered community and a collective consciousness about the value of their work, providing them the space to strategize together, literally lightening one another's loads. Rather than outbidding one another, they set base prices collectively, and at holidays came together to take time off. With their nickels they founded mutual aid societies that buried the dead and paid out when a member was sick. And every so often, they would come together to strike for better treatment and pay. Sadie Hornsby saw what Sarah Hill did *not* have that February day in her spare and trampled yard, but that makes sense. Washerwoman was her job, not who she was.[24] The power of what Sarah had could not be seen by white onlookers, but it was there, simmering beneath the surface, blurred by black skin and the shining, iridescently white suds.

———

THOUGH MOST WHITE AMERICANS COULD ONLY DIMLY PERceive it, washerwomen, or laundresses, occupied a central place in Black life, history, and culture. Harriet Tubman was not only a freedom fighter but a skilled washerwoman. With the funds she earned "keeping an eating house," she paid for the construction of the washhouse at Beaufort, the first Southern city captured by Union forces during the Civil War. There she helped coordinate women who had fled from plantations and set them up as a corps of independent workers who did the crucial work of washing the uniforms of Union soldiers and the linens for the army hospital.[25] Booker T. Washington worried that their skills would not be passed down to new generations of young people striving for professional success and greater distance from a slave past. The brilliant Black educator Nannie Helen Burroughs sought to professionalize washerwomen's training and increase their pay.[26] The most beloved poet of the Harlem Renaissance and chronicler of the Black experience, Langston Hughes, wrote an elegy to them commending the way they turned the small proceeds earned from their washtubs into enough money to build homes for their families.[27] The people's historian and founder of what eventually became Black history month, Carter G. Woodson, wrote an essay that doubled as a historic praise-song for their contribution, chronicling their work as free Black women in the antebellum North and as freedwomen in the postbellum South. He credited not only the washerwomen's cash in a cash-poor economy, but also their collective consciousness for enabling Black families to buy homes, educate children, erect church houses, and start businesses.[28]

Perhaps the keenest insight into the culture of laundresses can be found in the work of the novelist, short story writer, and anthropologist Zora Neale Hurston, who spent years gathering together the stories of working-class Black southerners and chronicling the sound, feel, and beliefs of working-class communities like the one in which she grew up in Eatonville, Florida. Hurston captured a bit of the fierce and dangerous independence of the "wash-woman" in one of her most iconic tales, "Sweat." The short story, first published in the Harlem Renaissance quarterly magazine *Fire!!*, introduced Delia Jones, a Florida woman seemingly broken by her abusive and philandering husband, Sykes, who resents her and "the white folks' clothes" she sorts in piles around her home in preparation for wash day.[29] We learn that Delia was once beautiful, but hard work and Sykes's violence have left her once vibrant face drawn with pain. In spite of, or perhaps because of, her brokenness, Delia begins to stand up to Sykes, resisting his insistence that her home is rightfully his and that he can do what he wants with it, her, and his mistress.

The crucial moment in the story arrives when Sykes leaves a laundry soap box on the front step. Thinking that he is finally contributing to her work rather than castigating her, Delia is horrified when she looks inside the box to find not white flakes, but the thick stripes on the back of a large poisonous snake. For several days Sykes uses the creature as a tool of intimidation and terror, going as far as to leave it in the laundry basket in their darkened bedroom. The story ends with Sykes dying from a bite from the very copperhead he hoped would kill Delia, as she listens from the yard. The washerwoman's quiet and deadly determination to be free from work inside white folks' homes, and from living under an abusive man's thumb, is the lesson of Hurston's Black feminist tale.

Although it's difficult to imagine now, given that laundry is a domestic task done in our homes by computerized washing machines, in busy commercial laundromats, or in technologically advanced dry cleaners, at one time hundreds of thousands of Southern Black women washed the overwhelming majority of clothes in the region by hand. Most Southern cities had white-owned industrial laundries, which dealt with large-scale orders of linens for hotels and restaurants, as well as perhaps small storefront hand laundries owned by Chinese immigrants, who were pushed toward laundry work when they were prevented by racist bosses from working in other industries. But Black women did well over 90 percent of the laundry. By 1900, had it been considered a single industry, laundry would have been the country's third-largest employer of Black women, behind agriculture and domestic work. Black women who migrated to other parts of the US or whose ancestors had once been enslaved in the North also did laundry work; in fact, Black women were overrepresented in laundry work everywhere, including in regions where they were only a tiny minority. The statistics are remarkable: Black women made up only 11 percent of the women in the US in 1900, but they constituted almost 65 percent of the washerwomen.[30]

W. E. B. Du Bois accurately noted all the ways in which freedom had the ironic consequence of effectively de-skilling Black workers. Even though many Black men were skilled workmen, trained as blacksmiths, bricklayers, or carpenters when they were enslaved, after the Civil War, as free laborers, they were unwanted competition for white men. Cut off from opportunities to work in trades as higher-paying opportunities for skilled workmen and artisans were increasingly set aside for white men, the majority of Black men working in the cities of the South and the North were limited to manual labor or personal service.[31] Although Du Bois's observation was made about working men, the traditional frameworks that have defined skilled and unskilled labor were shaped by gender as well as by race. While most observers classified laundry work as menial and unskilled, the work of a laundress actually required immense skill. As enslaved women, that skill made them valuable on the auction block, but as free women it was systematically discounted.

Laundresses were largely dismissed as women who just picked up dirty clothes from their clients and returned them cleaned and pressed by the end of the week; most Americans did not consider the expertise that went into their labor. The art and science of washing clothes was passed down from one generation to the next. Sarah Hill had learned from her sister-in-law, who raised her after her parents passed away; Sarah recalled that she was a "mighty good trainer."[32] The work of a laundress was hard; it required toting heavy loads of dirty clothes from white

"Mrs. Annie Albrittan, who does washing in her home in Woodville, Greene County, Georgia, November 1941." Using irons heated in a bucket of coals or on a woodstove, skilled washerwomen pressed nearly every garment they laundered.

JACK DELANO, *SCHOMBURG CENTER FOR RESEARCH IN BLACK CULTURE, NEW YORK PUBLIC LIBRARY DIGITAL COLLECTIONS*

customers located all over the city, drawing several buckets of water from well pumps or pulleying heavy buckets to wash and to rinse, bringing that water to a boil, then washing the clothes at just the right temperature. Laundresses managed large loads of clothes without the benefit of technology other than a washboard and a clothesline. They rendered fat and potash to make lye and used that lye to make soap. They devised homemade concoctions of clay or alcohol to raise stains, and added bluing to whites to get them as bright as possible. In the decades before most homes had electric or hand-cranked mangles to squeeze water from wet laundry, they created handmade twisting devices to wring the water from sheets. Boiling wheat bran, they extracted starch to make pressed shirts crisp, smoothed by irons they heated in open fireplaces or in buckets of smoldering charcoal. Racial barriers left the majority of Black women among the lowest-paid workers in the urban South, but they should not be remembered as "unskilled." (The same can be said about other work, as we will see.)[33]

In addition to their skill, laundresses had real independence. That was worth something, too. The fact that they didn't work under the watch of a white person could be heard in the laughter that filled back alleyways, the chatter and fuss that buzzed in the air as they worked alongside neighbors doing the same work. As they hung the clothes to dry, they could treasure the opportunity to work for themselves. As they pressed the garments with hot smoothing irons heated in fires in their kitchens, they weren't isolated from family and community, working alone in white folks' houses, as many domestic laborers were. So, while the women who picked up dirty clothes often did not make more than a few dollars per load, their independence was a valuable resource, not only for themselves but for their families and communities. That independence, and their recognition of their own collective power, made them an integral part of the working class.[34]

———

BOTH OF SARAH'S PARENTS DIED WHEN SHE WAS JUST THREE, so it is most likely that she could only remember little things about them, perhaps the feel of her mother's hands while being tucked into bed next to her siblings under the heavy quilt that kept her still, or sitting on her father's knee when they gathered to eat after working in the field. So, it would be from her sister- in-law that she would learn how she might survive in a terrible world. She was born in December of 1878, the daughter of freed slaves in Elbert County, Georgia, the same rural county where my maternal grandfather's ancestors had been enslaved, about 35 miles northeast of Athens.[35] Had my grandfather known her personally, he probably would have thought of Sarah as homefolks. While the scant records that still exist make it impossible to know for sure, Joseph "Squire" Rucker, who owned my ancestors, had twelve separate plantations and vast holdings of property and people, so it is not hard to imagine that he may have held some of Sarah's ancestors in bondage, too.

After her parents were gone, her adult older brother and his wife took her in, so it was in their household where Sarah learned laundry work. She recalled that her sister-in-law taught her how to get clothes truly clean and how not to burn "cat face" marks with the hot iron on white clothes and sheets. It was vital to make items perfect for exacting white customers. As a child, any mistakes she made resulted in a beating with a switch. Beatings were a terrible legacy of enslavement that lived on through Black parents, who believed that punishments had to be serious, painful even, in order to impart a lesson. Being entrusted with the clothing of a white household was a tremendous responsibility, particularly in a world where white Southerners were empowered to punish Black people in any way they saw fit. A misunderstanding or

SARAH AT HOME, WORKING ON HER OWN ACCOUNT

accident could be met with deadly reprisals. Young Black girls learning laundry work knew early on that mistakes could cost them their lives.

When as a young woman Sarah moved to Athens, Georgia, transitioning from one brother's home to another's to look for better opportunities, she took these valuable skills with her. While East Athens wasn't far from where she was born, in terms of the freedom of everyday life for Black people, it was an improvement.[36] The small home on East Broad Street where Sarah lived with her brother, his wife, and five of his seven kids was crowded, but it was situated in a pleasant, tight-knit Black community. Even in the shadow of the segregated University of Georgia, Sarah was hopeful about the life she might build for herself.

Between the 1880s and the 1900s, hundreds of thousands of Black workers who grew frustrated when landowners defrauded them of the value of their crops year after year began to migrate to Southern cities. This was not yet the era historians now call the Great Migration, a term used mostly to describe the movement of Black southerners to the North; this was decades before, but it was nevertheless the beginning of the movement of Black life from predominantly rural places to urban ones. A life in cities like Atlanta, Richmond, Durham, Montgomery, Houston, Athens, and Memphis allowed Sarah's generation to have more control over their time and more say over their daily lives. But even as urban residents, their employment options were circumscribed by racial prejudice. Thousands of Black men were employed in the construction of the infrastructure of these New South cities, doing the heavy labor of ripping up cobblestones in order to lay streetcar tracks, constructing electric grids and city drainage and sewer systems. Over time, these skilled Black workmen were increasingly cut off from opportunities in trades, as most higher-paying opportunities were set aside for white men. By 1890 more than 75 percent of Black men working in cities of the South and the North did manual labor or personal service. For women the figures were even higher; more than 80 percent of Black women in the nation's cities worked as maids, cooks, or laundresses. Only a tiny elite of Black women and men could be described as a middle class of teachers, doctors, nurses, typists, and shop or business owners.[37]

In spite of the limitations cities presented, Black migrants must have felt marginally safer and freer. There was no landholder to demand that your children leave their schoolwork to harvest cotton in the fields; instead, they could finally attend schools that weren't determined by the agricultural calendar. White landholders could not demand that you clean their home, pick their crops, or tend to their crises; urban spaces created a buffer of privacy—a porous one, but a buffer nonetheless. While Black working-class folk in cities may have appreciated the physical distance cities provided from their white bosses, they still had to negotiate with violent police and charges of vagrancy that might land them on the chain gang or in a labor camp when legislators or industrialists decided they needed unpaid Black labor. And they had to manage one another in close quarters, leading to quarrels and drunken fights. The cities held new dangers, but the rows of whitewashed shotgun houses with clean swept yards held out the promise of new benefits, too.

The urban communities that Black folks lived in emerged from their own efforts. There was no public aid to help them get established. It was Black determination that created Black neighborhoods, and with them greater safety from the threat of violence and rape by night riders. They built not only homes but also small businesses and independent institutions, meaning they could shop at Black-owned stores that had fair prices, and commune in spaces that were their own. While nothing could fully insulate Black people from the threat of racial violence— there were attacks on both the prosperous and the poor in these new urban hubs, and the constant specter of injustice hovered over their daily lives—the Black cities that grew within larger, white-controlled cities made things a little safer.

The Athens where Sarah settled as a young adult became one of these urban landscapes packed with Black southerners on the move, seeking the opportunity for a life away from the men and women who had held them in bondage. Out of the informal hush harbors that had been founded in the countryside, Black Athens built church congregations; by 1915 there were twelve Black churches within in the city and seventeen more in the surrounding areas of the county. The Black church in turn founded schools, mutual aid societies, and Masonic lodges, and helped to launch new leaders. By the time Sarah moved to Athens, there was an established safety net of mutual support that allowed working Black folk to thrive.

Sarah did begin to flourish. She met Whitman Hill after she arrived in Athens, and the young couple joined in holy matrimony on a hot and clear June day in 1907. Their families made their way to Ebenezer Baptist, a few blocks from Sarah's brother's home, to witness the ceremony, fanning themselves as they sat on the hard wooden pews of one of Athens's most important independent Black churches while the Reverend J. H. Horton presided over the ceremony.[38] Eventually Whit, as Sarah called him, also got the call to the ministry and became a preacher, a fitting choice for a carpenter. The couple had a long, and apparently loving and supportive, marriage. Sarah's WPA interview quietly hints at their losses, too. Although she told Sadie "I have just two girls and two boys," the couple had five children together—the "just" spoke to the shimmer of the memory of her firstborn son, Lorham, who died before the age of ten. At the time of the interview, her other four children—Mary, Marion, Whitman Jr., and Caroline—were still living.

The census also records Sarah Hill's thirty-year stretch of work as a laundress. Each census year Sarah was recorded as living in Athens,

Georgia, listing her occupation as "laundress," her industry as "at home," and her employer as "working on own account."[39] As Sarah recalled, washing was a choice that prioritized her children. She told Hornsby that after she married and started having children, "I couldn't do no good at working out. So, I stayed home and [took] in washing." Sarah's choice made her part of the 68 percent of Black working women in Athens who took in laundry. Even a racially biased 1915 sociological study of the condition of Black life in Athens, Georgia, noted that:

> Laundering is evidently much more popular among the negro women than cooking. The explanation of this fact is that as cooks, most of the time of the negro women is controlled by the employer, whereas as laundresses the women are able to remain in their homes, securing in this way that freedom of movement which they all prize so highly, and finding time to give more attention to their children and housekeeping.[40]

When asked, most of the women who worked folding and bundling clean clothes highlighted their ability to keep their eyes on their own children while they worked. This was well before the advent of public nursery schools. Indeed, laundry was measurably the favored work among both married and widowed Black women who were caring for children. While 53 percent of single Black women engaged in personal service did domestic work in white households, over 40 percent of married women took in laundry.[41] Blanche Davis, a Black woman from Montgomery, Alabama, recalled that "after [she] had small children, [she] couldn't go out on the job, so I was doing washing and ironing at home."[42] Children who were too young to be in school, particularly the girls, could work alongside their mothers, helping as they could and learning the trade for themselves.

In freedom, Sarah made a choice that her ancestors and my ancestors could not have made as chattel slaves in Elbert County. Stripped of power over decisions about their work, they could only labor for the benefit of landowners who made fortunes off their and their children's toil. A woman once held in bondage by Joseph Rucker, who also happened to be interviewed by Sadie Hornsby, recalled that when she was only a toddler—"just knee high to a duck"—she was already separated from her mother and forced to work, carrying buckets of water, gathering wood, and tending to the slaveholder's livestock. As laborers in cotton fields who worked from sunup to sundown, her mother and father had no say or control over her time. They could not raise her the way they saw fit because these choices were not their own. Sarah Hill had the power to make different decisions. She didn't make much money, but her choice was worth a lot. Prizing her time, her attention, her movement, and the lives of her children, Hill chose to work as a laundress and thereby delineated her existence from those of her ancestors who were not free to choose or allowed to move. The quality of her life and her children's lives would be better for her choice.[43]

Sarah was one of thousands of Black women whose working lives were hemmed in by the assumptions of a society governed by segregationists. White people attempted to put in place policies and practices, both legal and understood, that left working Black women with few choices. But when we look past the surface, deeper into Black women's lives, the story is quite remarkable. Again and again, working women like Sarah made choices, individually and collectively, that were space-making. They improved their working lives, securing time and havens for themselves and for their children. Washerwomen joined together to determine what their customers could demand. And although this work didn't allow them to change the rules of race or the violence that undergirded segregation, it did make them into some of the most consistently resistant members of the Black working class.

CHAPTER THREE

Resistant Washerwomen

We do not wish in the least to charge exorbitant prices, but desire to be able to live comfortably if possible from the fruits of our labor.

—WASHERWOMEN OF JACKSON, 1866[1]

We were always opposed to washer women. Between us and them there never was, and never can be any affinity.

—*YAZOO CITY DEMOCRAT*, 1870[2]

W hen she heard the insistent and strange knocking reverberate against the old wood of her front door that afternoon in August, Callie House knew it wasn't good news. She and the National Ex-Slave Mutual Relief, Bounty and Pension Association had been targeted for years for organizing people who had been enslaved and for petitioning the federal government to request that they receive a pension for their years as unpaid laborers. Although Americans have the First Amendment right to petition their government, the government did not seem to think this right, like so many other rights, really applied

---

"Washing day."
A. W. MOLLER, COURTESY *GEORGIA ARCHIVES, VANISHING GEORGIA COLLECTION*, TH0176

to working-class Black people. It certainly did not think a protest should be led by a washerwoman like Callie.[3]

Callie believed she was probably born in 1861, but like thousands of men and women born in bondage she did not know her date of birth; plantation owners did not record the birthdates of enslaved children, just as they didn't record the dates that calves or foals were born. She was a child during what became the final years of slavery on a plantation in Rutherford County, Tennessee, just a few miles from Nashville. Callie Guy, as she was then known, was raised by her widowed mother, who worked as a laundress. Her mother struggled to support the family on her meager pay, and she only survived due to a community of support.

Her mother wanted young Callie to be educated, so even as local whites discouraged Black education during the day with political rhetoric and threatened it at night with arson attacks and night riders, she insisted that her children attend school. Callie received as much education as was available to Black children in Rutherford County, completing the eighth grade as a good reader and a strong writer. She was innately talented, an excellent speaker and an independent thinker determined to forge an identity for herself as a free woman and a citizen. But she didn't have the means to continue her education, so she married a man named William House and left rural Rutherford County for Nashville, where she worked in the trades her mother had taught her, as a laundress and seamstress.[4]

William House died young, leaving Callie a widow and mother of five. As she worked, picking up loads and returning freshly laundered linens and garments to white families at the end of the week, she grew frustrated seeing that so many in her community were poor in spite of how tremendously hard they worked. Although they were rich in connection to one another and had a measure of control over their lives that their forebears hadn't enjoyed, they had little to show for all the work they had done for the benefit of others as enslaved people or during the Civil War. Callie was a member of organizations in her church and neighborhood that provided for the sick and the elderly, but still she believed that the local, informal efforts at mutual aid were insufficient.

Then Callie came across a pamphlet called the "Freedmen's Pension Bill: A Plea for the American Freedman," written and published in 1891 by Walter R. Vaughan. The pamphlet explained that there was proposed Congressional legislation (H.R. 11119) that would give the formerly enslaved, like Union veterans, a pension. The idea behind the legislation was simple: the government would provide a pension to any ex-slave. Payouts would be dispensed on a sliding scale based on the pensioner's age, with the highest payout going to those seventy and above, while lesser amounts were designated for younger ex-slaves.[5]

Vaughan, the white, Selma, Alabama-born editor of the *Daily Democrat* in Omaha, Nebraska, and former mayor of Council Bluffs, Iowa, was no friend of the race. The son of a slaveholder, Vaughan was a reunionist, that is, a proponent of a turn-of-the-twentieth-century white supremacist ideology that recast the Civil War as a dispute among a white brotherhood. Vaughan wrote regularly that he wished he had been old enough to fight on behalf of the Confederacy, promoted a nostalgia for slavery in the antebellum South, and argued that white southerners best knew the answer to the "Negro problem" because they were the ones who had held Black people in bondage. Insisting that Northern whites should simply ignore lynching and the passage of laws instituting segregation and disenfranchisement, reunionists argued that limiting Black liberty was the cost required to politically reunify white men.[6]

Asserting that white northerners should take a hands-off approach to the question of race, reunionists usually opposed federal involvement on behalf of Black southerners. However, Vaughan viewed a pension for ex-slaves as a flow-through that would not stay in the Black community but would help boost the white South economically. He even went as far as to encourage his congressional sponsor, Nebraska representative William Connell, to call the bill he forwarded in 1890 (H.R. 11119) a "Southern-tax relief bill" rather than a pension. Eventually, when it was clear to Vaughan that the bill would not pass, he published it as a pamphlet, toured the country to promote the idea, and hired agents to promote its sale. With the marked exception of an elderly Frederick Douglass, who endorsed the pension movement, established Black organizations did not support the idea. However, Vaughan knew that the idea of recompense for the formerly enslaved would catch fire among Black southerners. Promoting sales of the pamphlet was an easy way for Vaughan to profit from African Americans' collective desire for just recompense.

But the idea of reparations for the formerly enslaved was bigger than Vaughan. More than ten thousand pamphlets of the "Freedmen's Pension Bill" were sold for a dollar each. In barbershops, churches, and front porches across the South, the pamphlet was shared thousands of times, and read aloud for the benefit of those who could not read it for themselves. Its reach multiplied dramatically by folks who passed it on to family and friends after reading it. Washerwomen like Callie, who moved about widely in their towns and cities each week, most likely carried copies of the pamphlet to share with other Black workers they met along the way, tucked discreetly between the piles of laundry.

Captivated by the notion that a pension for freedpeople was owed, Callie began to calculate the true cost of what Black people had done during slavery, comparing it to the desperation she saw among the elderly who had once been held in bondage. Believing that this effort ought to be Black led, Callie teamed up with Isaiah Dickerson, a former Black representative of Vaughan's campaign, to form the independent National Ex-Slave Mutual Relief, Bounty and Pension Association. As the voice of this movement, she discovered the cause of her life.

Chartered in 1898, the organization harnessed the spirit of the Black working class, transforming Vaughan's idea into a South-wide movement for reparations. Utilizing the mobility of Black workers from laundresses to hack drivers, the organization became a grassroots movement. Publications were distributed through Black churches, social clubs, and small Black businesses. Tapping into the networks of the Black working class, chapters of the organization grew up all over the South, with members committing small sums of money to sponsor advocacy of the legislation. This movement, led by a washerwoman, grew to be the largest popular cause of its time. The scope of the movement put Callie in the crosshairs of federal officials determined to silence a Black woman laundress who boldly advocated for reparations for the wrong of slavery.

Although the pension effort had been initially started by a white man, who was never prosecuted, the Black leaders who took up the cause were labeled con artists attempting to trick elderly former slaves into donating out of their meager funds. The funds they collected were for the mutual aid of their members and some of the costs of lobbying Congress; there was never any evidence of fraud. Even without clear evidence of wrongdoing, the federal government would lead a decades-long campaign to stop a washerwoman simply for advocating what it perceived as a dangerous idea. In retaliation for House's activism, the post office cut off her mail, at the time one of the most important resources for organizing a movement, launching a ten-year-long investigation trying to connect her to fraudulent behavior.

Undeterred, Callie took on the accusations, writing directly to government officials to explain that the funds collected were used for advocacy and mutual aid. She was hopeful that a thorough investigation of the organization would find no wrongdoing and the Mutual Relief, Bounty and Pension Association would be allowed to continue. But eventually federal agents arrested Callie, charging her with using the mail to defraud a member. Even without sufficient evidence, the jury, angered at the idea that people like Callie House were demanding recompense for their lives in bondage, sentenced her to a year and a day in prison. While her organization formally ended, the demand for reparations continues.

After serving her sentence, Callie returned to South Nashville and to her work as a washerwoman. Never able to revive her organization, she died of uterine cancer ten years later. Remembered as the first Black woman to rise to national prominence as a leader in the fight for reparations, Callie House's national stature made her unusual; that she was a laundress with a resistant spirit did not.

SARAH HILL'S WORK, CALLIE HOUSE'S WORK, INDEED, ALL BLACK women's laundry work was born both in compliance with and defiance of white authority. After slavery ended, white southerners attempted to construct a racial order very similar to what had existed before. They wanted to see Black women laboring at the bottom of a nominally free society; for a washerwoman, this meant laundering for a single family and under the supervision of "the lady of the house," for low pay. Black women needed to work to survive and care for their families and, in some surface ways, laundry aligned with an image of subservience and service. However, these women not only insisted on determining how the work would be done—away from the gaze and control of employers—but also figured out how to work in service to their own households. Women like Sarah prized their mobility, the opportunity to set the pace of their own work during the week, the ability to make more money by taking in wash from several families, and to labor away from white supervision. Founded in this spirit of independence, laundry work ended up taking on a fundamentally resistant form. Under slavery, Black southerners had learned to lean on one another to survive. As emancipated people, those networks of mutuality and solidarity helped them survive as a class.

Washerwomen's independence made them a source of fear and fascination to their white customers. They were mocked by minstrels who portrayed them as slow, ignorant, and careless, while at the same time fear of them would drive urban policy-making; police, sheriffs, and judges would target laundresses, labeling them as vagrants because of their refusal to work within white households. Their independence made them into the good help that was so hard to find. Lawmakers would try to keep tabs on them, hoping that registries and licenses might keep them under control. But even with all these measures in place, white authorities would have a hard time exerting complete dominance over their bodies, their labor, the pace of their work, and their time.

This resistance was a collective effort. Together, laundresses could take off for holidays or special occasions in their own lives by simply not showing up to pick up a laundry load, without having to commit to quitting their job or begging permission for time off. As a group, they could bring cities to a halt just by not showing up. The power of their collective consciousness would give root to movements—for fair pay, boycotts against segregation, and, like Callie House's movement, calls for reparation—and strands of fervent Black working-class resistance. Washerwomen were primed for the fight.

As we have seen in the story of Sarah, laundry was hard work. As historian Tera Hunter put it, "laundry work was the single most onerous chore in the life of a nineteenth-century woman, and the first chore she would hire someone else to perform whenever the slightest bit of discretionary income was available. Even poor urban women might send out at least some of their wash."[7] Not only was it laborious; it was also by nature very public. To clean clothes required being outdoors, as one boiled wash pots and hung clothes on a line across the yard. For white women striving to attain a better standing in their community, doing their own laundry wasn't an option. As one Southern white journalist noted, "white women who have been dependent upon the Negroes for this sort of labor and who have come to look upon washing and ironing as a lowly menial task certainly are not going to do their own washing."[8]

For generations, laundry work in the American South was associated with the labor of enslaved women; indeed, white observers from all backgrounds characterized it as "nigger work" and not something a white woman of any standing would want to do for her family, and certainly not as work she would perform outside her own household. Even during the Civil War, elite white women went to great lengths to avoid washing their own dirty clothes. When white, Northern-born Amelia Lines set up a household in wartime Georgia, she took on the "thinking of a plantation mistress." Even though she could barely afford to hire a laundress or a domestic servant, she believed that "hiring out her wash and keeping a house servant were absolutely vital accoutrements." If she did her own domestic labor, she wrote that she "could never look nice" or effectively keep her "baby or house clean."[9] So stigmatized was the labor of washing clothes that during Reconstruction one aged former slaveholder did his family's laundry just "to spare his daughters."[10] For respectable white women, the cost of the laundress was small in comparison to the cost in status they would have suffered by doing their own laundry. While not every white household could afford a domestic worker to clean—work that took place behind closed doors—most did what they could to pay for laundry. The artificial standards of white femininity—the real status of a household notwithstanding—were dependent on Black washerwomen.

After Reconstruction, this color line governing women's labor kept even some of the poorest white women from doing their own laundry or taking in wash to supplement their income. Elite whites looked askance at the idea of poor white women washing their clothes. Even as one Southern white woman, Mrs. George Ward, complained about the work habits of the Black women she employed, she would not hire white servants, whom she dismissed as "inferior" and the most "hopeless, helpless, trifling set of people in the entire South." Ward suggested that poor white women also believed that all domestic work was Black women's work: "Even if they have no homes, they are so very much opposed to going out as servants. They think service is synonymous with slavery. They make no distinction between free domestic service and compulsory servitude—regular old-time slavery."[11]

Wholly dependent on Black women's labor, white employers attempted to coerce Black women to work on their terms. The schedule of washing—which began every Monday—was established during enslavement; one former slaveholder testified that her family "would always have in one of the cabins close by the house one or two washerwomen who took the clothes out on Monday morning and washed them straight through the week."[12] After the war, Black washerwomen maintained the tradition of starting the wash on Mondays, but complied with little else.

White women wanted washerwomen to clean clothes in white households under white supervision, but after the Civil War washerwomen pushed back, collectively insisting that they would do this work on their own timelines, in their own yards. They set limits so that they could care for their own households and children, worship, and participate in school or church activities.[13] The physical distance also allowed for the "separation of tasks that had characterized prewar forms of domestic labor." If washerwomen were hired to wash, they didn't want to also cook or clean, and working outside their employer's home allowed them to maintain that division.[14] By systematically avoiding labor in white homes, they could avoid having all the domestic duties added to their labor. Any downtime could be used in service of their own households.

Washing outside white homes also provided a buffer against unwanted assaults. In the homes of white employers, Black women were vulnerable to sexual and physical violence, as they had been under slavery. Abuse could come from both women and men, but the threat of rape loomed large. Black women, in the antebellum era, were characterized as hypersexual, unfaithful to their partners, and open to sexual liaisons. As free women, these stereotypes lived on, making them frequent targets for white men who felt that they had a right to Black women's bodies. Given that white men were the police and lawmakers, Black women had little means of fighting back, particularly if the attacker was also their employer. Cleaster Mitchell, a Black woman who worked cleaning white homes as a teenager, "learned very early about abuse from white men." She recalled that "it was terrible . . . and there wasn't anybody to tell."[15] So, Black women and girls who worked in white homes had to constantly strategize about the best ways of protecting themselves from the ever-present threat of sexual violence. Washing laundry at their own homes was part of a broader strategy to maintain their own space and, by extension, a measure of personal, bodily security.

Across the South, Black women could be seen at the beginning of the week toting home dirty clothes bundled on their heads, to be returned clean at the end of the week; their movements were even memorialized in printed calendars advertising laundry soap. But their mobility was notable as a sign that things had changed. They were not paid well, yet they had won the battle to be not employees but independent workers who completed a service for the households they selected on a week-

"Louisiana, carrying washing on head, 1912." Continuing the practice of their African forebears, Black women, who often walked great distances with laundry, balanced the loads on their head.
*WALTER P. REUTHER LIBRARY,
ARCHIVES OF LABOR AND URBAN AFFAIRS,
WAYNE STATE UNIVERSITY*

by-week basis.[16] As enslaved women, washerwomen had been tethered to the plantation, but as free workers they could move, choosing their customers as they went, adding new rules to existing customs to better accommodate their lives.[17] Their resistance allowed them to stop short, on the back porch, just at the edge of the danger of white households, to pick up and drop off their loads. They won this first labor war.

Given their resistance, the image of the Black washerwoman took up space in the white imagination as a figure of great attraction, fear, and resentment. In any Southern city there were thousands of Black women who did this fundamentally intimate work; taking all the clothing of a household, literally white Americans' dirty laundry, to Black households to be cleansed, dried, pressed, folded, and returned like new. Many white people assumed that Black laundresses overestimated the work required to wash a family's laundry, that they padded their time or perhaps even used the family's clothes for themselves. One white southerner reported "a great many of them have been living . . . around in these little cabins, where they take in two or three days washing and ironing a week and have all the rest of the time at their command. . . . And that mode of life has some advantages, because they can take out a day's washing and keep it away seven days and wear the clothes in the meantime."[18]

Indeed, the very act of taking clothes away to be cleaned became the subject of vivid fantasies about what happened to the clothes when they were out of sight. White southerners believed that Black men, women, and children would don the clothing of their laundry customers, flaunting themselves in the wares of the white elite. The mobility of the Black working class was a subject of broad consternation. Black church groups and mutual aid societies hosted excursions: train trips to conventions, parks, Black fairs, and church events in neighboring cities. These trips facilitated Black folks' ability to explore, travel, and move freely in ways that they could not when they were held in bondage. The very sight of Black men and women who were agricultural laborers, maids, and laundresses dressed in their best traveling clothes, freely enjoying community and communion, infuriated white observers. Mrs. George Ward of Georgia recorded her disgust with such excursions:

They will go and engage a train of cars from the railroad company and agree to pay, perhaps $135 for a train to take them to Chattanooga. Then for a week before hand they are sent around advising and urging everybody to go on the "scursion." . . . They will get down here to the depot at 6 o'clock in the morning, headed by a brass band, and the noise they make is perfectly awful . . . and the crowd will hang around here on the platform and all about the cars trying to get sufficient to make up the required sum.[19]

To white observers, most if not all demonstrations of Black freedom were offensive—and they imagined that such excursions were made up of laundresses sporting white women's finery. As Mrs. Ward insisted, "when our servants go on these 'scursions' we generally know that the larger part of our week's washing is gone in the 'scursion,' too."[20]

White anxiousness about the temporary loss of control over their garments was almost institutionalized as law in South Carolina when one state legislator "introduced a bill ... prohibiting washer women from wearing their patrons' clothes." Complaining that it was common that the "'white lady' sees her embroidered skirt walking around on the person of the washer woman ... or the master finds his shirt on the back of the washer woman's husband," the bill threatened high fines or imprisonment for washerwomen accused of sporting customers' clothing.[21] These claims were so common that some well-dressed Black families recalled being accused of thievery for wearing their own clothing. In 1910 in Charleston, South Carolina, Mamie Garvin Fields remembered that that her mother, a talented seamstress, was publicly accused by a white woman stranger of being a thieving laundress because the dress Mamie was wearing, crocheted and interlaced with yellow ribbons, was so beautiful.[22]

In spite of white southerners' perennial desire to have more control, the washerwomen continued to work on their own terms, but there were limits to their autonomy. During every transaction, they were at risk of being cheated by customers who refused to pay the amount agreed upon when the laundry was first picked up for cleaning. Knowing that washerwomen would have little ability to challenge the word of a white person, some customers feigned displeasure with the condition of their clothes and linens. Like the family that accused Sarah Hill of losing a garment, they might demand that laundresses purchase new garments to replace something that was said to be missing or damaged. Unlike others engaged in business transactions, laundresses who were cheated could not go to court to demand fair pay or just treatment; they were frequent victims of mass arrests, regularly charged as vagrants for their refusal to work inside white homes as domestics. There would be no easy justice for them inside a courtroom. In this context, it could be perilous for Black women to try to negotiate the value of their work.

Stories of violence against washerwomen were common. In Nashville, two laundresses accused of "improper conduct" were stripped naked, tied to trees, and beaten by White Caps (white supremacist night riders) in front of their home.[23] Also in Nashville, a washerwoman named Eliza Jane Ellison was viciously beaten, then fatally shot by a white customer for insisting on fair pay for extra loads of laundry.[24] When any argument could lead to death, laundresses were forced to placate the whims of white customers. Their primary recourse for abuse was not to wash again for families that were unfair or aggressive, and to let other women know to avoid them in the future. For many malicious white families, good help was indeed hard to find. Black women learned to protect themselves, to a degree, through their racialized monopoly on washing clothes.

WHEN WE THINK ABOUT LABOR ORGANIZING IN AMERICAN history, we tend to think first of white men's resistance on factory production lines. Fewer historians and commentators have characterized Black women's work in the same light. Conventional historical accounts have leaned toward emphasizing the menial status of their labor, while neglecting the rich history of Black women's class consciousness. Washerwomen are a reminder that those assessments are incomplete at best, misguided at worst. Even during the nadir of lynching, women throughout the South continued to organize to improve their pay. Historian Tera Hunter's groundbreaking 1997 text *To 'Joy My Freedom* chronicled the best known example of laundresses' collective power, the Atlanta Washerwomen's Strike of 1881, when three thousand of the city's laundresses organized a "trade association" to demand better wages and conditions on the eve of the Atlanta Exposition, leaving city leaders little choice but to negotiate.[25] Although this was probably the largest coming together of laundresses in American history, smaller-scale efforts similar to the 1881 strike were not uncommon.

From the first moments of freedom in the postwar South, laundresses determined to unite in ways that would benefit them all. One of the first efforts to organize was that of the Washerwomen of Jackson, freedwomen in Mississippi who in 1866 sent a resolution to the city mayor that declared: "We join in charging a uniform rate for our labor." Policing one another, the union also warned that any woman violating their prices "shall be liable to a fine." Driven by the "desire to be able to live comfortably if possible from the fruits of [their] labor," these women moved to set collective terms under which they would work.[26] An Alabama newspaper reported that the Washerwomen of Jackson were charging "$1.50 per day; $15 per month for family washing; $10 per month for single individuals"—something approaching a living wage for a laundress who washed for four or five families.[27]

The same year, 1881, that the famed Atlanta laundresses launched their labor strike, washerwomen in the growing industrial hub of Charlotte, North Carolina, went on strike in response to a report that a newly instituted city charter was going to impose a tax targeting laundresses. By refusing to accept laundry from their elite white clients, including the households of city commissioners, washerwomen let their opposition to the proposed law be known. After a few brief weeks of protest, the *Charlotte Observer* clarified that the tax proposal was just a rumor; no new tax would be levied. The protest had stopped a policy that would have made all their work worth less, and taught city leaders that laundresses would mount a collective response to punitive policy changes.[28] Fearing additional strikes, the local newspaper editorialized that before they passed new laws, city officials needed to establish their own white-run commercial laundry to ensure a steady supply of clean laundry for white residents.[29] No such laundry was founded in the 1880s.

Across the South, white newspapers were filled with regular laments about the need for more washerwomen and domestic laborers, a reflection of ongoing contests between white authorities and Black women for control. One North Carolina paper, complaining about the paucity of Black women workers, said it plainly: "How are we southern people going to get our clothes washed?"[30] In 1870 in Little Rock, Arkansas, the local paper lamented that "during the past five years . . . cooks, washerwomen, nurses, etc. . . . have become scarcer," decrying the fact that "negro women who can be depended upon now have obtained homes of their own." Blaming Republican politicians who, many white southerners claimed, advised Black workers that they were the equals of white people and should not work for low pay, the paper proposed a scheme to import white immigrants from Northern cities.[31] They were looking for an outside solution to end their dependence on organized, and often defiant, Black women.

In 1904 the *Paducah Sun* sounded the alarm about resistant washerwomen in their town by asking, "Are the washer women on a strike?" The writer went on to explain that it was difficult for families new to the Kentucky town to find a washerwoman, and claimed that he did not "know what is responsible for the state of affairs, whether it is the fact that the regular washerwomen have all they can or want to do, or whether the number who desire to do that . . . work is gradually diminishing." The writer also complained that laundresses who were working in Paducah were charging "an exorbitant price"—unwilling to recognize that Black women could, like white people, follow the principles of capitalism and charge higher prices in tighter markets. In fact, there was so much concern about Black laundresses that city businessmen spoke of starting their own laundry service for white families, reminiscent of the proposal that had been advocated decades before in Charlotte, North Carolina. It would be set up somewhere on the outskirts of town, and would provide "the long-needed relief" for white families. Hoping to employ white women, white leaders argued that the laundry would "furnish work for scores of deserving white girls and women who will be only too glad to get work of any kind to make an honest living." However, given the long-standing racialization of laundry work, the article was quick to clarify that white women working at the laundry would be working for hourly wages and "consequently it would be nothing like 'taking in washing,'" awkwardly attempting to draw an artificial line between Black women doing laundry and white women doing laundry.[32] In any event, there was little hope for their plans.

Calls to hire poor white women or to arrest Black women were constant. Even as Black workers operated under the constant possibility of violence, Black working-class unity, first born on the plantations of the South, prevented white leaders from establishing complete control over Black washerwomen. A 1908 editorial in the *Charlotte Observer* spoke to white fears that were common across the region. "There is always one spectre as to the unionization of labor, this being that the negroes may some day be organized, it being declared that if this were done and the blacks, male and female, welded together in a sort of organization which would be effectively mainly through their churches and various societies, the whites would be . . . at their mercy."[33]

Even though white civic leaders across the South contemplated making end-runs around them, the fear of organized Black women was a constant. Within the decade, news of washerwomen organizing in the mountain towns of Lenoir, Hickory, and Morganton, North Carolina, caused local officials to fear that a planned washerwomen's convention in Hickory would lead to a "trust," invoking language usually reserved for companies that illegally collude to set artificially high prices, rather than a union of individual workers.[34] Protests continued in the new century in Morganton, North Carolina, where white housewives complained of "trouble with the 'colored ladies' who have been doing the cooking and laundry work." They recounted that "many families find themselves without servants and cannot get them for love or money." More than a decade after Black women first banded together in the town, officials suspected "that there is an organization among the cooks and washerwomen" and that they were "acting in concert."[35]

More definitive confirmation of an organization of washerwomen was reported in the timber town of Brewton, Alabama, the self-described "richest little town in the South."[36] Demanding that some of the town's wealth be reflected in their pay, the town's laundresses went on strike in 1900. The local paper, the *Laborer's Banner*, accurately reported that they had been "work[ing] for practically nothing, and take pay in 'chips and whetstones.'" In contrast with many other journalists, the writers at the pro-union weekly sided with the women's cause, claiming that "it is said by conservatives that their demands are reasonable."[37]

Such strikes were not always strictly about pay. In Albany, Georgia, in December of 1905, washerwomen, most likely including a young Sarah Hill, united in order to secure time off and "notified their customers that no family washing will be done during the week of Christmas." The laundresses, working in solidarity with the city's Black welders, took a week off that they dedicated to rest and fellowship with their families.

When individual white housewives in Athens went on a search to find alternative workers for the holiday week, they "discovered that an agreement had been reached among practically all the washerwomen of the city." The *Atlanta Constitution* angrily lamented that "the novel ultimatum will have to stand." Standing together, laundresses briefly upended the household economies of white residents, forcing entire cities into "economizing . . . in the use of linen."[38]

Washerwomen were also participants in wider labor movements of the era. In 1873, when workers in Raleigh, North Carolina, organized a general strike of workers in different industries, Black washerwomen joined that interracial, citywide effort. Although the demands for a ten-hour day had little to do with their work culture, calls for improvements in pay resonated. More important, perhaps, is what their move to join the city's striking men represented: Black women workers were delineating themselves as part of the community of workers, and as essential as workers in skilled industries. Even as one local paper found it "curious" that "the washerwomen have struck," their efforts aligned not only with a long history of Black women's organizing but with Black workers seeking solidarity across the color line. This moment of unanimity would not be the last.[39]

Protests led by Raleigh's Black women laundresses would continue for the next several decades. In 1885, the local labor organizer for the Knights of Labor, printer John R. Ray, wrote an urgent message to Terrance Powderly, the national head of the union, asking what to do about "the colored women (washerwomen and domestics)" who were pressing him to organize their own Assembly of the Knights. Both men were white. Although the order was said to be open to anyone who worked for a living and "no distinction was to be made of race or sex," Powderly encouraged the labor leaders in Raleigh to "postpone the organization of the colored women until the men (of both colors) are more thoroughly enlisted in the movement." Powderly saw labor organizing as primarily men's work and feared that organized Black women would be a hindrance to recruiting white men.[40]

In response, Ray lamented the prejudice in Raleigh, noting that "there is a continual cry of '*nigger! nigger!*' in politics, society, labor organizations, and everywhere." He went on to argue that "the order is intended to protect all people who work, the poor ignorant underpaid and overworked cook as well as the skilled mechanic." Although he too characterized Black women workers as "very ignorant and illerate [*sic*] as a rule," Ray insisted that they "need organization in some way to protect them from the avariciousness of some of the brethren (?) and they shall have it, if I am forced to remain here long enough to accomplish it." (Emphasis and question mark in original.)[41] The labor organizer seems to suggest that Black women workers were seeking union representation not just for better pay, but also to protect themselves from sexual assault. Indeed, although washerwomen worked outside of white homes in part to escape sexual violence, they too lived with the threat of rape by white customers as they moved from house to house, and neighborhood to neighborhood, alone. For them, the labor movement had to respond to the particularities women faced. In turn, they hoped that collective efforts to organize with other workers would lead to a recognition of the unique burdens they bore as women laborers.

The efforts of Black washerwomen to formally unionize, like those of the women in Raleigh, were realized when "fifty-four negro women organized a washer women's union at Kansas City" and "obtained a charter from the American Federation of Labor." The *Florence Herald* reported that it was "the first union of the kind in the country," but, more accurately described, it was just the first of such efforts that was officially recognized by the AFL. Black women had long been leading organizations that were effectively labor unions, and in doing so created pathways for future generations of Black women workers.[42]

Working-class women, laundresses in particular, were also at the heart of resistance against urban segregation. As more and more Black people moved to Southern cities in the late nineteenth and early twentieth centuries, white legislators pushed to pass laws designed to stigmatize them and restrict their liberty. New state laws and ordinances divided streetcars with demeaning signs, rails, gates, and even seats that faced backward to separate Black and white passengers.

Targeting the conveyances was not arbitrary; streetcars were essential to Black working people. The cars that traversed ever-expanding cities like Richmond, New Orleans, and Nashville made far-off places of employment accessible and reduced the time of commutes. Black women workers in particular benefited from better access to transportation; domestic workers could work in households far from their homes, and laundresses could seek out customers in distant neighborhoods. Streetcars made their work less physically arduous. Rather than having to carry their burdens in their arms or on their heads, often across hilly terrain or in the heat of the summer, washerwomen could set their bundles down in the cars. Streetcar systems meant that as white suburbs expanded, so too could the territory of washerwomen. So, when the South-wide movement to segregate the cars began, it was seen as an intrusion on Black mobility. Marking them all as inferior, Jim Crow segregation was designed to control Black people and replicate the totalizing control of rural slavery, but in urban spaces. Southern segregationists hoped to institutionalize second-class, inferior treatment for all Black residents who traveled in the public square.[43]

In response to the new laws, Black residents of more than twenty-five Southern cities organized to protest streetcar segregation with boycotts. Washerwomen were at the forefront of the protests. When

Maryland state representative William G. Kerbin introduced a segregated streetcar bill, the two Black women he employed as a cook and a washerwoman quit.[44] In Houston, Black laundresses "organized and [began] fighting the innovation with all their might." Not only did the city's laundry workers participate in the boycott, they also led a strike in support of the boycott in order to push white public sentiment toward their cause. They leveraged their monopoly on laundry to "induce their white patrons to advocate a change in the car system."[45] Strikes were a ready tool in the arsenal of organized washerwomen, which they could use to amplify a different, or larger, cause.

———

IN 1904, RICHMOND'S BLACK WORKING CLASS ORGANIZED ONE of the most successful streetcar boycotts. Led in part by Maggie Lena Walker, a leading businesswoman and the daughter of a washerwoman, and buoyed by the support of the city's more than 2,500 Black laundresses, the boycott of Virginia Passenger and Power made news throughout the nation. Maggie Lena was an outspoken advocate for the boycott and for full citizenship for Black Richmonders. Centering the voices of Black working women in the fight against segregation, Maggie Lena countered white notions that women who took in laundry were just vagrants or sex workers in disguise. She insisted that working women were "noble, and true and clean," and that their labor was essential to the survival of Black families. She described Black washerwomen as venturing "out into the world—not for name, not for glory and honor—but for bread, and for [their] babies."[46] Reminding working Black women that "the fact that we are at the very bottom of the ladder should not dishearten us," Maggie Lena, a Black feminist visionary, went on to defend those who did engage in sex work, reminding her audience "that ninety-five percent of our women who go astray, do so from absolute need, selling their souls to clothe their bodies!"[47] Speaking in defense of all Black women, she told Black male leaders that "instead of scoffing at the efforts of your women, instead of criticizing them, every Negro man, every Negro Newspaper, every Negro preacher should be extending the hand which helps and giving forth the words which encourage—for the path of the colored women is dark and thorny."[48]

Born in 1876, in the decade after Emancipation, Maggie Lena didn't grow up with "a silver spoon in [her] mouth: but instead with a clothes basket . . . upon [her] head." Her mother, Elizabeth Draper, had been held in bondage by a white woman who was a Union spy. Maggie Lena's biological father was a white abolitionist who disappeared not long after her birth. With her father long gone—and her stepfather killed when she was just a girl—Maggie Lena's widowed mother worked hard as a laundress in order to provide for her young daughter and son.

Some of Maggie Lena's earliest memories were of College Alley, of being surrounded by a bustling community of women, born in bondage, now free and hard at work on the laundry in front of them. At first, she was just a small girl playing with the other children, running in between the rows of sheets to hide and seek, never far from the sharp eyes of her mother. To Maggie Lena's young ears, the women's banter and arguments were a cacophony of rhythmic sounds, laughter, stories, teasing, remembering, sometimes all at once. Their tones would drop to a somber register when they spoke of their troubles at home, of death, of loss. Together they laid those burdens down, praying, crying, and testifying, laying down the garments to lay hands on one another.[49] Like the generations before them that had survived slavery, they were a community. Now, their possibilities in freedom were a bit greater. They made plans, they organized, they decided on what might constitute a fair wage. They talked about which families paid well and which should be avoided. And they would strike if their employers started to make unreasonable demands. They had a vision of what their freedom should be, a vision of what their citizenship could mean. Not all, but many of their plans would be realized in an education for their children, the purchase of their own modest homes, and the organizing of political movements.

Maggie Lena learned how to organize at the feet of the washer-women in that alleyway.[50] She first came to know her city's largest Black community, Jackson Ward, from underneath a basket perched on her head, picking up dirty clothes, then delivering them back clean at the end of the week. Maggie Lena also came of age in what Black histori-ans term the Women's Era, a time when leading Black women formed women's clubs in their local communities, built to address the challenges Black communities faced in the age of Jim Crow. Those local clubs came together in 1896 to form the National Association of Colored Women's Clubs, with the motto "lifting as we climb." Even as she rose to promi-nence as a business owner, banker, and clubwoman, the experiences Maggie Lena had among the washerwomen were never far from her mind. She never shied away from advocating on behalf of the women folk who raised her.[51] As an adult she recalled how work had shaped her:

I have worked from a child ... worked before I was married, worked after I married, and am working now harder than I ever worked in my life. And the great all absorbing interest, the thing which has driven sleep from my eyes and fatigue from my body, is the love I bear women, our Negro women, hemmed in, circumscribed with every imaginable obstacles [sic] in our way, blocked and held down by the fears and prejudices of the whites—ridiculed and sneered at by the intelligent blacks.[52]

Centering the importance of Black working-class women in her leader-ship of a mutual aid society, a dry goods store, and a bank, she described herself first as a Black working woman, a distinction that for her had as much to do with race as with class. These lessons gleaned from a community of working women were foundational, guiding the way in which she would lead one of the most formidable streetcar boycotts in the turn-of-the-twentieth-century South.[53]

With 77 percent of the more than eight thousand Black working women in Richmond listed in the 1900 census working as laundresses or household servants, the boycott could only be possible with the enthusiastic participation of those women, "who, by virtue of their employment, had to traverse and were seen as 'belonging in' the widest range of spaces."[54] By traveling far afield, they encountered people in all parts of the city and could quickly communicate plans for protests throughout the community.

Maggie Lena saw segregation as an attack on the livelihoods of Black workers. "We are being oppressed by the passage of laws which not only have for their object the degradation of Negro manhood and Negro womanhood, but also the destruction of all kinds of Negro enterprises." Indeed, the washerwomen's need for free access to streetcars, to maintain and expand their businesses, was threatened. An attack on the cars was an attack on their livelihoods. For washerwomen, boycotting the cars cost them time and dramatically shrank the territory they could cover, so participating in the protest came at a cost. As Maggie Lena asserted, though, the independence and prosperity of Black people of all classes would allow them to more effectively contest segregation and degradation.[55] Most laundresses sacrificed what little they had to join the boycott of segregated streetcars. The boycott was successful; by 1905, the working women and men of Richmond had bankrupted the city's main streetcar company, forcing it into receivership. However, streetcar officials were willing to face severe reductions in Black patronage to uphold segregation. Eventually Richmond's segregationists won out, but the spirit of staying off the cars was not forgotten within the Black community.[56]

The inability to stop the passage and enforcement of segregation laws and the lack of recognition from national unions did not stop washerwomen from continuing to form effective protests outside recognized structures. For example, in Durham, "washerwomen [were] as scarce as hens' teeth" when they went on strike to protest a police officer who attacked a laundress after she told him that she was not employed by any white family. News of her arrest for vagrancy and the rumor that all washerwomen would be forced to pay a city license tax in order to take in laundry drove the women to demonstrate their disapproval.[57]

In nearby Wake Forest, North Carolina, washerwomen, without any outside assistance, waged an effective campaign to raise prices on college students at Wake Forest University from fifty cents a week to $1.25. The *Charlotte Observer* reported outrage among students who felt "that the colored women have formed an organization to get all they can." Although the paper said that the price increase wasn't exorbitant, the young men on campus protested "the principle of the thing," complaining that the "negroes are so independent." There were also signs that the washerwomen's organizing had spread to cooks working in the town of Wake Forest. The *Charlotte Observer* noted that local household cooks were insisting on set hours so that they could spend the evenings with their own families. Employers who refused the set hours suddenly found themselves without help with their meals. When local white families attempted to bring in Black women "imported from the country," these working women from neighboring counties also soon "jine'd the organization." The fear of a general strike of laundresses and cooks during Wake Forest's commencement week was so great that the journalist who reported on Black workers' labor conditions was afraid of publishing additional articles on the protests for fear of making their effort even more successful.[58]

White critics were right to recognize the power of Black working-class organizing throughout the Jim Crow South, though their "solutions" were largely ineffective. Whether aligned with other workers or not, washerwomen carried a legacy of resistance along with the bundles on their heads in launching both grand protests and spontaneous everyday battles for control. Building on the traditions first fostered by their enslaved forebears, they made space for their families, for their rights, for their dignity, and for one another.

CHAPTER FOUR

The Jeremiad of the Porter

"For, I know the plans I have for you," declares the Lord, "plans to prosper you and not to harm you, plans to give you hope and a future."

—JEREMIAH 29:11

The first time Cottrell Laurence Dellums rode the train alone, he was traveling to see if his older brother was dead. William Dellums had been living and working in Tulsa, Oklahoma, when on May 31, 1921, mobs of white men seeking revenge against the prosperous working- and middle-class Black residents in the oil-boom town descended on their community. A Black teenager, Dick Rowland, had been arrested after a white woman elevator operator, Sarah Page, accused him of assault after he accidentally stepped on her foot as he boarded the car. In reaction to the overblown news that a Black man had assaulted a white woman, a lynch mob organized outside the courthouse, demanding custody of Rowland. Armed Black men, including many veterans of the First World War, sought to protect Rowland and surrounded the

"Family photo." William Warren, a Pullman porter, and his family pose on their front porch in Fort Worth, Texas, in 1930.　*SHADES OF L.A.: AFRICAN AMERICAN COMMUNITY, LOS ANGELES PUBLIC LIBRARY*

building to prevent him from being taken. When the lynch mob could not reach Rowland, they turned their anger on all of Black Tulsa.[1]

White Tulsa residents had clearly been searching for a reason to mount an all-out offensive on the Black neighborhood of Greenwood, which was heralded as the Black Wall Street of the Midwest. Gangs of armed marauders went house to house, stealing the possessions of Black citizens, then setting their homes on fire. The attackers even placed machine guns in the middle of the central thoroughfare, mowing people down as they attempted to escape the flames. Over two fateful days, Black residents fled in terror as their homes and businesses were razed by their white neighbors with the complicity of local law enforcement.[2]

When W. I. Brown, a Pullman porter on the Missouri–Kansas–Texas Railway, locally known as "the Katy," rode into the depot in Tulsa on June 1, 1921, he could see crop dusters circling in the sky above Greenwood from the windows of the railcar—not trying to extinguish the flames, but rather feeding the fires. The porter noticed that two of the planes were dropping what were reported to be turpentine bombs on Black-owned residences and businesses in the commercial district, filling the air with the shocking sound of percussive explosions and sending debris flying hundreds of feet. A photograph of a bombed and burned-out city block, reminiscent of war-torn Europe, was captioned by the state's Black newspaper: "Not Belgium, but Greenwood Street."[3] By the time the massacre was over, hundreds of African American residents were dead or unaccounted for, and thousands more survivors had been beaten, shot, and burned. The destruction of property was astounding: more than 1,200 homes, nearly every church, and dozens of businesses were left in ruins. When news of the violent race massacre made headlines throughout the nation and word had not come from his brother, twenty-one-year-old Laurence set out from Corsicana, Texas, to find him.[4]

Arriving in Tulsa a few days later, Laurence found a tense situation.

City officials were still holding Black residents captive; they had been herded at gunpoint by the National Guard into the local ballpark after the mob violence finally ended. Officials refused to provide any information about the Black Tulsans killed by the mob or arrested as suspected rioters. They also prevented Black outsiders from entering the city to check on the whereabouts of their family and friends. Witnesses reported seeing hundreds of Black victims buried in secret in mass graves or thrown into the river. For those who did survive, justice would never come. No white men were ever arrested for the rampage of murder and destruction, and the city has still not made recompense to the survivors for the loss of life and property.[5]

Because he could not get into Tulsa, Laurence waited for news of his brother for more than two weeks in nearby Muskogee. Eventually, he learned that his brother had survived. William Dellums had been arrested and was being held on $10,000 bail, accused of being one of the leaders of the Black resistance. Laurence would later recall that along with relief that his brother had survived, he felt pride knowing that he had been among those who had fought back to protect Greenwood. It was what their father, William, had taught them both.

The senior William Dellums was born in the closing days of chattel slavery in Texas, the child of an enslaved woman and a member of her slaveholder's family. William Sr. was fiercely independent and determined to assert his political rights in spite of the racial oppression of Jim Crow Texas. He was a barber, and owned a small, four-chair shop that also served as a place where Black men could speak freely about what they thought of the world and their place in it. Dellums's shop became a hub of political conversation in Corsicana, where Cottrell Laurence grew up. His mother, Emma, was also a profound influence on her children, raising them to be confident and outspoken, and she instilled such a love of literature in young Cottrell that he adopted the middle name Laurence to honor his favorite poet, Paul Laurence Dunbar, adopting it as the name he preferred.[6] He was a talented student and a gifted orator, but after witnessing what his brother and thousands of others had faced in Tulsa, he had little doubt that there was no safe future for a young, educated African American man in the region. After his father's death in 1922, Laurence took to the rails again, this time with a one-way ticket to California, guided by his father's directive to "be angry, but not bitter."[7]

He didn't know anyone in the city, but Laurence's goal was to go to San Francisco. Most of the Black migrants from Texas to California whom he knew had gone to Los Angeles, but he was independent and wanted to do something different. He had read about San Francisco in high school, and thought it would be "an ideal place for a Negro to live." Always interested in expanding the possibilities for justice for his people, he hoped to study law at the University of California after he found a job and saved up a bit.[8]

The confidence he felt as he boarded the train waned during the long journey. At just twenty-three and leaving home for the first time, he had never undertaken such a journey before. And his plan to go to San Francisco was vague; he didn't know what life in San Francisco would entail, where he was going to stay, and who in the city might be hiring Black men.

There weren't many Black people on the train other than Laurence and the Pullman porters, so on his break the porter assigned to his car sat down with Laurence, and, sensing that the young man's nerves were on edge, he struck up a conversation about his plans. When Laurence said that he intended to go to San Francisco, the porter began to quiz him, asking who he knew in the city and where he was going to stay. Laurence replied that he expected to get a taxi to take him to a "rooming house." The porter responded that there were no "rooming houses" in

San Francisco, just hotels. The porter then offered his unsolicited advice. He said, "Get off in Oakland," explaining that "there are not enough Negroes in San Francisco for you to find in order to make some connections over there." The porter knew that those connections were necessary for Laurence to find a job and locate a safe and affordable place to live. Across the bay from San Francisco, in Oakland, there was a growing Black community and people who could help a young migrant discover his way.[9]

The porter suggested that he get off at the Sixteenth Street station, within walking distance of Eleventh and Wood Streets in West Oakland, where he knew "a very fine lady" who he thought might have a spare room to rent. Laurence got off the train and walked through the Southern Pacific Station's grand arches and down its wide marble steps, carrying his baggage, light with his few possessions, and found, on the corner of Eleventh and Wood, a small but lovely stick-style home with big windows, ornate woodwork, and bright paint, which looked a lot like a smaller version of the grand Victorian homes he had seen in pictures of San Francisco.[10] The porter's information was spot on: the cottage did indeed have a garden apartment for rent, with a separate entrance. As he walked through the town that day, the Black men he encountered nodded and the Black women smiled, noting the suitcase in his hand and the hesitancy of a newcomer in his step, perhaps thinking of their own first days in the city.

West Oakland became Laurence's home. He found his first job working as a steward on the Pacific Coast Steamship Company, waiting on passengers traveling from Seattle to Los Angeles, serving their meals and cleaning their rooms. The work quickly frustrated Laurence: the pay was low, so he and the other stewards depended on tips; the hours were long; and the living conditions on the ship were horrendous, with all the Black stewards housed in the bowels of the ship, in a single room they called the

Glory Hole. So, Laurence decided to follow the footsteps of his informal mentor on the train and applied to the Pullman Company to work as a porter, receiving one of those coveted jobs in January of 1924.[11] There in West Oakland, Laurence found not only a job and a place to stay; he also discovered a community and, eventually, a cause that would become the purpose of his life. The work for his people would keep him angry, but not bitter, and hopeful about what might be possible.

THE GREAT MIGRATION WAS TRANSFORMATIVE FOR THE LIVES of working Black folks. In just a few short decades, this massive movement of people created a new Black America, distinct from the experience of the majority who had long lived in the South. While there had always been Black northerners—the descendants of those enslaved in Northern states who found their way to freedom through purchase, manumission, war service, or escape, and those freed by gradual emancipation before the Civil War—the Great Migration changed the region. Black migrants traveled great distances to find new lives for themselves and their families, leaving behind the rural Southern communities where they had worked in a rigged system of shares on the same land where their ancestors had once been considered property. Some Black people, of course, had already moved to Southern cities. While many found solidarity and improved conditions—Sarah Hill and many thousands of other washerwomen would have said as much—they also found that segregation consigned them to poor housing, and that racial violence and exclusion in the labor sector limited what work they could do. The movement north and west was the next step in their journey to seek better circumstances. In total, more than six million Black southerners chose to leave the South for the cities of the Northeast, the Midwest, and the West.

Although historians have debated whether it was the pull of good jobs and schools that attracted Black southerners to the North, or if it was the horror of lynching, the lack of citizenship rights, and the limited job opportunities that pushed migrants out of the South, the words of migrants remind us that most were simply seeking something other than the limits they faced in their Southern homes. The journeys along the thick steel and wooden ties of the railroad lines that originated in the former Confederate states and wound their pathways north landed most in the first- or second-closest major Northern city where they had kith or kin. Those from Virginia's and Maryland's Eastern Shore and the Carolinas landed in Philadelphia and New York City. Those from Upper South states like Tennessee, West Virginia, and Kentucky made their way to the Midwestern hubs of Chicago, Detroit, and Cleveland. The train from Mississippi to Chicago may have been the most well-worn migration route, with hundreds of thousands of Black Mississippians fleeing the Delta for the Windy City. Folks from Louisiana and Texas most often took trains west, building new lives in Los Angeles and Oakland.

If the railroads were the pathways of the migration, the Pullman porters were its lantern-carrying guides. Easily the most well-traveled Black folks in America, the Pullman porters provided assistance to people seeking opportunity in the North and West, connecting porters' home folks with jobs, and offering their knowledge about the cities where migrants planned to settle, including information about living spaces for rent. Porters were also beacons of resistance; like the porter who saw the atrocities in Tulsa, they bore witness to the violence of lynchings and racial massacres, and also carried copies of Northern Black newspapers to sell to Black residents in the South. Papers like the *Chicago Defender* and the *Pittsburgh Courier* served as guidebooks on job possibilities for Black workers, and on the organizations that provided services to help new families settle in and learn to navigate the city. Porters themselves had already navigated migration and its pitfalls. They had already found safe places to stay in cities segregated by custom and violent force. Many purchased modest homes in Philadelphia, Chicago's South Side, West Oakland, and Los Angeles. The importance of the porters' informal work far outweighed the daily tasks assigned by their employers.

Even as African American populations in the North and West grew exponentially during the first half of the twentieth century, family and community ties maintained their strength. As working-class Black southerners moved, they brought their beliefs with them—not only their faith ways, but also the practices of community and connection that had helped them withstand violence, exclusion, and segregation. They would still band together to provide mutual aid in the North and the West. They would still share stories about which employers to seek out and which to avoid. They would still worship on Sunday and sing God's praises. They would still dance and drink brown liquor, moving their parties from Southern jook joints to Northern speakeasies, block parties, and Chitlin' Circuit clubs. They would still watch each other's children and make sure that they got to school and were learning all that they could. They formed clubs based on the state or town where they were from so they could stay connected to news of home and folks they knew growing up. They maintained the spirit of solidarity and the willingness to fight for their rights that they had displayed in the South. That worldview would continue to shape them as they came north and west. Although life in Northern and Western cities presented a whole new set of challenges, from poor housing to urban police violence, the massive networks of family and community traveled on those trains too, moving Black Southern resistance and determination northward. Southern-born porters who lived in the cities of the North and the West were leaders in the process of maintaining the networks of home even in new places. After decades of struggle, the Pullman porters would turn these patterns of mutual support and community into a union, and then use the power of their union to reshape what was possible for all working-class Black Americans.

IT SOUNDS TOO BIBLICAL, BUT OSCAR SINGLETON MIGHT NEVER have migrated if not for a lethal bolt of lightning. If his father had not been struck that day, perhaps Oscar would have worked as a longshoreman or, like his father, as a carpenter, in the small town of Beaufort, South Carolina, where he was born, but the storm that day carved a different path for young Oscar's life. Head down, working hard on a project in the shade of a tree, Oscar's father must not have seen the ominous clouds. When lightning struck, the current split the mighty tree into two fiery pieces and then passed through his body with such force that it left him instantly breathless, stopping his heart and rendering his strong body as limp as a piece of cloth. The passing of his father meant that Oscar would not grow into manhood in rural Beaufort, but would be sent to live with his aunt in Savannah, Georgia, where a young Black man might have more opportunity for education and certainly for better employment. Savannah also happened to be a hub for the Central Georgia Railway and the home of several Pullman porters, including some of his uncles. Circumstances of place and time drove him away from the rural community of his birth and toward a position that could be a life-changing step for him and his family, a job in which he could earn a decent living and be respected as a man. Porters had to work hard in serving their passengers, but it was a job Oscar really wanted for both the mobility and the pay. He felt he could do a little tipping of his hat for the opportunity of a new life.

Just as it was for Oscar, for thousands of those who moved north and west the Great Migration was about more than just employment; it was a search for everyday dignity. Astounded by the massive flow of Black southerners moving north, Emmett J. Scott, a journalist and administrator at Booker T. Washington's famed Tuskegee Institute, began to chronicle the letters from migrants that poured into Black newspapers like the *Chicago Defender*, the *Pittsburgh Courier*, and the *New York Age*, removing the writers' names in order to protect their privacy. Notable in the content of these letters is not just a desire for work but for better treatment for themselves and for their families. One man from Charleston, South Carolina, wrote on February 10, 1917, that he sought work in New York because to him "the times in the south is [sic] very hard and one can scarcely live." A letter dated April 27, 1917, came from a man in Sanford, Florida, who wanted help finding a small town close to Chicago and to know about "treatment, work, rent and schools." An April 20, 1917, letter came from a man in Houston, describing his desperate desire to "leave the South and Go any Place where a man will Be anything Except A [cur]," then a common phrase for a despised and cowardly man. An experienced dockworker, he explained that he had no preference about where he might go, just a drive to leave the South. As he wrote, "Chicago or Philadelphia But I don't Care where so long as I Go where a man is a man."[12]

Oscar had a desire to be perceived as a man, too, and putting on his Pullman uniform got him closer, as he saw it. However, the corrosive politics of race still shaped his everyday experience in his new job. Indeed, each time Oscar Singleton heard the word "boy" ringing out of the mouths of what he called his most "segregated passengers," the word hit like a punch to the chest. His first thought was always, "Who did they think they were calling?" He was clearly a man; his crisp black uniform only emphasized his broad shoulders, and his polished demeanor was that of an educated man. His very stride was a clear reminder that he was no boy. That word, "boy," was a remnant of slavery, and the language of those striving to keep the color line alive in a changing world. White men used the term to degrade, emasculate, and dehumanize.[13]

Oscar's uncles who had worked the rail lines before him warned about that aspect of the work, the daily insults that he'd have to face without any outward show of anger. Their generation of porters were often called "George" by passengers, as if they were no more than the property of company founder George Mortimer Pullman. Most of Oscar's passengers did not disrespect him in this way. Most frequently he was called simply "porter"; he would have preferred Oscar or Mr. Singleton, but he could tolerate the generic title of his job. After all, he was a Pullman porter and part of the job was respectfully and patiently serving customers who might not exhibit the same patience or respect for him. But there were always the bad routes—from Cincinnati to Jackson or from St. Louis to Tampa—where customers would insist on disrespect.[14]

Over time, Oscar learned how to tolerate the intolerable. He learned to "wear the mask that grins and lies" that the poet Paul Laurence Dunbar so aptly described. Generally, he wore it so well that his passengers could not discern his true thoughts. When a passenger would say "boy" a few too many times or with too much enjoyment, he'd suddenly pretend that he couldn't hear them, activating the bell that passengers could use to call him and taking a seat in the next car. Oscar found that these breaks helped his "segregated" passengers learn that the call of "boy" didn't result in the best service. More importantly, such breaks gave him time to breathe and a moment for the tide of his anger to recede. So, for Oscar, the most difficult challenges of being a Pullman porter weren't the long hours or obliging passengers' every request, but summoning the patience to accommodate people beckoning him with words other than his name.[15]

However, one day Oscar's tolerance bucket got a little too full.[16] As Oscar was serving drinks to a group of women passengers, a man walked in and demanded immediate service. Oscar responded that he would be right back to assist, and the irate customer loudly demanded his drink immediately, swearing and calling him a "black son of a bitch." Oscar decided that he would tell that man exactly what he thought, in words that he refused to repeat to an interviewer more than forty years later. His unfiltered response drew the attention of every other passenger in the car. The offending passenger reported Oscar to a white conductor, demanding that he be fired. That kind of demand was common. Oscar must have known that, as one porter wrote, "many men have lost their tempers and sometimes their jobs for the want of tact."[17] When the train arrived in Chicago, Oscar was told to report to the main offices of the Pullman Company, and that he would most likely be fired. But he would not be alone: the Brotherhood would join him.

The Brotherhood's formal name was the Brotherhood of Sleeping Car Porters, and it was the porters' union. At the station that morning, Oscar was met by the union attorney, who insisted that they stop to get a hot breakfast before reporting to Pullman. The meal was good, and more importantly it calmed Oscar's spirit. Working on the rails, there was generally little time to eat, so this sit-down breakfast complete with a cup of piping hot coffee was a relief for his appetite and his mind.

When they arrived at the company offices a few minutes late, Pullman officials angrily asked why they were not on time for the appointment. The Brotherhood attorney firmly pushed back, insisting that any man who worked all night deserved the chance to eat a hot breakfast in the morning. That set a tone of respect for the meeting, something Oscar found to be a pleasant surprise. There, in Pullman's offices, Oscar had the opportunity to share his side of the story, and provided the business cards of passengers who had witnessed the man's provocation and profanity. In the end, with the assistance of the attorney and other Brotherhood officials, Oscar was reinstated with back pay.

In the 1930s, a Black man responding in kind to the insults of a white man could be killed for violating the etiquette of racial segregation. But as a Black man who was part of the Brotherhood of Sleeping Car Porters, Oscar felt empowered. Laurence Dellums, the Texas-born migrant who became a Pullman porter and then a stalwart organizer for the Brotherhood, recalled that the union made a big difference: in securing "the standard eight-hour day," "the 240-hour month," overtime, and a "lay-over rest period" between assignments. However, Dellums noted that perhaps "the most important thing of all was that it established the Pullman porter as a human being and a worker and gave him some respect and some rights that the owners and managers of the Pullman Company, and even the traveling public itself, *had* to respect! Up to then, Negroes didn't have such rights."[18] The fight that Laurence Dellums and thousands of others had waged throughout the 1920s and 1930s would substantively change what it meant to be a working Black man, so much so that Oscar Singleton could defend his dignity and his name, knowing that his union had his back.

The Brotherhood of Sleeping Car Porters, which was founded in 1936 after more than a decade of continuous campaigning for a union by porters, stood for Black Pullman car workers as a fierce and honest advocate for justice. The first of its kind, as an all-Black railway union, the Brotherhood became a clarion voice not only for decent working conditions for men like Oscar Singleton and the thousands of porters in their ranks, but also for justice for Black workers throughout the nation, including federal workers in the post office and employed in the defense industry during the Second World War. Bound under the motto "Service, not servitude," the Brotherhood of Sleeping Car Porters became more than a union; it was a shared cause and, at its height, one of the most powerful organizations in Black America. It used its platform to call to task not only corporate greed but also a nation whose wealth had been and continued to be built on the backs of Black workers. The union critiqued capitalism, fought for fair pay, and insisted that the federal government provide equal protection and equal opportunity. The radical truth-telling of the Brotherhood under the leadership of its president, A. Philip Randolph, brought together whole communities determined to forge a more just world.

IN 1900, CHARLES F. ANDERSON, A MIGRANT TO CHICAGO, TOOK a job as a Pullman porter. He did not have the position long before he decided that it was "not the 'easy job' that it is generally thought to be, but on the contrary, was one that called for the endurance of many real hardships."[19] With no union to represent him, Charles discovered that being a porter meant that he would be fatigued from working ungodly hours on his transcontinental route; he frequently worked past utter exhaustion, staying awake and on duty for twenty-four to thirty-six hours on trains that were often delayed. In spite of his tiredness, it was still his duty to be a pleasant source of knowledge for his passengers, "a sort of 'walking encyclopedia' and a bureau of information" about the timing of the train schedule, the flora and fauna outside the railcar's window, and the architecture of each of the small towns they passed.[20] Even as he worked without sleep, he risked being written up if he didn't "look fresh" while tending to his passengers on the berth. Anderson recounted the constant surveillance he and other porters labored under while working the rails; any tiny infraction could lead to a formal reprimand. Anderson had seen porters written up or fined for having a button missing on a jacket, for sneaking away for a brief moment to eat, for lying down to sleep, for wearing a winter cap on a cold night, or for getting dust on their uniform.

While there were myriad ways for the company to police porters' every move, at the same time there was no formal mechanism for vetting the complaints of Pullman employees. Complaints to the company—then run by Robert Todd Lincoln, Abraham Lincoln's son—about working conditions went unaddressed. Anderson said that "petition after petition" appeared to have been "consigned to the waste basket," given the silence of company officials.[21]

In August of 1903, Anderson decided that the Pullman porters should form a union, to better address the coercive work culture. Organizing in secret, he wrote a circular letter that was to be shared only with brother porters, calling for a meeting on State Street in the Bronzeville neighborhood in Chicago. Upon learning of the planned meeting, Pullman fired Anderson without stated cause while he was out of town, just eight days after he first circulated the notice. Angry about the suppression of his efforts and disgusted with conditions on the cars, Anderson decided to publish an account of his frustrated efforts to organize. The resulting pamphlet, "Freemen Yet Slaves Under 'Abe' Lincoln's Son or Service and Wages of Pullman Porters," detailed his efforts to organize a national union to represent the then "six thousand or more porters in the service as so many slaves to be used in whatever way they can be made to bring the company the most money." Though Anderson had not been successful in this early effort, he reminded his readers that "by their refusal to give labor a fair reward in return for its service, capitalists are really the first cause and do create unions, while labor simply gives them birth."[22] The fight to contest working and racial conditions on the rails would be a long one.

The Pullman Company was fueled by the dramatic expansion of

America's rail system. In the decades before the Civil War, a railroad boom saw the expansion of railroad lines between the Northeast and the South, connecting small towns to bigger cities and dramatically expanding the nation's capacity for regional trade along the East Coast. After the Civil War, existing routes in the South were rebuilt and Indigenous peoples in the West were violently removed from their lands, which they had long held by tradition and treaty, in order to expand the railroad from coast to coast. Through war and illegal land seizures targeting the Cheyenne, Lakota, and Pawnee, and through the exploitation of Chinese immigrants who labored to lay the tracks, the US Congress and railroad industrialists used the railroad to more thoroughly colonize North America, in a process that one historian characterizes as a form of "continental imperialism."[23]

By the 1880s, rail travel was accessible to more white Americans, not just for practical reasons, including work, but also for leisure. As rail lines extended, trips grew longer, necessitating spaces on the train for passengers to sleep. Traditional sleeping berths on trains were more like bunks in a cabin on wheels. They were plainly appointed—simple and practical, and frequently dirty and uncomfortable spaces.

Industrialist and company founder George Mortimer Pullman built the Pullman Palace Car Company to tap into the American traveler's increasing appetite for luxury. More elaborate, comfortable, and pleasing to the eye than conventional cars, Pullman Sleepers were ornate cars designed to be a well-appointed alternative for discerning travelers. They featured carved woodwork, expensive velvet seating, and clerestory windows that let in additional light. These beautiful daytime cars would then be transformed into luxurious sleeping berths, to provide the comforts of the finest hotels on the rails. Cushioned shock absorbers made the ride smooth and restful. After the Pullman "Pioneer" car was selected to be on the train bringing President Abraham Lincoln's casket from Chicago to Springfield, it became a national sensation. As one Pullman Company historian noted, "the beauty and elegance of the sleeping car became a visible symbol of the material promise of American industry and ingenuity."[24]

Almost obsessive in his control—from the manufacture of the cars to the thread count of the sheets for the beds—George Pullman called his approach to industry the Pullman System. Characterized as "uniformity in production, design, and service," this system meant that every aspect of passengers' experience on his cars was held to an exacting standard. This was, to him, the best way to make sure that his customers would pay more for their experience.[25] Every aspect of production and service was carried out by the company; cars were leased, not sold, to rail lines so that Pullman could ensure consistency of performance in all of them.

An essential part of Pullman's vision was a high standard of personal service on the cars. The first Black porter was hired in 1867, with

"African American waiter Pullman Co. Car on the New York Central Railroad Line."
ALBANY INSTITUTE OF HISTORY AND ART

the plan to have one porter assigned to each car. George Pullman did not want Northern-born Black men to work on his cars, and instead sought out men who were freed after the war. He believed that emancipated southerners were best suited for service "and by nature adapted faithfully to perform their duties under circumstances which necessitate unfailing good nature, solicitude, and faithfulness."[26]

Harkening back to the mythic, romanticized slave past of the white American imagination, Pullman, the son of a tradesman from upstate New York, wanted rail journeys in his cars to evoke stereotyped images of white life on Deep South plantations, where white people would be served by Black manservants at their beck and call, day and night.[27] Ironically, these porters would therefore have to be educated, but not too educated. Men who would be elegant, yet humble and unassuming, and above all else happy for the opportunity to serve their passengers. The imagined past of enslavement even extended to the practice of providing these Black workers as part of the lease of the cars to regional railroads, in much the same way that enslaved workers and then, later, Black prisoners in the wake of the Civil War were leased to work by their owners or the state. They would be as unknowable as any Black servant was to the white elite, their black skin signaling an anonymity and privacy that would allow passengers' indiscretions to go unchallenged. Just as an enslaved manservant would never report on a master's drunken night or adulterous affair to white strangers, neither would a Pullman porter. To white passengers, the porters' names and identities weren't important; only their presence as servants mattered. The historical archive reaffirms this racialized anonymity; although company archives catalogue many company firsts in great detail, the name of the first Pullman porter was not preserved.[28]

In practice, the Pullman Company was controlling of both Black and white workers, but it segregated its paternalism. Pullman built a

"Pullman porters, 1940." On Pullman Palace Cars the conductors were always white, while the porters were Black and sometimes Asian American.

PULLMAN PALACE CAR COMPANY COLLECTION, ARCHIVES CENTER, *NATIONAL MUSEUM OF AMERICAN HISTORY, SMITHSONIAN INSTITUTION*

company town on the outskirts of Chicago, providing not only homes but also theaters, churches, and a hospital, in order to encourage "good order" among employees. The company town provided a psychological wage as well, affirming white supremacy by limiting the town of Pullman to white workers only. Pullman subsidized some Black institutions in Chicago, too, but maintained a strict color line on and off the job.

On the rails the porters were distinct from the conductors, and like other Pullman employees they were separated both by race and assigned tasks. Conductors were the bosses of the cars; they sold and collected tickets, announced the stations, and enforced the rules of the rail lines, including racial segregation of passengers. Only white men were hired as conductors, while Black men were hired as porters. Advertisements for porter jobs stated that applicants must be "American Negro." This

773890

1234567890

1234567890

racial division of labor was a lasting one. As one Brotherhood historian noted, "the porter's job was a black man's job and by the end of the [nineteenth] century the term 'porter' raised an image of a black person while the term 'conductor' raised the image of a white person."[29] The Black Pullman porter, featured in both advertisements and Hollywood films, became integral to the brand. Pullman's predominance eventually meant that, by the 1920s, over 35 million passengers annually traveled in a Pullman car, served by one of the 12,000 Pullman porters, making the company "the single largest private employer of African Americans in the United States."[30]

According to Pullman, porter applicants had to be physically strong and willing to travel at short notice. They also had to be literate—educated but not too educated; the company preferred high school graduates over college grads, perhaps assuming that education would add more politically radical organizers to the ranks. They required applicants to submit a photograph, which many men thought was a way to ensure that porters were discernibly Black and not too light-skinned or white-passing, which might blur the racial boundaries on the cars too much for the company's liking.[31]

Porters were assigned the technical tasks of shifting the cars from daytime sitting to nighttime sleeping spaces and back again. Porters also made the beds, cleaned every space, and waited on the passengers.[32] In addition to attending to the sleeping quarters, the porters were also in charge of maintaining a comfortable temperature in the cars with heating or air-conditioning, as well as seeing to proper lighting, water, and any needed supplies. Serving the traveling public on a Pullman car was complex work; the company manual was "over 120 pages."[33] Beyond the trials of the physical labor involved, patiently serving passengers may have been the biggest challenge, as Charles F. Anderson found. As another porter put it, "first, [the Pullman porter] must obey the company's instructions; second, he must not displease passengers; and thirdly, he must have the goodwill of all; even [when passengers] wanted something that seems unreasonable, there is where the Porter is called upon to show discretion." In the end, the work of speaking with "tact and diplomacy" meant that while on the job porters were called to bring "all reasonable energies to bear" just to work in a cool and calm manner each day.[34]

The company also employed a small number of Black women as Pullman maids. Maids were not assigned to every Pullman car, but only to specially advertised "de-lux" limited-run trains and chartered trains. They waited on women passengers and cleaned the cars. The company boasted that "these maids are expert manicurists, they can sew and can care for children, babies, and elderly people." In 1926

"Porters preparing bed in Pullman Sleeper." Pullman porters were responsible for transforming daytime seating into nighttime sleeping berths.

PULLMAN PALACE CAR COMPANY COLLECTION, ARCHIVES CENTER, *NATIONAL MUSEUM OF AMERICAN HISTORY, SMITHSONIAN INSTITUTION*

there were approximately two hundred maids working for the Pull-man Company on the rails.

The work culture of Pullman porters and maids was contorted by the irrational fear of Black male sexuality. Indeed, the fear of Black men raping white women guided company policy; Pullman porters were not allowed to physically assist white women climbing in and out of cars or sleeping berths. Only white male conductors or Black women maids could hold a white woman passenger's hand to help steady her balance. Porters were even forbidden to touch a white woman passenger to wake her. Instead, they were instructed to vigorously shake the curtains on the berth to signal that it was time to rise. On the special trains, maids provided particular forms of assistance to white women and children that the twisted racial etiquette of the United States dictated that Black male porters could not.[35]

Indeed, historically, rail travel in the United States was shaped by white notions of Black men as a sexual threat and Black women as unrapable by white men. In the nineteenth and early twentieth cen-turies, first-class cars were called "ladies' cars," and set aside for white women and their gentlemen companions. Black women contested the limitations on these cars in the 1870s and 1880s, but by the 1890s, laws segregating the rails in most Southern states kept Black women and men out of first-class accommodations. Segregated ladies' cars mimicked "a domestic sphere where Black women were accepted only in servile capac-ity."[36] Pullman maids fit that tradition; their presence as servants was welcome where their presence as passengers was not. Ironically, it was Black women, both passengers and Pullman maids, who were most vul-nerable to sexual assault by white men who saw them as unprotected by the company and by the law.[37]

Despite enduring working conditions governed by the contra-dictory and pernicious stereotypes of both Sambo and brute, porters became a powerful force. These Black southerners who had grown up under the threat of lynching and the pressures of de jure segregation had the opportunity, through their work, to leave the South. Mobility gave them new eyes. Outside the South, they could respond to the conditions that threatened Black life and organize to confront those injustices.

The porters forged a community among themselves, one that was not necessarily based in the localized communities, given that porters found themselves working with other men from across the South. Still, their far-flung community fought for better pay, mobility, knowledge, and access, and aimed to benefit Black society as a whole. Porters used their buying power to purchase homes and educate their families. They remained firmly working-class, but they were highly esteemed within the Black community, imbued with the responsibility to help the race.

While the Pullman Company actively relied on the tropes of enslavement, assuming that Black folk were servile and disempowered, its leaders knew nothing about who the formerly enslaved and their descendants truly were. The porters, and their forebears, had survived the system of chattel slavery by building durable networks of resistance. They knew how to make the most of what they had. They had always made a way out of no way, and as Pullman porters they would continue that resistance work. They took advantage of the tips, the mobility, and the connections between the North and South and West to build something new for themselves and their kith and kin. They used their labor as the groundwork for change. They made the pathway for the migration of millions of Black southerners. Most formidably, because they were systematically blocked from joining white unions, they ended up building the most powerful Black labor organization in the country's history. The Pullman Company had no idea that Black men and women had created a community of workers, before and after Emancipation. Pullman porters and maids drew on their community's prior fights for liberty and citizenship to change what was possible.

———

THE PULLMAN COMPANY USED A VARIETY OF MEANS TO SUBDUE workers who looked likely to agitate for better pay, investing in efforts to keep porters from formalizing complaints about working conditions on the cars. Pullman hired people to monitor not only conditions on the cars but also the conversations of their fellow workers, serving as a corps of active spies; the company spent to suppress dissent rather than to improve pay and working conditions. Pullman sought to keep porters compliant and subservient, ruled by a climate of fear, in the belief that this was the only way to force them to provide the highest level of luxury service to passengers. The Pullman Company became "accustomed to the notion that the black porters [were] not entitled to the same working conditions and manly treatment [as] other workers."[38] Conductors not only received higher pay and better hours, but the pleasure of knowing that such prerogatives were only available to white men.

As the Great Migration accelerated and the era of the "New Negro" began, heralding a new, organized movement determined to improve the lot of African Americans, Pullman stood by its commitment to silence Black dissent. The door to union organizing and improved conditions opened a bit during the First World War, when the federal government took control of the railroads to create efficiencies in order to support the war effort. In addition to streamlining routes, standardizing service, and restructuring ticketing, the federal government decreed that Pullman employees had the right to demand better pay and decent working hours, and to form their own unions. Immediately, Pullman porters took advantage and testified before the federal Board of Railroad Wages and Working Conditions—part of the United States Railroad Administration—which governed nationalized railroads during the First World War.[39] The Board found that the "peculiar conditions under which the sleeping-car service is operated" made it "impractical to apply the principle of the basic eight-hour day in the case of the sleeping car conductors, porters and maids, orders have been issued that such employees shall have reasonable and proper opportunity for rest and sleep while actually on duty." Unfortunately, what was "reasonable and proper" was not defined.[40]

Even in this new window of opportunity, organizing a porters' union would prove to be difficult. Pullman conductors organized the all-white Order of Sleeping Car Conductors in 1918, with the requirement that members be white men written directly into their charter. Efforts by the porters to organize were divided, and a series of smaller unions came into being. The largest of these, the Brotherhood of Sleeping Car Porters Protective Union, which started as an independent effort, was later co-opted by the Pullman Company.

After 1920, when the railroads ceased to be under federal control, the Pullman Company created the Employee Representation Plan, a "company union" that was a union in name only. Pullman spent liberally on a set of bogus efforts in order to tamp down worker complaints and put those most interested in protesting workplace conditions under the scrutiny of an official appointed directly by the company's chairman. As one journalist from the Black, pro-union newspaper the *California Eagle* explained, "although the company had a paper plan of representation which claimed to offer the porters a method of handling their grievances, long, bitter years of defeat and disappointment under this company union had proved to the men that it was indeed a company union and not a porters' union." Indeed, "it was organized by the company for the company and could never function for the porters."[41]

The company union resembled earlier schemes to quell discontent.[42] For example, the company had started the Pullman Porters Benefit Association in 1915, mimicking Black church organizations and mutual aid societies. Sponsored by company funds, the Association provided death benefits and a sickness payout for porters who were ill, and also hosted annual conventions and holiday fetes, as well as formal ceremonies to honor porters who had passed away. It was led by porters who were hand-chosen by company officials. Among the porters chosen was George Pullman's "private car attendant and personal assistant," Arthur A. Wells, who became the Association's president. Pullman also funded efforts to purchase the silence and favor of Black businessmen and clergy, particularly on the South Side of Chicago, where many porters resided. Pastors, newspapermen, and business leaders participated in the festive events and received sponsorship and donations in exchange for discouraging the porters from organizing their own union. Chief among the Black anti-union businessmen was Chicago's Jesse Binga, owner of the Binga Bank, who was a former porter and a reliable supporter of the Pullman Company. Binga benefited personally from the company's largesse when $10,000 was deposited by the Association in his bank.[43] Sponsoring parties and social events, the faux mutual and union organizations were really an attempt to substitute benevolent paternalism for fair and equitable treatment and pay.

In 1925, dissatisfied with the Employee Representation Plan, porters sought once again to found their own independent union. That year, porters made just $67 a month for 400 hours of work, traveling 11,000 miles on the rails. Pullman maids made even less, a flat $50 a month. In addition, they were not paid for the hours they spent "deadheading," that is, riding to the location of an assigned route. By 1925, the white conductors were unionized, and the differences in the treatment of white conductors and Black porters were stark: "Porters were compelled to work up to 400 hours a month for a rate of pay less than one half that of the conductor, who only work[ed] 240 hours a month."[44]

Their low wages forced porters to be highly dependent on tips; they had to maintain an exacting standard in order to make a real living. Many skilled and experienced porters could earn thousands in tips each year.[45] Decades after his retirement, Oscar Singleton was hesitant to share with an interviewer just how well he did in tips, worried that the Internal Revenue Service would be interested in retroactively collecting some of his unreported earnings. Maids had a harder time with the tip system, given that etiquette dictated that a cultured white woman should not be an extravagant tipper. While the majority of porters did extremely well on tips, the practice was also highly racialized. John Gilmer Speed, the Kentucky-born managing editor of the *New York World*, wrote in 1902 that tips were a "token of their inferiority," insisting that "Native [-born, white] Americans do not as a general thing accept tips."[46] Indeed, the performance of servility, or what they might have called putting on for the white folks, became a requirement if one hoped for a tip. Porters were not simply required to do the work of making customers comfortable, but also needed to feed the egos of their passengers. They were actors who had to perform the part of the polished but inferior caretaker. They were tipped not just for the tasks they completed but also for the way they made their customers feel during the journey. No matter how skilled any individual porter was at securing the highest gratuities from passengers, in the end, the tip system left Black men dependent on the whims of white people for their wages.[47]

The circumstances porters faced made organizing both an attractive possibility and a fundamental struggle. As a massive all-Black labor force, the porters had a form of accidental power, clout that George Pullman surely did not imagine when he conceived of the position. Although the Pullman Company threatened to hire white porters, and

"Photographic postcard of Pullman Porter
T. R. Joseph circa 1930." Working as a
Pullman porter and being a member of the
Brotherhood of Sleeping Car Porters was
such a point of pride that porters often posed
in their uniforms in personal photographs.

*SMITHSONIAN NATIONAL MUSEUM OF AFRICAN
AMERICAN HISTORY AND CULTURE*

"Photographic postcard of Pullman Porter
Omer Ester and his wife, Jean." Based out
of Minneapolis, Missouri-born Omer Ester
served as a porter for decades.

*SMITHSONIAN NATIONAL MUSEUM OF AFRICAN
AMERICAN HISTORY AND CULTURE*

did in fact begin to employ Filipino immigrants in the job, Black porters had become so essential to the luxury brand that it would have been impossible to replace them. On the other hand, the lack of good jobs for Black men meant that working as a Pullman porter was an immensely appealing opportunity in a world with limited options. Far from the fields where most of their ancestors had toiled, porters made decent wages through pay and tips, while seeing much of the country and building lives away from the harshest expressions of segregation and disenfranchisement, and further from the threat of lynching. Yet, Pullman took advantage of the diminished stature of the Black American worker. The company institutionalized the porters' separateness from higher-paid white conductors and factory workers, and provided minimal pay. Although they were esteemed within the Black community, porters still faced "long hours, lack of adequate rest on trips, lack of bargaining power, and job insecurity." Indeed, as one observer noted, "through long years of custom [the company] could only regard the black Pullman Porters as inferior individuals deserving inferior treatment." Though the job was an improvement on the worst positions under white supremacy, the ongoing inequalities left porters little choice other than protest. As one porter explained, "The Pullman Porters organized because they were overworked, underpaid, and treated as menials when they wanted to be treated like men."[48]

ASA PHILIP RANDOLPH WAS A PREACHER'S KID. HIS FATHER, James W. Randolph, an AME pastor, received his call to ministry as a young man. Serving a small congregation in Jacksonville, Florida, and preaching once a month at smaller churches that did not have a full-time minister as a "circuit rider," Reverend Randolph had a ministry for the Black working class. The worshippers in his churches were the descendants of the enslaved who still made a living by their hands; many were workers who moved from farm to farm picking Florida's oranges, grapefruits, berries, and melons. Others were household workers or day laborers. Having grown up poor himself, Reverend Randolph knew that their poverty did not extend to their minds. Under the pastor's teaching they were steeped in a Black faith, a belief that the Black poor would indeed one day inherit the earth. Above all else, Reverend Randolph taught his congregants to take pride in what Black folks had accomplished despite the oppression they faced. Each Sunday, he would remind them that the racial subjugation that kept them at the bottom of society's economic ladder meant little in the end. They, with bronzed skin and woolly hair, were God's people, made in his image.[49]

Reverend Randolph's parenting mimicked his ministry. Drawn to the AME church because it was "the first black militant institution in America," he raised his two sons to be race men, in the tradition of radical Black resistance. They learned history lessons about Toussaint Louverture, Nat Turner, and Frederick Douglass by the fire in the evenings. Along with history and literature, they read anti-segregationist Black periodicals like J. Max Barber's *The Voice of the Negro*. And their father taught them a uniquely Black faith, and a cosmology based in the power in their collectivity.

Asa Philip Randolph would not be called to be a preacher like his father. He was an ardent socialist; he claimed that he first read Karl Marx "as avidly 'as children read Alice in Wonderland.' "[50] After migrating to Harlem in 1911 at the age of twenty-two, he wasn't a regular churchgoer. But even outside the walls of the church, he drew heavily on the lessons he had learned in the pews of New Hope. Randolph had been raised to be a fiery truth-teller, and he used his rhetorical inheritance to powerfully exhort passersby on Harlem's busy sidewalks with his message about Black liberation.

Randolph's message moved from the spoken word to print when he founded the *Messenger* with a fellow migrant, Chandler Owen, and support from the Socialist Party. The national magazine was widely read, presenting Randolph's brand of socialism coupled with a sharp critique of white supremacy. In the pages of the *Messenger*, Randolph argued that race was the ruse that distracted the white working class from seeing the common bond of exploitation both white and Black workers faced. A collective of Black workers could improve circumstances not only for themselves but for all working-class Americans. The training he received while traveling with his father as a circuit rider would reverberate in his baritone voice as he preached the good news about a new day for Black workers in America.[51]

In August of 1925, a group of Harlem-based Pullman porters invited Randolph to meet with them and discuss the possibility of heading up their efforts to organize. While he had never been a porter, he was, by that point, a longtime journalist and labor organizer, and, like many porters, he was a southern migrant. His brother had once worked on the rails, so he was familiar with the harsh treatment these men received. Ironically, his most important characteristic may have been the fact that he was not a porter; he could not be fired for his seemingly radical stance and his desire to build a Brotherhood for change.

Randolph had already thought through many of the challenges facing Black men working on trains. He had written about the struggle to organize across racial lines in the *Messenger* in 1924, saying that "white railroad workers fear the Negro as a strikebreaker, but still refuse to take him into their unions because of the social pressure that decrees that Negroes are inferior to white men, and hence should be religiously denied contact."[52] Randolph believed that labor organizing could be transformational and a crucial first step in deconstructing the bonds of race and capital on all Americans. He willingly took up the porters' cause.

So, beginning in the fall of 1925, Randolph and the porters began their campaign, traveling nationwide to increase awareness about the "exploitation of the Pullman Porters" and their efforts to unionize. From the very beginning, Randolph framed the cause of the Brotherhood of Sleeping Car Porters as a fight not just for better pay and decent hours, but for the betterment of Black America and America as a whole. Porters would continue to serve as ambassadors—this time for Black equality. Early in their struggle, Randolph wrote that "Negro workers have a distinct spiritual contribution to make to the American labor movement," arguing that "more than any other group of wage earners they have drunk deep of the bitter dregs of economic exploitation." But "out of the tragic depths of their suffering," Black workers had the capacity to "bring forth a new, vital, stirring message for industrial peace with justice which will enrich, ennoble, and inspire the life of labor, thereby advancing the cause of humanity."[53]

Randolph was a powerful and convincing orator, and in the early days, his speaking engagements were some of the best chances to recruit new members and broaden support.[54] The outspoken anti-lynching advocate turned women's suffragist Ida B. Wells-Barnett became one of the Brotherhood's earliest boosters, after she hosted a Women's Forum featuring Randolph in her home in December of 1925. Wells-Barnett led the Alpha Suffrage Club, a women's voter organization that became influential in city politics by backing the election of Chicago's first Black alderman, Oscar De Priest. Wells-Barnett was curious, and more than a bit skeptical, about the opposition to the union that many of the city's leading Black men expressed. She wanted to give the city's Black women leaders an opportunity to make their own judgment about Randolph and the Brotherhood. Randolph did not disappoint. Indeed, his talk successfully convinced Wells-Barnett and the Women's Forum to endorse the efforts of the Brotherhood, which they described as a "great movement." The group's positive opinion helped seed crucial support for the union throughout the city of Chicago, counterbalancing the silence of community leaders who were beholden to Pullman.[55]

The fight to build the union was a long and vicious one. Pullman, of course, had a well-established reputation as an anti-union company. Perhaps the most striking example had occurred during the economic depression of 1893 and 1894, after Pullman drastically cut the pay of white workers who lived in the company town but did not reduce rents as well. When workers organized a group to represent their concerns about low pay and unfair policies, George Pullman would not meet with the delegation and instead fired them. Their harsh treatment sparked nationwide strikes and violent clashes between the American Railway Union on one side and rail companies and the federal government on the other. In the end, Pullman, not the workers, won out. Decades later, as the Brotherhood began to organize, they first had to consider what it meant for Black men to organize a union at a company that was more than willing to violently suppress *white* workers.

Much of the work of the Brotherhood had to be conducted in surreptitious ways. In the pages of the *Messenger*—which they knew very few white people read—the porters could share news of their organizing efforts and talk about what they hoped to change with an independent union. Porters who worked on the routes between New York and Chicago who supported the union cause became "underground couriers, delivering bundles of *The Messenger* with its description of the porters' grievances and its presentation of the brotherhood's program. They carried leaflets and confidential communiqués to the brotherhood nucleus already operating in Chicago."[56] Membership rolls and votes were kept truly secret—that is, out of the pages of the *Messenger*—so that company spies could not as easily target the active leaders.

As the porters worked to create consciousness about the union cause, Randolph spoke at a labor forum at John Wesley AME Zion Church in Washington, DC, that featured Senator Royal Copeland of New York as well as Mary Church Terrell, a leading Black clubwoman, suffragist, and race advocate who had recently announced her support for the Brotherhood. After the forum Terrell accompanied Randolph to the White House to meet with President Calvin Coolidge.[57]

Randolph's high-profile trip to the White House was such a threat to Pullman that the company had him trailed by Perry Parker, a former parlor car porter who had been promoted to be a company representative and grand chairman of the Pullman Porters Benefit Association.[58] In response to Randolph's work, Parker hosted a dinner in Washington, DC, paid for by the company, "in order to send out resolutions condemning Randolph and the Brotherhood." Pullman porter and union field representative S. E. Grain characterized Parker and other Black company spies sent to attack the Brotherhood as "spineless, unsophisticated stool pigeons [or] barking dogs . . . carry[ing] out their master's voice." Describing them as worse than white segregationists, Grain was disgusted by the way Parker was determined "to keep down the progress of his own people." Even with the company doing its best to stop them, the membership drives of the Brotherhood were successful from coast to coast. Grain reminded the readers of the newspaper the *New York Age* that "fourteen thousand Pullman porters, armed with organization in the holy cause of liberty . . . are invincible."[59]

The porters hoped in the long run to be invincible, but first there would be more than a decade of struggle while they battled for recognition. The Oakland migrant turned porter Laurence Dellums, who now went by just his initials, C.L., joined the Brotherhood early on, in 1925. Fervent for change, later that year he was elected head of the Oakland chapter. Dellums knew there would be a price to pay—consequences for his public stance on behalf of the union.

One day in 1927, C.L. was on an intrastate run in California with just three passengers in his car. On his break, separated a bit from his passengers, he was reading the *Messenger* and the *Pittsburgh Courier*. One passenger passed close by, close enough to see the masthead of the paper, then took a seat near Dellums and soon after rang the call bell. When C.L. asked what he needed, the passenger requested a couple of pillows, even though he had refused pillows earlier in the day. When C.L. returned from the next car with the pillows, the passenger had moved to the porter's seat and was reading his copies of the *Messenger* and the *Courier*, holding them high in the air. He commented that he "had never seen a magazine or a paper that seemed to be published by Negroes," and asked, "Are they?" Dellums explained that they were indeed Black-owned publications. The passenger acted as if he was impressed, saying that it was "excellent" and that the papers appeared to have "brilliant articles . . . written by [A. Philip] Randolph, Chandler Owens, and George Schuyler." Dellums was suspicious, but hoped that this very curious passenger just happened to want to chat that day about labor and race.

His suspicions were confirmed when he was called in and told that a passenger had complained that he had "propagandiz[ed] . . . about the union and [shown] him these papers." The Pullman superintendent who was interrogating him grew angry when Dellums denied the claim. The superintendent alleged that the Brotherhood was "Bolshevik propaganda" and accused Randolph of being on "orders from Moscow!" Seeing that his discharge slip was already on the superintendent's desk, Dellums laughed and called his superior's bluff, asking, "Where is that?" and "What's a Bolshevik?" mispronouncing it the way his supervisor had, as "Boolsheevik." The superintendent turned red with anger when he realized that Dellums was mocking him and not fearful about losing his job. He fired Dellums and told him, "Now you remember one thing . . . you're being discharged for unsatisfactory service only." The union leader snapped back that he knew why he was discharged and that his service didn't "have a damn thing to do with it!"[60]

Dellums walked away from Pullman that day, still fully invested in the union's cause even though he would never work as a porter again. For the rest of his career, C.L. never stopped organizing on behalf of the Brotherhood. In fact, his main concern the day he was discharged was making sure that the men he represented didn't lose faith in their cause. He knew that his firing was probably the first of many, designed to intimidate and discourage. He activated the Oakland chapter's "grapevine" to call a meeting. And the Oakland porters did meet several times; Dellums encouraged them to stay calm and stay in the union, and that the retaliation from Pullman could only work if they collectively panicked and backed down. Even as he had lost his own job, he told them that "there never was a war without some battles, and there never was a battle without casualties." He had always worked, and had faith that he could find employment somewhere else. He framed his own firing as a "small sacrifice" needed for the bigger cause, and he hoped to be an example for others, arguing that it was "worth the effort to stay." His father's lesson to be angry, but not bitter, kept him focused on what he could still do to move the cause of the Brotherhood forward, even as a former porter.[61]

Dellums was not alone in this regard. Even after men and women were fired for participating in the union, members continued to pay dues and support its organizing efforts. What they were building was not predicated on employment, but rather constructed out of the faith that their cause was more important than any one individual. Collectively, they saw what they were doing as having the power to improve the lives of the Black working class writ large. Dellums's firing did not have its intended effect. On the contrary, it led him to redouble his efforts and gave him a platform to remind the porters that even in the worst-case scenario they could still be an essential part of the cause. It also impressed the union leaders, who brought him on as a full-time organizer.[62]

Firing Dellums was the first shot in Pullman's battle against the union in Oakland, one of the most successful cities for Brotherhood organizing. Along with Dellums, several men were fired in the next week and a half, all on thin and farcical charges. The following year, 1928, saw an all-out assault by Pullman in Oakland, when forty-five men were fired and an additional forty-five were suspended. So many were fired, in fact, that the company had a hard time staffing the trains and was forced to transfer assignments to districts in other regions of the country. In spite of it all, most of the men remained loyal to the union cause.

In the months after his firing, C.L. began his life as a full-time organizer, traveling the rails coast to coast to encourage union members to continue the fight. Like Randolph, Dellums was a powerful speaker, and became a leading figure of the union on the entire West Coast. He recalled that in those days his trademark was to encourage an audience by asking, "What do you have to lose? You've only got four things anyway: a hard job, low pay, long hours, and a mean bossman! That's all you've got. What if you do lose it?"[63]

Firings and suspensions were just part of the company efforts to silence the union. Pullman also funded a campaign of misinformation directed at Chicago's leading Black newspapers.[64] After a Pullman Company attorney purchased a controlling interest in the *Chicago Whip*, the paper embarked on a campaign against the Brotherhood, while copies of the paper were mysteriously distributed for free to the porters at Chicago train stations. The main organ of the Great Migration, the *Chicago Defender*, led a campaign of discouragement targeting the Brotherhood from 1925 to 1927. Randolph took the *Defender* and its editor Robert Abbott to task in the pages of the *Messenger*, renaming the weekly the *Surrender* and rebutting their calls for caution point by point.[65]

Beyond firings and seeking to purchase influence, the Pullman Company's tactics put lives at risk. One porter and union organizer in Jacksonville, Florida, was charged by local police with the crime of "preaching racial equality." Pullman Company officials had alerted local officials that the porter was distributing copies of the *Messenger* to Black residents. The porter was told to leave the state or be sentenced to labor on a chain gang.[66] The employer that conservative Black people characterized as a benevolent friend of the Negro was willing to unleash the power of southern lynch mob injustice to silence union efforts. Southern porters would continue to share information and newspapers secretly, but with additional caution.

While seeking to increase their numbers and the wider movement for support, the porters attempted to utilize the levers of government, including the Railway Labor Act, enacted in 1926, to force the company to recognize the union and negotiate for better terms. Given that the law called for "the prompt disposition" of disputes and active negotiations, Randolph and the Brotherhood hoped that the government would force Pullman to the negotiating table. They also attempted to lobby the Interstate Commerce Commission to institute just wages and sanction the company for its practice of pointing to tips as compensation when porters were hired, in violation of the Interstate Commerce Act. However, both government agencies sidestepped intervention on behalf of the porters, while the company refused to come to the bargaining table.[67]

The Pullman porters reached a true low in their struggle for recognition when Randolph called for a strike in 1928 in an attempt to force the government, and the company, to finally act. The Brotherhood voted to support the strike in overwhelming numbers; however, as the moment when the strike would begin grew closer, Randolph feared the level of retribution in store for the porters who walked out. Taking note of the ongoing unwillingness of the government to act on their behalf, the Brotherhood leadership called off the strike. Many people who had once been committed supporters lost faith.[68]

Randolph was insistent that the best way for the Brotherhood to be recognized as a union would be as part of the American Federation of Labor (AFL), even though the AFL had long ignored the systemic exclusion of Black workers from the ranks of its unions. Many hoped the Communist Party would provide an important alternative to the racism of the AFL. But Randolph, an ardent socialist, was anti-Communist, and felt that the best way to push the white labor movement in the country was from within. The Brotherhood applied for recognition from the AFL, while Randolph waged war on the racism within American unions as a member of the AFL himself.[69]

The Depression and the resulting downturn in train travel rocked the relatively secure place porters had in the economy. With less and less leverage, the porters' cause seemed to be headed to inevitable failure. Initially there was little reason to hope that the New Deal would provide a pathway for change for Black workers. The 1933 National Industrial Recovery Act, which was intended to guarantee living wages, ended up institutionalizing inequality by honoring existing pay scales that provided systematically lower wages for Black workers. In industries where Black wages *did* go up, many Black employees were fired to make room for white workers. The majority of workers, those doing agricultural and household labor, were exempted from the protection of the legislation altogether. This initial salvo of the New Deal left Black workers worse off than where they started, with discriminatory wages or exclusion from protection inscribed into federal law. Pullman porters, the most organized of all Black American workers, were initially also excluded from protection, based on the argument that they should be categorized as "employee[s] of a carrier engaged in interstate transportation" and covered under the Emergency Transportation Act. In fact, porters were not covered under that act, since they worked for a company that was technically not a railroad.[70]

In the end, the Brotherhood finally obtained federal recognition. Pressure on federal officials by porters and their advocates led to a breakthrough, under a 1934 revision of the Railway Labor Act. This crucial change brought the Pullman Company and all of its employees under the jurisdiction of the legislation. Withering criticism of the racial biases within the New Deal and the failure of the federal government to advocate on behalf of Black citizens had made a difference. For the first time, government officials used their power to force the Pullman Company to meet and negotiate new terms with the all-Black union. After more than a decade of organizing, it was an incredible breakthrough.[71]

In August 1936, the AFL awarded the Brotherhood of Sleeping Car Porters an international charter. One year later, the Pullman Company would sign a deal providing a dramatic reduction in monthly hours from 400 to 240 and $1.25 million for higher pay for porters and maids. The Brotherhood became the first federally recognized Black union in American history. Though they had endured more than a decade of frustration, the union members had "the determination to win." Just as the *California Eagle* had noted almost ten years earlier, a "new spirit has been born, a new Pullman Porter has come to be. Service not servitude is the motto of these brave men. . . . Square shoulder, clear-eyed, unassuming and unafraid. No favors does he ask, but justice he demands. Truly the spirit of America is represented in this man, and surely the true Americans will support their cause."[72]

THE EXISTENCE OF THIS HARD-WON UNION MADE A SIGNIFIcant difference in Oscar Singleton's life. In addition to helping him deal with the insults of his segregated passengers, the decent wages and good tips he earned allowed him the ability to fund the college educations of his own children and those of a few of his relatives. He had the financial freedom to purchase his own home, and to purchase nice cars. But the Brotherhood could not change the larger circumstances of the world around him. When Pullman forced Oscar and several other porters to settle in Salt Lake City, Utah, in order to provide better coverage for a route, he was confronted with a city full of people who had been taught that Black people were less than in the eyes of both God and man. No matter how hard Oscar tried, he could not get local white residents to properly accommodate his family. He could not rent a decent apartment; when he found places where he and his wife would have wanted to live, white landlords would say the apartments had suddenly been rented out. When the couple passed by days later, the "for rent" signs had magically returned. When Oscar attempted to purchase a home for his family, white realtors would only show him properties in the worst part of town, ironically on land that directly abutted the railroad tracks. When he found a nice home in a different neighborhood on his own, he and his wife's attempts to buy it were rebuffed.

Eventually, after all the union porters based in Salt Lake City demanded change, company officials began to put pressure on town officials to accommodate its Black employees, and Oscar was allowed to purchase a home he wanted, in spite of a petition organized by the neighbors. When the couple finally moved in, they discovered that their neighbors refused to speak to or make eye contact with them. This lasted for several years, eventually cracking when the neighbors realized that the Singletons had not "come out of the jungle." As much as the economic gains that came from organized labor mattered, Black workers' ability to live as free people and make their own choices was still hindered by the corrosive logic of race that had made the battle for union recognition such a formidable challenge in the first place.

AS THE LEADER OF THE FIRST FEDERALLY RECOGNIZED BLACK union, A. Philip Randolph was invited to attend a meeting with President Franklin Delano Roosevelt at the wartime White House, alongside NAACP leader Walter White and the head of the National Urban League, T. Arnold Hill. The three Black leaders were there to ask for the equal inclusion of Black people in the armed forces and defense industries. At the time, the armed services were still segregated and the Marines excluded Black men altogether. Meanwhile, the ramped-up wartime defense industry was turning Black workers away. The nation was being asked to come together to support the fight for democracy abroad, while Black Americans suffered under the burdens of second-class citizenship. Randolph, White, and Hill were hopeful that the president might recognize that change was urgent.

The meeting was a shocking disappointment. Throughout their conversation the president referred to Black men as "boys," suggested that serving as a mess attendant was actually a good position for a Black soldier, and then offered the idea that the Navy start "a colored band on some of these ships, because they're darn good at it." After closing the meeting with vague promises to investigate the question, the president released an official White House statement reaffirming the armed services' policies of segregation and exclusion, falsely implying that the union and civil rights leaders had agreed with the tepid statement continuing the status quo.[73]

Refusing to be called boys and tired of being forced to quietly accept second-class citizenship, Randolph and the members of the Brotherhood were determined to make good on their promises that their hard-won platform would do more than just assist the porters. Frustrated with the president's unwillingness to move, Randolph called for a march that would "let the Negro masses speak." He organized the March on Washington Movement to demand equal access to home-front defense jobs during the Second World War, after fruitless lobbying behind the scenes that included meetings with Eleanor Roosevelt and New York City mayor Fiorello La Guardia. His call for the march grabbed the attention of the federal government.[74]

Black communities around the nation responded, with porters once again becoming movement ambassadors, this time for citizenship. They organized in New York, Detroit, Oakland, Los Angeles, and Chicago to gain grassroots support. They sold march buttons and distributed bulletins explaining their demands. The porters canvassed in Black neighborhoods, recruiting people who would be willing to travel to the capital. Unlike their earliest union organizing, their efforts had nearly universal support in Black newspapers and from Black ministers. In just a few short weeks, the response to the campaign indicated that it was a resounding success. Over 100,000 people committed to marching in Washington.

Randolph and White's next meeting with the president would be very different, with the president on the defensive, fearful of how 100,000 Black protesters in the nation's capital would look to the world. When they refused to back down in exchange for promises to negotiate and for the president to "reach out" to defense officials, Roosevelt conceded to Randolph's demand to desegregate defense employment. Randolph took the opportunity to push for the desegregation of all federal employment, pointing out that the government was the "worst offender" in enforcing segregated employment. The president's fear of an all-Black march suddenly made the concerns of the Black working class a national security matter. He agreed to make the change.[75]

Over the next few days, Randolph reviewed drafts of what would become Executive Order 8802 until he and the White House found clear and unequivocal language for the presidential decree. The executive order was the first of its kind, an anti-discrimination action that provided new access for Black workers to defense industries and government employment. The cultural shift caused by the executive order, coupled with a tremendous demand for workers, opened new opportunities for Black folk in every major city in the North.[76] Randolph would become the nation's foremost Black labor leader, meeting with every president until his death in 1979. The power of Black working people's collectivity, independence, and determination had secured recognition: from the president, from the federal government, and from one another.

C. L. Dellums, who had lost his job as a porter years before, became Randolph's right-hand man within the Brotherhood. Much as his father's four-chair barbershop had served as a haven for political decision-making in Corsicana, Texas, his pool hall, with an office on the second floor, became a hub of Black activism in West Oakland. Dellums was also an active member of the civil rights cause and encouraged men in the Brotherhood to join as well.

Among the men organizing in Dellums's Oakland community was H. T. S. Johnson, a minister whom young Laurence had first met when he went in search of his brother in Tulsa in 1921. C.L. recalled his great admiration for, and political partnership with, Johnson, who along with William Dellums was among those arrested for leading Tulsa's Black men in resistance to the mob. C.L. remembered that Tulsa officials had demanded that those seeking bail and wanting to live in Tulsa should find a white man to vouch for them, and then register under the name of the white man and white employer in order to stay free. Even though a white Tulsa resident who knew Johnson offered to vouch for him, Johnson refused to be vouched for. He was no slave. Johnson joined the diaspora of people who left Tulsa and never returned, unwilling to reside in white supremacy's cage without protest.

C. L. Dellums organized within the vast networks that were established during the Great Migration, remaining connected to the community where he was born, the community where his brother had suffered unthinkable violence, and a Brotherhood of labor that spanned the nation. Their achievements, built solidly on the structures their forebears had left for them, would make new things possible for the Black working class.

CHAPTER FIVE

Minnie and Bruce

They were getting ready for a cakewalk that sunny day in May—not the turn of phrase that means something easy, but the elaborate dance invented by enslaved Africans that joyfully mocked the ways of white people in plain sight. As a free people, the descendants of the enslaved had continued to pour their unique frustrations and creativity into the dance, so much so that by the turn of the twentieth century the cakewalk included a modern ragtime beat to measure their steps.[1] However, this particular cakewalk, meant to be a fundraiser and a moment of fellowship at a little church in rural Accomack County, Virginia, ended up being one dancer short. Sixteen-and-a-half-year-old Minnie Savage was supposed to dance, but that day she had other plans.[2]

Sitting on a hard wooden pew waiting for everyone else to arrive for the cakewalk, Minnie whispered to her uncle to pass along the message that she had a headache and needed to go home. She knew her daddy

"During the church service at a Negro church in Heard County, Georgia, April 1941."
JACK DELANO, *SCHOMBURG CENTER FOR RESEARCH IN BLACK CULTURE,*
NEW YORK PUBLIC LIBRARY DIGITAL COLLECTIONS

was on the way and she wanted to be long gone before he arrived so that she wouldn't have to lie to his face. Normally she loved a church day, particularly Sundays. The Lord had commanded that everyone have a day of rest and Minnie looked forward to the one day of the week with no weeding, tending, or bending low to pick beans or dig potatoes. She would sit with her cousins and friends during service, enjoying the songs and the fellowship, and she liked waiting to see who would lead the spontaneous shouts of praise and hearing the preacher bring the Word.[3] On this day, however, she was preparing to slip out before the day's events began.

As soon as her uncle gave her permission to go home, Minnie moved, almost silently, head bent toward the floor, one finger slightly raised in reverence to the Lord, sprinting as quietly as she could on the balls of her feet on her way to the door. As she stepped outside, she slowed for a second while she adjusted to the midday sun. She saw her cousin's lanky friend in the distance.[4] Minnie Savage had lied. She didn't have a headache; she had a train ticket to Philadelphia.

Riding briskly along in the wagon that was taking her to the train station, she was sad that she had to deceive her folks to get away, particularly in God's house, but it was the only time when she knew for sure that both her parents would be occupied and distracted. She was defying her parents' wishes; Minnie had asked them about the possibility of moving north many times before, but her father, Thomas Savage, was dependent on her labor and wanted her to stay close to family and home, to continue working on the farm with him. Despite his protests, she felt she had to leave.[5] Some of her relatives and classmates had gone, some venturing out on their own, others sent north to mind the children of their sisters who worked jobs as live-in maids in fancy mansions.[6] Many of those sisters made enough money that they could send some home to their folks. The migrants would return back home each fall to visit in

Seeing migrants return home with new clothes and cars made Black southerners want to go north.   "NEW CAR (SOUTH RICHMOND, VIRGINIA), FROM THE PROJECT
THE NEGRO IN VIRGINIA." ROBERT H. MCNEILL, COURTESY OF SUSAN MCNEILL,
SMITHSONIAN AMERICAN ART MUSEUM

high style, the girls sporting satin-lined, dropped-waist dresses, bobbed hair, and arched eyebrows, the young men driving home in pretty cars with big whitewalls, dressed in pinstriped city suits and sharp shoes, all of them bragging about a freedom that Minnie wanted too.

It was 1918. Minnie couldn't have known that she was near the front of a grand exodus that would change Black life and transform the nation. She just knew that at sixteen and a half, she felt as though she had no future in Accomack County, Virginia. Hundreds had already left her small community; hundreds would leave in her wake.

By happenstance, among those leaving Accomack in this era was my father's father, Theodore Brooks Murphy, who was called Brooks as a child but as an adult preferred to go by the name Bruce. Known in our family for his incredible memory, which made him an exhaustive storyteller and, occasionally, a good gambler, he surely spun a rich and detailed narrative of his journey whenever he told it. He died years before I was born, yet I feel like I know him from the stories my family has shared, even if with the passage of time some of the details of his journey are lost.

Strikingly, Bruce and Minnie were born just months apart, both in 1902. Family lore suggests that he also migrated at the age of sixteen, in 1918. From the archival record, I can see that his journey north must have occurred prior to the arrival of the 1920 census taker at the Murphy home in Pungoteague, about 15 miles south of Lee Mont, where Minnie lived with her family.[7] Only one train route from Virginia's eastern shore connected to Philadelphia. These two teens in search of a freer life must have followed the same path. I cannot know if the two ever spoke to each other, but both Minnie and my grandfather came from the same ground and followed a similar trajectory, even if the opportunities available to Black women and men at the time were very different.

———

ACCOMACK COUNTY SITS ON THE NARROW SOUTHERN TIP OF the peninsula that is comprised of present-day Delaware and the Eastern Shore of Maryland and Virginia. The flat and fertile land bordered by the Chesapeake Bay on the west and the Atlantic on the east was named by the Indigenous people who lived there for countless generations before British colonizers arrived. It was the site of one of the first white settlements in Virginia, and one of the first places where Minnie's and my African forebears were held in bondage, beginning in the 1620s. The county's enslaved had been brought directly to the port of Accomack to be sold, or were purchased from traders during travels across the bay. The county's elite white plantation owners grew wealthy on the backs of enslaved laborers, who did the arduous work of clearing very old trees, digging canals to drain the swampy land, and carving plantations out of the natural landscape. But holding people in bondage was not reserved for the wealthiest whites on the Shore; small farmers were also slaveholders, and almost 50 percent of white families in the area held enslaved people by the 1750s. By that point, enslaved people made up almost half of the region's population.[8]

Their work made the fertile land and its surrounding waters productive for the men and women who held them as property, even as the physical separation of the peninsula kept them a land apart from the rest of Virginia—it was, for generations, difficult to access. The train changed things. Expanding into the Eastern Shore in the 1880s, the New York, Philadelphia, and Norfolk Railroad (NYP&N) was originally built to move coal from Virginia to Philadelphia and then on to New York City while bypassing Washington, DC. Although Accomack had always traded across the bay with Baltimore, the railroad fueled an agricultural boom in the county as well as the founding of the Eastern Shore Produce Exchange in 1900.[9]

The Produce Exchange was led by William A. Burton, an Accomack County–born son of a slaveholding family that had been in the region since colonial times. Burton, who had moved to New York City as a young man to trade produce for a Commission house there, was tapped by white farmers on the Eastern Shore to help found a cooperative that would allow for collective marketing of their sweet and white potato crops all along the East Coast.[10] Modeled after other cooperative farming efforts of the time, the Produce Exchange made the isolated Eastern Shore the hub of potato production for two regions, as small farmers banded together to create greater market security and shared wealth. Unsurprisingly, the Produce Exchange was a whites-only cooperative. In spite of the fact that Black farmers were purchasing their own land

and making efforts to be independent, they would not be able to realize the full potential of their efforts. From independent Black farmers to tenants and sharecroppers like the Savage and Murphy families, Black Accomack was completely shut out of the local boom, barred by company bylaws from purchasing shares. The region's Black farmers could sell their crops only at the arbitrary prices set by the white farmers of the Exchange—well below market value—even as the labor of thousands of Black workers was essential to the profitability of the venture and the entire region.[11] It was Black men and women, boys and girls planting, maintaining, and harvesting the crops, but those laboring at the bottom of the economic pyramid would not benefit from the windfall.

Although the white stakeholders of the Produce Exchange viewed the Black farmers of Accomack County as expendable, unskilled labor, they were in fact immensely skilled. My grandfather, Bruce, was taught at a young age how to cultivate potatoes by his father. They would begin by placing small seed potatoes from a previous year's crop in a hotbed—a rich, nutrient-dense soil of chicken manure—to encourage the tubers to root. Taking care to regulate the warmth and moisture of the bed so as not to burn or dry out the plants, they would maintain a watchful eye as the potatoes sprouted. Carefully disentangling the "slips," or beginnings of vines sprouting from the potatoes, they would keep the young plants in plentiful water until they rooted. When it came time to plant the growing vines in the earth, they would dig a hole deep enough to pull groundwater, use that water to moisten the mound, and place each slip into the soil. Throughout the season they would make sure the crop was weeded and watered; not too wet, which could cause the potatoes to molder, and not so dry that they would grow long, because potatoes that had grown long looking for water would be more stringy and less sweet. At the end of the season, they would harvest the potatoes, after their lush vines began to yellow but before they turned frost-bitten black. Accomack's Black farmers could look at those vines and know by sight the ones with the best and biggest potatoes. Their quick hands were tasked with digging them dexterously from the earth without scarring the sensitive skins and spoiling the harvest. Their horticultural knowledge, passed down over generations, if properly applied in a year when the weather complied, would yield a perfect crop—sweet, round, and as full of rich sap as possible.[12]

Despite the riches Black workers cultivated in bondage and after Emancipation as free people, Black workers in Accomack—skilled farmers who owned their own land as well as sharecroppers and laborers—were some of the poorest residents in the state, ruled strictly by the small white elite in the small town of Onancock, who attempted to wield absolute power well into the early decades of the twentieth century. But by the turn of the century, in response to white violence and low pay in a prosperous economy, hundreds of Black residents on the Eastern Shore were beginning to leave, seeking work and a better life in Baltimore or Philadelphia. In fact, so many Black residents left the county that there was a labor shortage that had local white landowners complaining that the "negro population [was] drifting toward the cities and towns" and that those who remained were "thriftless and not to be depended upon," an ironic claim given their own status as landholders loath to labor in their own fields.[13]

Denied the profits of the cooperative Produce Exchange and leveraging their power as workers in the midst of an agricultural boom, Black workers who stayed in Accomack sought to become more independent. Although no records of an organization are extant today, what was touted as an anonymous account of a meeting was published in Accomack's local white newspaper, the *Peninsula Enterprise*, as an alert to local white farmers. According to this breathless report, Black laborers in Accomack met in secret at night pledging to "only accept employment from the white people when no other means of a livelihood was open to them," "to charge always the highest price for wages they could possibly get," and "to do as little as possible for those employing them."[14] Evidently, this is what Black people striving for landownership, fair wages, and set work hours sounded like to a white observer. Black efforts at independence were just as threatening as their efforts to become equal participants in the Produce Exchange.

News of Black people deciding to purchase from Black stores and to demand fair wages made headlines nationwide; even the *New York Times* caught wind of the organizing efforts in Virginia, publishing a front-page story claiming that the "oath" not to work for white employers was "equivalent to saying that they will not work at all," as if self-employed Black farmers and businesspeople were a complete impossibility.[15] The threat of the Black working class organizing in the same ways that white industrial workers were organizing around the country was unimaginable to many, if not most, white observers. It is in such reactions that we can see evidence of a powerful network of mutuality within Black life on the Eastern Shore. We can imagine all the ways that Black workers came together: meeting in churches and fraternal halls, talking in lowered tones while shopping in town, sharing ideas in the fields as they weeded or on the waterways as they fished, frustrated at being locked out of the opportunities that were making white farmers prosperous. We know that these organized workers, often one by one, demanded higher wages when negotiating the price for their labor at harvest. And the organizing was clearly feared by the white establishment: by the fall of 1906 the *Peninsula Enterprise* began to demand that white farmers plan reprisals against the growing number of Black workers insisting on better pay.[16]

SAMUEL L. BURTON AND JAMES D. UZZLE REPRESENTED WHAT the descendants of the formerly enslaved could do on their own, even as white residents actively blocked equal access to new opportunities. They would pay a price for their spirit of independence. Samuel Burton, who, probably not by happenstance, shared a surname with William Burton, was the first son of James and Maria Burton to be born into freedom. As a free man, James worked as a waggoner and a farmer; his wife Maria was listed in the census as "keeping house."[17] Samuel would be among the first generations of newly freed Black southerners to earn a college degree in the 1890s. After graduation, he returned to Accomack, serving first as a schoolteacher and later, in 1897, opening a successful grocery store for Black residents in the town of Onancock. Samuel was not only a businessperson but also an active member of the community. He joined Black fraternal orders in Accomack, serving as president of the local chapter of Prince Hall Masons and the Odd Fellows.

The impact of Samuel Burton's grocery store must have been significant for Black folk in Accomack County. For Black tenant farmers and sharecroppers, the ability to buy or seek credit from a Black grocer provided a crucial opportunity to upend the totalizing financial hold white landholders had on the people who worked their land. Most Black sharecroppers and tenants were doubly subjugated by white landholders who not only paid out less than a fair share for crops they grew, but also charged exorbitant prices in their stores and extended credit, in a cash-poor economy, on terms that bordered on usury. Fair credit rates from a Black grocer could make all the difference in the profitability of Black farmers' labor. Beyond the financial independence was the joy of having a Black-owned space, a meeting place where Black folk could catch up, laugh, and talk about the goings-on away from white people's earshot. It was not just a store; it was a community space.

James D. Uzzle, for his part, was the Hampton Institute–educated principal of the local Black public school and the owner and editor of the only Black newspaper in the county, the *Peninsula Times*.[18] Although no editions of the newspaper have survived, it is easy to imagine the importance a free Black-owned press had on organizing in the county. Black newspapermen like James Uzzle were at the forefront of campaigns against segregation, disenfranchisement, and economic inequality across the South. Independent Black presses were an essential component of black organizing. Together with Samuel Burton, Uzzle sponsored the Tasley Fair, the region's largest Black agricultural event, which annually drew an estimated 4,000 participants, demonstrating the depth and power of their network and influence on the Eastern Shore.[19] Even in a place as rural and remote as Accomack County, Samuel and James represented the independence of "new issue Negroes."[20]

In 1892, independent Black journalist Ida B. Wells-Barnett had to flee Memphis, Tennessee, after chronicling the lynching of Thomas Moss, Calvin McDowell, and Will Stewart. Moss's store, the People's Grocery, undercut the prices of a white grocer, who was angry at losing his Black clientele; Moss and his two employees were brutally killed to stymie Black independence.[21] When Wells-Barnett asserted in the pages of the *Memphis Free Speech* that market competition, not the rape of white women, drove white men to lynch Black men, she too became a target. The *Memphis Commercial Appeal*, the local white newspaper, demanded that Wells be lynched and her business partner, J. L. Flemming, be castrated and burned at the stake. The two escaped with their lives, but their press was burned to the ground and the People's Grocery did not reopen.

Fifteen years later, in the fall of 1907, a similar dynamic began to play out in Accomack County. Local whites started targeting Burton and Uzzle in the belief that they were behind the efforts to organize calls for a minimum wage and were perhaps using the all-Black Tasley Fair as one of the spaces to discuss Black agricultural independence. They feared that the agricultural fair was actually a movement center for the Black working-class labor resistance.[22] Local officials drummed up false charges of theft against Sylvanus Conquest, a twenty-two-year-old Black man employed by Burton as a clerk. Although Conquest has once been a farm laborer, Burton's business gave new opportunities for independent employment and a wage not determined by local landholders.[23] When Burton came to his young employee's defense, he became embroiled in the legal fight and was physically attacked inside the county courthouse after giving his testimony. The assault on his business partner Uzzle was even more straightforward: that same day, a mob of angry white men beat him in the town square. Fighting to escape the onslaught of blows, Uzzle shot one of the attackers in the thigh in self-defense. Word of the shot sent the county into mayhem.

Uzzle and Burton escaped the initial attack by hiding in the wilderness, just as enslaved people trying to avoid capture had done in prior generations. As more and more white men and boys gathered to find and kill Burton and Uzzle, Black Accomack prepared for the attack they knew was sure to come. One group organized a nighttime roadside defense to try to keep armed marauders away from Black residences. The defenders fired on a mail wagon that had been commandeered by the mob. After the roadside firefight, those Black defenders who had fired scattered into the woods. Unable to find them, local authorities charged Burton and Uzzle, both of whom were still in hiding, with attempted murder, even though there was no evidence that they had even been present. A mob of "one hundred white men, fully armed, marched" through Onancock, firing "hundreds of bullets" into Burton's store. Black residents had used the store as a meeting place, so the mob poured oil and gasoline and torched it, in the vile hope that the two, or other Black people, were hiding in the building and would be burned alive. When no one emerged from the burning building, hundreds of white men set about terrorizing local Black farmers and shooting into the homes of Black sharecroppers. Three Black women reported to the governor's officials that they had been raped or sexually molested by white invaders and had to flee their homes.[24]

Local officials did nothing to stop white vigilantes and instead cracked down on Black mobility. Passing an ordinance demanding that all Blacks leave Onancock by eight o'clock each night, they turned it into a sundown town. Additionally, the town council banished fifty landholding Black families from the county, forcing these "bad negroes" to leave at gunpoint. Most left permanently, forced to abandon their land and property, moving to Baltimore, Norfolk, and Philadelphia. Some of the most prosperous Black residents were targeted; among those told to leave were the county's only Black doctor and the pastor of Accomack's African Methodist Episcopal church, the latter targeted for encouraging Black women domestic laborers not to work on Sundays in order to keep the Sabbath holy. The reverend was threatened directly with a "notice . . . posted on the door" of his home "telling him that he would not live to remember the consequences if he did not leave Onancock by . . . Monday morning."[25]

Local whites used rabid violence to attempt to undermine Black success and independence and to stop organizing efforts demanding fair pay and decent hours. One Black man who was shot, captured, and jailed by the mob was forced to inform on Burton and Uzzle. The captive said, under duress, that the two men insisted that Black laborers be paid at least the small sum of a dollar and a half a day for their work. This was not an extravagant amount; it is equivalent to just four dollars an hour for a ten-hour workday today. It was not much to ask for as white farmers were making millions in dividends.[26]

Hiding in the woods for more than a week, Samuel Burton and James Uzzle survived. The two men surrendered to the state militia sent by Governor Claude A. Swanson, who was determined to suppress the violence and deliver the men to court without a lynching.[27] Virginia had built a record of avoiding lynchings by mustering state forces to protect Black people accused of violence against whites. The state did not necessarily act for moral reasons—lynching was bad press, and discouraged the industrial investment so desperately desired by state leaders. In most cases, unjust courts could more quietly enact the violence sought by mobs.

However, in this case, neither the mob nor the courts took Black lives. Black Virginians across the state rallied on behalf of the two men, pointing out that they had not started the violence. The state capital's Black weekly newspaper, the *Richmond Planet*, followed their cases closely, heralding their innocence and describing them as "the new type of Negroes": "educated, industrious and ... of positive benefit to the community in which they lived."[28] Eventually, the advocacy seemed to make a difference. Sylvanius Conquest, the clerk falsely accused of theft, was eventually released and settled in Philadelphia, where he worked as a tailor.[29] James Uzzle was freed on appeal and moved to Norfolk, Virginia, where he revived his career as a newspaperman.[30] Samuel Burton not only avoided the lynching rope but after serving a year and a half of a ten-year prison sentence got his bogus convictions overturned. Banished from Accomack County, he moved to Baltimore and began working as a store clerk. What Burton did next was even more extraordinary. He hired W. Ashbie Hawkins, one of the first Black attorneys in Baltimore, to file a $100,000 case against the town of Onancock, the mayor, and four other white men, including the young white man who struck him during the riot.[31] Astoundingly, in 1913, Burton won a $3,500 judgment, which was small in comparison to the value of what he had lost; nevertheless, it was remarkable that a court recognized that the "riot" amounted to an unjust seizure of his property. Burton invested the settlement, opening a clothing store serving Baltimore's Black community in 1917. In 1920, his successful business was cited in the pages of the NAACP's *Crisis* magazine for making $60,000 in profit that year.[32]

Burton's story was in the end triumphant, but his survival and success prompt the question of what happened to the other fifty Black families banished from Accomack County in the wake of the riot. They did not sue for the value of the land and property they lost. Burton was determined to sue the city that once organized to lynch him, but the lawsuit, and its outcome, were an anomaly in the Black experience in the Jim Crow South. There would be no justice for the rest of those forced out of Accomack for their expressions of Black advocacy, or merely for their prosperity.

And what did it mean to stay in Accomack County after the explosion of white mob violence and the suppression of the Black movement for better pay? This was the climate in Accomack County when both Minnie and my grandfather were young. They grew up in the place where their ancestors had lived in bondage, and they watched, just children, a peaceful Black working-class rebellion get crushed by a mob backed by corrupt lawmakers.

AS MINNIE ENTERED HER TEENAGE YEARS, SHE DISCOVERED that her temperament didn't match her life as a Negro girl in Accomack. Like others who stayed after the tide of racial violence, Minnie's family lived a life hemmed in so tightly by white-imposed limitations that she felt that they could never get ahead. Her father was a sharecropper and she was girl number two in a family of older girls and younger boys, so she had toiled all her growing-up years as if she was her father's second-born son. Each year they worked hard to feed themselves and make their shares, but, because they were dependent on fair treatment at the time of settlement from the white landowner, her family's hard work never led to progress.[33] Each year her father hoped to do more than break even when he went to the exchange at Onancock to settle up on the value of his sweet and white potato crop, so that he could put some money away for his children's future. However, there was no means by which he could demand an accurate accounting of the value of the crop he produced.

After the riot, Accomack's racial hierarchy left little space for Minnie's father to safely advocate for himself in setting the price of his labor as an individual or collectively with other sharecroppers. He was not allowed to speak freely, ask questions, or challenge the amount offered to him at the end of the year. Minnie thought that these injustices embedded in the system of sharecropping represented a new kind of bondage. She recalled:

> You know there was a rule they say that whatever the white man would tell them, they [had to believe] him. And if he says, well, you didn't earn but $5, this year, they [were] still . . . living under their bondage of slavery . . . what could they do? Sometime I used to see my father look very downhearted.

This process was hard on Minnie too. She was tired. Tired of bending low to carefully pick crops worth less and less every year. Tired of seeking out jobs picking sweet-smelling strawberries or blueberries, only to make a handful of coins at the end of the day. She was tired of toting the dusty bags of sweet potatoes she dug out of the soil, tired of the heavy cabbages she cut from their bed of leaves on the ground with her favorite sharp knife—it was food to feed her family but fed little else.[34] Her father and uncles were skilled on the water in the boats they owned or rented, bringing in crabs and fish from the bay or oysters from the beds in the estuary, but it seemed that they could never do enough to make the family anything but poor.[35] Minnie put it best when she said, "I worked and I couldn't share in nothin'."

And then there was the constant second-class treatment in every other aspect of their lives. Minnie had loved school, but each year there were fewer teachers at the not-much school provided for Black students in the rundown building Black parents had built themselves, and she

"Negroes picking tomatoes. Homestead, Florida." Fieldwork required knowledge, strength, and endurance. MARION POST WALCOTT, *FARM SECURITY ADMINISTRATION, LIBRARY OF CONGRESS*

could only attend during the four months when she wasn't working on the farm.[36] When Minnie was a teen there was no high school for Black students in Accomack. She hated watching her strong-willed father submit to going to the back door of an Onancock restaurant because she got hungry on a trip to town. Standing in the white-owned grocery with her eyes downcast so that no one could see her anger, tinged with anxiety, waiting for every white person who walked in after her to be served before her.[37] Painting on a fake smile and looking at the ground as she said "yas sir" and "yas m'aam" to any and every white person who addressed her. Physical deference extended to the roadways in Accomack. Minnie remembered that "if they meet you on the road . . . [even] if you was there first, you better wait till they come by driving." And above all else, she hated watching her family accommodate every ridiculous request of the man who owned the land her family farmed or face his violent wrath. Minnie recalled a particularly painful moment when her father was brutally beaten because a relative visiting from the North dared to claim that he was the equal of a white man. Resistance to white authority was often met with swift retribution.[38]

My grandfather's experience was somewhat similar. It might have been just his personality, or it could have been his frustration with the circumstances that limited his opportunities, or both—but Bruce Murphy's father, John Jr., or Jude, was not a reliable parent to his children or a reliable partner to his wife, and he would leave his family in dire need, gambling away the proceeds of their collective labor at the fair. Given his disappointment in Jude, Bruce looked to his grandfather as his model; he was a Civil War veteran, a skilled and knowledgeable farmer, and a successful waterman. He had settled in Accomack after the war as a young man, married, and built a family and a life there. He was a sharecropper but was truly gifted in the fields; his potato crops and kitchen garden were bountiful. His farming and fishing made him a hub of support not only for his own household but also for his grandchildren and daughter-in-law; most years he had more than enough even for other families in need in the community. Bruce recalled with pride that his grandfather, John Sr., earned enough fishing to have two boats in the water. Most of the time Bruce had to work on the farm, but he loved to fish; he recalled running to the inlet to greet his grandfather coming in laden down with such bounty that the boat slung low in the water.

John Sr. was so successful, in fact, that he wanted to purchase his own land. But when he talked about the possibility of buying land with the man who leased him his family home and owned the land he farmed, the white man assured him that he need not do so, that he would always be welcomed on that land. So John Sr. held on to his savings, trusting that he'd be able to save and provide. However, the one year when he fell ill and was too sick to manage the labor of the full crop, the land-holder ejected him from the home and the land. There was little that John Sr. could have done to enforce a white man's promise, in a county where white men's desire to suppress Black success was backed up by violence. Having learned this painful lesson as a child, as a man Bruce would never trust in the word of a white man when it came to providing for his family, seeking always to own his own land and home, and to feed his children with the fruit of his own labor.

In spite of this climate of repression, sparks of Black resistance remained. Bruce recalled that when he was growing up there was one large Black family, full of men, whose brothers and cousins would travel to town collectively whenever they had to trade. Each man was armed with a long gun. They didn't seek any trouble, but demanded respect. My grandfather noted that white residents spoke calmly and carefully to them, giving them wide berth when they moved through town. This family's homeplace was well protected, and no one sought them out; their reputation for taking no mess provided them with a buffer. This family that my grandfather recalled with pride served as a reminder that even after the events of the fall of 1907, Black families and communities found ways to defend themselves against the ever-looming possibility of white hostility.[39]

For Bruce and Minnie, as young people, existing in this place that required either submission or constant vigilance, or both, was a challenge. Minnie's family had been in Accomack for generations beyond what anyone alive could accurately remember. Her grandparents were born into slavery but she felt that her parents were "still in ... bondage, they was still living under some of the slave rules."[40] Minnie dreamed of living in a place where it didn't feel like they were slaves anymore. A place where she could be paid fairly for her hard work. A place where she could safely join with others to demand fair treatment. She had to leave Accomack to "get freed from 'freedom.'"[41]

Bruce's drive to leave was probably the result of a combination of disappointment in his father and the sense that he could never fully protect his own family from chaos and harm. When he boarded the NYP&N he was about the same age as his grandfather had been when he escaped enslavement. Bruce would tell the story of John Sr.'s escape frequently to his children, calling up a vivid image of the teen riding toward Union lines on a horse repossessed from the man who had held him in bondage. At just sixteen, Bruce sought a similar freedom. So, in 1918, it seems that both Minnie and my grandfather were seeking a place where the injustice and insult of everyday life might sting a little less. Philadelphia was their chosen destination.

AS MUCH AS THEY WANTED TO LEAVE, THEIR UPBRINGING ON that land and the things they learned in its Black community would be imprinted on them. For the rest of their lives, they could recall the shape of the tidal creeks and ponds, the feel of the sandy loam under their feet. They carried the knowledge gleaned from their fathers, mothers, aunts, uncles, and grandparents as part of them. This place and its people, particularly those who loved and nurtured them, lived on inside. It would be the way that they mapped meaning into their Philadelphia lives.

Indeed, the years spent in Accomack made young Bruce Murphy a skilled farmer and fisherman, much like his grandfather. For the rest of his life, my grandfather would love the water and the soil. He applied for and received a plot of land for a Victory garden in Philadelphia during the Second World War, but after the war, the land he had cultivated was taken back by the government to build housing for white GIs returning home. Bruce had used the harvests of his city garden to provide food for families on his block on Norris Street and to keep his son working hard and out of trouble. Through his network of Accomack County

Bruce and his firstborn daughter, Sarah Jean Murphy, a decade after he migrated to Philadelphia.

homefolks in Philadelphia, Bruce had heard of a man who had acres of farmland, hidden from the road behind some pines in Pennsauken, New Jersey, that he was not using. He met the man, whom he did not know from home but who had grown up in the same community on the Eastern Shore, to ask if he could rent some of the land or take a share of his crops at the harvest. The man refused to rent it or take shares, but instead insisted on providing an opportunity for my grandfather to grow whatever he wanted free of charge, pleased to see the young father make the land productive.

None of this was exciting to my father, Leroy Murphy, a preteen who dreaded rising before dawn for early Saturday morning bus rides to a plot of South Jersey land. There he and his father planted mostly corn and sweet potatoes, the same crops Bruce had learned to grow in Accomack. As a teen my father often wondered why they worked so hard to carry their harvests of fresh fruits and vegetables back home just to give them out for free to their neighbors on Norris Street, a bounty to this community in exile. My father's only pay after the long days would come in the form of some of his favorite Nestlé coconut cookies from the corner store back in the neighborhood.

While most of the harvest was shared with others, my grandfather would always keep a stash of his own sweet potatoes to store in a rat-proof basket hanging from the rafters in a corner of the cool basement. There they would keep all year, growing sweeter by the day. The previous season's potatoes would be baked with meals or made into sweetly irresistible pies by the skilled hands of my Nana, Sarah Jane Murphy. They were the staple that kept the large family fed.

To Bruce they were something even more. After a day at work and a good supper, he'd go down and select a fat sweet potato that shone golden under its dusty skin. Roasting it in a hot oven until its sweet sap caramelized inside its burnished skin, he ate the bright, smooth flesh, unadorned by sugar or cinnamon. Its smoky, sweet flavor was a memory—a taste of home in a new place.

———

THE TRAIN THAT INCREASED COMMERCE IN THE REGION ALSO ended up expanding opportunities for Black folks on the Eastern Shore, providing the means for Black Accomack County residents, and more broadly Black people from Virginia and Maryland's Eastern Shore, to escape to Philadelphia. Within a few decades people began moving by the thousands. Any day of the week there were families, loaded down with their belongings, boarding the train for one-way journeys north.

Minnie left with no suitcase. Except for a sandwich of leftover country ham in a paper sack she was empty-handed, sneaking away to claim a seat in the train's hot and crowded colored car, excited that she was going to a place where, she'd heard, colored cars didn't exist. Until the very last second before she boarded the train, she worried she wouldn't make it, fearful that her father would come in search of her. At the first stop on her journey, the Parksley station, Minnie hid in the colored ladies' room on the train until the train departed, bound for Philadelphia.[42]

The anticipation she felt in her bones made the hours in that steaming car drag on like days, but when the train finally arrived at Broad Street Station, Minnie smiled as she strode with just the clothes on her back through the massive, smoky station as if she had been in Philadelphia all her life. She loved the idea of moving away from her small cart-and-buggy town to the streetcar city. She didn't know what it would be like, but she imagined that there was a lot a hardworking young woman could do in a city as big as this one.

Beyond the coincidence of my grandfather and Minnie both migrating from Accomack is another, lived connection between Min-

nie and the story of my family. My maternal grandmother, Brunell Raeford Duncan, also migrated to Philadelphia. Although she was born far
south of the Eastern Shore in Newberry, South Carolina, she would end
up walking a very similar path as Minnie. Minnie and Brunell left the
South in search of greater opportunity. They wanted a fair shot at better jobs, a life away from the strict boundaries of segregation and subjugation. Both ended up working in Philadelphia as maids, hemmed in
by stunted views about what was considered Black women's work but
buoyed by networks of community that made their lives both within
and outside the South possible.

CHAPTER SIX

The Maids of the Migration

During her first days in the North, Minnie learned some of the ways that Philadelphia was different from Accomack. One migrant who moved to the city in 1917 sketched those differences in sharp relief:

> I am now housekeeping again ... I make $75 per month. I am [carrying] enough insurance to pay me $20 per week if I am not able to be on duty. I don't have to work hard. [I] don't have to mister every little white boy comes along. I haven't heard a white man called a colored a nigger ... since I've been in the state of Pa. I can ride in the electric street and steam cars anywhere I get a seat. I don't care to mix with the white ... I mean I am not crazy about being with white folks but if I have to pay the same fare I have learn to want the same acomidation. ... If you are first in a

"Negro maid, Washington, D.C., 1941." Black women household workers were often required by white employers to clean floors on their hands and knees, even well after the advent of the mop.   JACK DELANO, *LIBRARY OF CONGRESS*

place here shopping you don't have to wait until the white folks get through tradeing. . . . The kids are in school every day . . .[1]

However, when Minnie arrived in Philadelphia in 1919, the majority of white factory managers would not hire Black women, even as the factory economy was booming.[2] For white male workers, twentieth-century Philadelphia was a site of opportunity in a formidable industrial center. In addition to sugar and oil refineries and heavy industries in iron, steel, and coal processing, the city was also a textile hub, with thriving cottage industries in the production of clothing, hats, upholstery, draperies, and carpets. Given the breadth of soft goods production, there was plenty of work for women, particularly those with dressmaking skills. Yet most Black women were not afforded opportunities in these industries, despite the absence of legal restrictions preventing employers from hiring them.[3] White employers had created a de facto color line in Philadelphia's industries that pushed African American women toward domestic service.

At first Minnie reveled in her distance from the toughest aspects of life in the South. Thanks to the help of her cousin, she already had a job cleaning a family-owned drugstore on 41st and Girard Avenue waiting for her. She was excited to start, but soon learned that she alone was responsible for cleaning all the way through the massive building and into the store. The woman who employed her was exacting, and every morning she was given a long set of tasks to complete, along with specific directions about how to go about doing each task. Like the work she had done for her father on the family farm in Accomack, it was hard; but now she was also isolated and closely supervised with suspicion.

She dreaded cleaning the floors. Black "girls" who cleaned were forbidden the convenience of a mop, lest they miss a spot.[4] As customers traipsed in and out with city grime on their feet, her employers gave her just half an hour to wash every inch of a thousand square feet on her knees with her bare hands dunked in a caustic combination of lye and water so hot that it felt like it might tear away her skin and fingernails. Although a Black inventor, Thomas W. Stewart, had secured the first American patent on a yarn mop well before the turn of the twentieth century, the convenient tool was thought to be less precise than the hands of Black women. Perhaps the restriction on mops was also a way to physically emphasize the racial distance between Black women workers and their white employees. Scrubbing mirrored the iconic anti-slavery image of an enslaved woman asking, "Am I not a Woman, and a Sister?" There would be no sisterhood between white women and the Black women they forced to work on their hands and knees. Daily humiliation was a job requirement.

"Washington, D.C., Negro maid, in the home of a government worker."

JACK DELANO, *LIBRARY OF CONGRESS*

As she spent her days literally on her knees, Minnie started to feel that Philadelphia "was no advancement... at all." After her first few weeks, the only significant change from her life in the South was the pay, which allowed her to send two dollars a week home to her worried parents, who stopped searching for her when they started receiving help from their willful daughter.[5] Frustrated, she looked for other jobs, but soon discovered that she could find no work outside of serving as a maid. She applied to various places, and even visited an employment agency, but she was always told "there was no other sorts of job" for Black women, only cleaning and cooking in white people's homes. The jobs downtown for "Negro girls" were jobs cleaning offices, not serving as clerks or secretaries. The jobs in doctor's offices were cleaning jobs too, not work assisting physicians. Minnie had found that while the differences between Accomack and Philadelphia were meaningful, the white-imposed limitations that circumscribed her life in the rural South as a working woman had simply taken a new form in the urban North.

MY MOTHER, FRANCES GERALDINE DUNCAN MURPHY—JERRY, to her family—was very particular about many aspects of her household. Near the top of the list were her rules about how she cleaned her kitchen floor. On weekends, when she'd clean the house from top to bottom, she insisted on doing the kitchen floor on her hands and knees. Perched on a pillow she reserved for just this task, she would scoot along, wiping every inch of linoleum, her nicely manicured hands tucked into high rubber gloves to protect her long, painted nails from the water and chemicals. She told me that using a mop meant you'd miss cleaning or waxing places that you just couldn't see standing up. As a little girl, I never thought to ask why.

She was also particular about her Waterford crystal and her Lenox china, glasses too fine and plates too detailed for us to drink or eat from more than three or four times a year. Every few weeks she'd take them out of the china cabinet and wipe them with a clean, dry, soft cloth. Every few months she'd get out her good silver—heavy forks and knives and massive serving spoons—and she'd lay it all out, then polish the pieces one by one. I'd sit by her side, wiping them down, not realizing that she too had once sat next to her mother, polishing the silver of the white family my grandmother worked for when my mother was a little girl.

At the time, I didn't know that my grandmother Brunell Duncan had been a maid, and that my mother was the daughter of a domestic worker. I didn't know that my mother and grandmother swore that the best way to clean their floors was on their hands and knees because that was the way my grandmother's employers had insisted that she clean their floors. I didn't know that seeing the china, crystal, and silver of the woman who employed my grandmother was the reason my mother was so driven to own china herself, perhaps an insistence that our family deserved all of what her white employers took for granted. In an unbroken silence on the subject, I lived with how those years as a household worker shaped my grandmother's life, and through hers, my mother's.

When I was growing up, my mother and grandmother would frequently tell me stories. Stories about my mother being a picky eater as a child, about my grandmother's job at the Philadelphia Navy Yard, about my mother's work in the typing pool in summer during her college years. They told thousands of stories, but when I was a child neither of them mentioned that my grandmother had been a maid. My mother did talk about spending time with her Aunt Sis, a hairdresser who owned her own beauty shop in North Philadelphia. I did not understand until I was an adult that Aunt Sis was not a relative, but a kind woman willing to watch and care for a little girl during the week, when my grandmother boarded in with her employers to be available to clean house at all times.

Worried that my mother would become more Sis's child than her own, my grandmother spent her days and nights on a job that paid a bit more, in the hope that she could save enough to make a real start for her young family. Even though she had moved North with her husband and her baby to make a better life, my grandmother was left doing domestic work after her migration, the same work she had performed before it.

This came at a cost. My mother recalled that once, as a tiny, not yet school-aged girl, she had visited her mother during her off hours at her employer's home. When it came time to return to Aunt Sis's home, my grandmother was forbidden by her employer to accompany my mother back from West to North Philadelphia. Still too young to read the street signs for herself, Brunell tied a piece of paper with the name of Jerry's stop to a silky, bright red ribbon and placed it around my mother's neck, telling her to find a Black woman riding on the car to sit next to and ask for assistance getting off at the right stop. My mother did as she was told and found a stranger, a Black woman with a kind face, and asked her for help. The woman sat with my mother, the way my grandmother would have if she could have, chatting and soothing her worries. At the right stop in her neighborhood, the sister stranger made sure my mother got off the car headed in the right direction. Watching her wend her way, she kept her eyes on the little girl as if she was her own.

FOR SOME WOMEN WHO HAD DONE DOMESTIC LABOR IN THE South, accommodating themselves to the work in the North was easier, relatively speaking. One migrant enjoyed her work in a large household that employed several Black women as domestic workers; she recalled, "I never had to go and just do all the cooking or all something like that, don't you know? . . . she had a cook, and I'd go there and me and the cook would be in the kitchen together and I'd help her. We'd do dishes or something like that." She had tried to work in a tobacco factory, one of the few areas of factory work open to African American women in the South because it was work white people didn't want to do; it was hard to tolerate the strong odors and noxious chemicals involved in tobacco processing. Although she knew that "perhaps the pay [was] better" in the tobacco factories, she still preferred to seek out nice employers and domestic jobs.[6] However, it is clear that for most African American women, household employment was not the work that they most desired. Driven to labor wherever she could because of her husband's chronic underemployment, one domestic worker reported that she did not have viable alternatives: "My husband and I were struggling and I had to help him some way. So, I made myself satisfied."[7] When asked to recall "pleasant experiences" as a domestic worker, another interviewee was blunt, stating, "None. Wasn't pleasant at all."[8]

The most immediate difficulty of domestic work was that it never ended.[9] One report noted that "low wages and long hours are characteristic of household service," finding that nationally "the typical hours were seventy-two a week." Some workers, particularly those living in, reported working up to eighty or ninety hours a week.[10] Domestic workers in the North polled in 1932 spoke of similar hours: on average, twelve- to fourteen-hour days, seven days a week.[11] One domestic employee noted that all holidays would be taken by her employers, with little consideration of her own desire to spend those days with her family. "They would never think of saying, 'Well, we'll have company this New Year's, later next New Year's we'll let you go to your family.' They never [thought] anything like that. They always [felt that] they come first."[12] A white woman explained that "my maids work until the dinner dishes are washed; this may be 8:30 or 10:30 p.m. They are then at liberty to go if we are in, otherwise one stays in to answer the phone." The day for her employees started at 7 a.m. Another white employer commented that she would "offer extra time off when it is convenient for me, and if it doesn't conflict, she may go out when her work is done." Domestic workers suffered from a "lack of freedom and of privacy" and were regularly forced to sacrifice their own time to the preferences of their employers.[13]

Although many household workers stayed in the job for years, most employers did little to get to know the women working in their homes. Most Black domestic workers suffered from a terrible anonymity. They labored in workplaces where their identities as women, mothers, friends, and individuals with interests of their own and aspirations beyond domestic work often were invisible to their employers.

That anonymity could have a tragic side. In December of 1945 the *Philadelphia Tribune*, the city's leading Black newspaper, reported that "an unidentified woman . . . collapsed" at 415 Mercy Street, a simple South Philadelphia row house. She "died an hour after she had been taken to the Mt. Sinai Hospital." Her employer, a Mrs. Nathan Sinelitsky, had hired the woman recently because "she had worked in the neighborhood before," but could not recall her name. In the effort to save her from burial in an unmarked grave in the paupers' field, the *Tribune* shared the deceased woman's physical description: "between 50 and 55 years old, brown-skinned, no teeth in the upper part of her mouth and about 125 pounds." They added the detail that the morning when she last came to work, she was wearing a "green coat, cream dress, red sweater, and tan shoes." The *Tribune* suggested that anyone who knew her could contact the coroner's office.[14]

While few domestic workers reported feeling ashamed of their work, they could not help but note the thoughtless behavior of their employers. One woman commented that she didn't think "domestic work is demeaning work," but did point to her second-class status in the household as humiliating, recalling that she was forced to "use the back elevators" and was not allowed to eat the meals she herself prepared for the family.[15] Although the constant refrain from employers was that domestic workers were more like family than servants, they were rarely given such privileges; a social distance was always maintained. Historian Kellie Carter Jackson recounted that although her grandmother's long-term employers claimed that they thought of her as a "member of the family," they never knew her last name, which had changed after marriage, until her funeral.[16] One interviewee recalled that her employer would refer to her as family "but [she didn't] feel that way." Her employer would invite her to have coffee while she "lay in the bed ... and you stand by the door and talk to them until you almost drop." She would "never ask you to sit on the bed or anything." Not every slight was blatant cruelty, but a day-to-day disregard for the humanity of women who were employed in their households was the unfortunate norm. Even employers who were relatively kind would treat these women workers "like a person would treat a maid ... they wouldn't go out of their way so much."[17]

For live-in household workers, like my grandmother, living situations were often as bad as the hours. A national report noted that "inadequate living and working conditions on the job were reported for many households. In a number of homes, no bathing facilities were provided for the workers; too often the bed was found to consist of a cot in the living room or furnace room." Damp and dank rooms lacking heat or a window were the norm.[18] In her employer's house down the shore in Atlantic City, my grandmother slept on a cot in the screened-in porch, even on rainy or cold nights.

No matter the circumstances a maid faced, what remained most difficult was the separation from family, particularly her children. Mothers doing domestic work often were forced to make the tough choice of leaving their own children unsupervised in order to watch other people's children. Many school-aged children, like my mother, wore keys around their neck; they would be charged with taking themselves home during the school day, letting themselves in to eat lunch, and then locking the door and making their way back to school. Some children would be tasked with chores, or starting dinner, before their mothers returned from work. Women with friends, spouses, or neighbors willing to look out for their children believed themselves fortunate; not everyone had such resources. One woman recalled that "we have to leave our children; sometime[s] leave the children alone. There's time when I [had] to ask winos to look after my children. It was just a terrible life."[19]

As the boom of the first postwar decade waned and the Great Depression began, the poor conditions Black women dealt with during good economic times only grew worse. The Women's Bureau, a New Deal agency within the Department of Labor, issued a 1938 report on "The Negro Woman Worker" that said: "The presence on relief rolls in 1935—the last date for which there is accurate information—of one in every four Negro women workers, and the fact that two-fifths of these unemployed women were the economic heads of families, constitute a situation that is of grave import to the citizens who must support these women and their families."[20] For women coming of working age during the Depression, their first experiences with domestic work were frequently corrosive and exploitative. Some Southern employment agencies that claimed to assist Black women in finding opportunities in factories in the North were really designed to funnel them into unpaid indentures. One informant recounted: "I was sent here by a minister. He was like an agency down there." The agency paid her fare north. When she arrived in the city she was "put . . . right on the floor to scrub or to mop. When he send you to that family it was like you was bought. . . . And you had to work until you pay the money back no matter what happened." Another woman migrant, profiled in the *Pittsburgh Courier* in 1935, was transported from Georgia and "subjected to conditions which represent slavery." For "payment" for her train ticket to New York City and the agency fee, she was forced to be the live-in maid for a family of six in a large apartment, and received no pay or time away for two months. The family even "farmed out" out this employee to two other households to clean and cook and then took the money she earned from those jobs.[21]

Extreme exploitation became common during the Great Depression. NAACP activists Ella Baker and Marvel Cook wrote a landmark exposé on what they called "The Bronx Slave Market" in the organization's magazine *Crisis* in 1935:

> Rain or shine, cold or hot, you will find them there—Negro women, old and young—sometimes bedraggled, sometimes neatly dressed—but with the invariable paper bundle, waiting expectantly for Bronx housewives to buy their strength and energy for an hour, two hours, or even for a day at the munificent rate of fifteen, twenty, twenty-five or if luck be with them thirty cents an hour.[22]

Women seeking employment would sometimes wait for hours for a day of work; some days they would be chosen, and other days they wouldn't and would return home empty-handed. The reality of such a loose labor market meant that white housewives who previously could not afford to hire maids suddenly had access to domestic labor, sometimes paying little or none of the pittance they had promised. These "slave markets" were common during the Depression. One Philadelphian recalled that "everybody in North Philly was standing on corners to get work." She claimed that these employers offered little pay for a lot of work. Clearly the nature of the "slave market" jobs was fundamentally hard. Employers had no interest in fostering goodwill or being even minimally decent; if today's employee didn't like the working conditions, they could hire another unsuspecting woman tomorrow. One domestic worker reported that she was paid with cash stolen from her own purse by her employer.[23]

These women seeking work faced graver dangers, too. Also taking advantage of their vulnerability were men searching for sex workers at a low cost. They too would frequent the corners where the "slave markets" appeared. Some young women were tricked into such arrangements, while others sought out sex work because the market for domestic work was so bad and they needed to provide for their families. Baker and Cook wrote that white housewives' "husbands, their sons, or their brothers, offer worldly-wise girls higher bids for their time." Some sex workers were indeed "worldly-wise," while others felt they had no other choice.[24]

Launched to create economic stability and help support the nation's workers amid the Great Depression, the New Deal represented a dramatic shift; increased government involvement led to improving standards for American workers. President Franklin Delano Roosevelt established the National Recovery Administration (NRA) in 1933 to stabilize industry and labor; under its provisions the Labor Department set base salaries, abolished child labor in factories, limited the hours in a standard workday, and provided protections for decent labor standards. Disturbed by the ways in which fair standards might empower Black workers, Southern legislators made sure that the protections did not extend to domestic laborers or agricultural workers. By excluding those professions with claims that the work cultures were too different to fall under regulatory standards, Congress made sure that the majority of Black workers and nearly 90 percent of Black women laborers were left unprotected. The professions filled overwhelmingly by white women— clerical work, retail sales, nursing professionals—were covered by "hour and minimum-wage laws, workmen's compensation provisions, the joint Federal and State social security program," and other protections.

Black women, who were much more likely than white women to have a job in the first place, were not so fortunate.[25]

Take minimum-wage laws, for example. The 1938 report on "The Negro Woman Worker" noted that minimum-wage legislation "set a bottom limit below which wage rates cannot fall; to assure to women wages adequate to meet the cost of a healthful standard of living; to end sweatshops and cutthroat competition among employers; to relieve the community of supplementing low wages by public and private relief; and to establish on the part of workers the purchasing power that is necessary to bring about and maintain industrial recovery." However, rough estimates that appeared in the same report indicated that "only about 1 in 10 of all African American women workers are covered potentially by minimum-wage legislation." The Bureau relayed the fact that "minimum-wage laws thus far have not been an important factor in raising the wages of the bulk of Negro women workers."[26] The *Pittsburgh Courier* put it more bluntly: "Domestic workers are the most exploited of American workers. With no [national] organization giving power to bargain collectively, they have always been at the mercy of unscrupulous employers. To these workers the NRA does not mean a thing. They are excepted from its provision. No boards of arbitration sit to adjust their wages and hours of work. Because of the downward pressure of unemployment their hold on their jobs is the most precarious."[27]

It wasn't just politicians from the South who supported the exclusion. Resistance to the inclusion of household workers in labor law reform went all the way back to the turn of the twentieth century, when Progressive Era reformers also excluded domestic workers from their calls for labor protections for American workers.[28] Then, too, government policies prioritized the affordability of "the help" over just treatment for Black women workers. As one white housewife complained, "it would be very expensive and difficult to employ a woman [for] regular hours with extra pay for overtime, as in the case of a factory or office worker."[29] Such blanket exclusions from federal regulation and oversight allowed white middle-class households to continue to afford—or afford for the first time—the privilege of domestic service at the expense of Black women. Assumptions about the privacy and sanctity of white households overrode any idea that the women who cleaned had rights to fair pay and standard hours. New Deal regulations gave racial bias the force of law.[30]

As the United States entered the Second World War, demand increased for Black domestic workers as white women took on new jobs. The nation's white Rosie the Riveters, entering the workforce for the first time, used the labor of Black women to maintain their households while they worked, benefiting from the household support and childcare they provided. The expanding opportunities for domestic workers did make the market for maids more lucrative than it had been in prior years. One maid recounted that "the war was going on when I came to the Lichtmans and they told me if I stayed with them, I would never miss my pay. You know the girls [were] very hard to get in those days. A lot of the people just [left] and went to work on other jobs."

The "other jobs" were opportunities at government worksites that after the March on Washington movement began providing opportunities for Black women to do industrial war work. With the boom in household labor and factory work combined, around 600,000 Black women joined the labor market between 1940 and 1944.[31] However, new opportunities in industry were temporary, particularly for Black women. This same interviewee recalled that "after the war, most [Black women] came back to domestic work."[32] As the wartime boom ended, Black women were the first to be laid off, leaving the overwhelming majority of Black women laborers firmly outside the nation's industrial economy until the 1950s.[33]

THE STORIES OF WOMEN LIKE MINNIE AND BRUNELL ARE NOT often at the center of histories of the Black working class during the Great Migration. The work of the migration is implicitly framed as men's work. We remember the Black newspapermen who heralded the call to the North, including Robert Abbott, editor of the *Chicago Defender*, whose proud clarion call to the "race men" of the South helped make his newspaper the voice of the Great Migration.[34] We remember Black factory workers, for instance, the meatpacking and slaughterhouse workers in Chicago or the men in Pittsburgh who poured hot steel beside immensely hot blast furnaces. In many of the other cities of the North, opportunities for Black men were even more limited. Often, they found industrial labor only at the lowest levels, in brutal, dangerous, or toxic work.[35] Frequently last hired and first fired and systematically blocked from joining all-white unions, Black men had a tenuous hold, at best, on industrial employment. Yet their work helped make the movement of millions possible.

We've framed the work of domestics as less important to the narrative of the Migration in the assumption that what happened in private homes could not be transformative or collective. We have not told many stories about the women who migrated north and worked as maids in the decades before they had access to better-paying industrial, government, or social service professions. We connect domestic work to the times prior to the Migration, when enslaved women were working in plantation households or when postbellum Black women served as "the help" for white households. In these ways and others, we've missed something essential about Black maids and about the Black working class more broadly. The South has been seen as the locus of racial oppression and the North the panacea. But Southern black women migrants found that although Northern cities held promises of higher pay and greater access to education for their children, they too were governed by Jim Crow employment patterns. The inclusion of Black women who worked as household laborers allows for the telling of a different story of the Black working class. From their knees they did the work to make survival and migration possible for themselves and for their families. Women workers were essential to the Great Migration.

Even if Black women were stereotyped as domestic servants before the turn of the twentieth century, they did not dominate the ranks of household workers in Northern cities. White women did; they tended to be younger than their employers and were often family friends, much like babysitters today. As households became more urbanized, complex, and wealthier, demand for specialized work grew, just as a large group of European newcomers immigrated to the United States.[36]

As the number of white immigrants employed as maids, cooks, and nannies increased at the turn of the century, so too did the social distance between household workers and their employers. The work of tending to someone else's house became stigmatized, and "native-born women refused to take domestic work, leaving employers with no choice but to hire foreign-born workers." Prior to the Great Migration, young, unmarried European immigrants made up a large part of the maids serving in Northern households: "In 1900, 41.2 percent of white servants nationwide had been born in Ireland." They were often subject to brutal conditions. In 1903 one white domestic worker wrote to the *New York Tribune* that a "servant is literally a white slave," lamenting that household workers with the privilege of white skin were still treated terribly.[37] Deemed by the pseudoscience of the day as racially separate from and inferior to their Anglo-Saxon employers, household workers were at least buoyed by networks of support in immigrant communities.[38]

When the First World War began, restrictions on immigration meant that there were fewer white newcomers seeking jobs as domestic workers. White Europeans were still favored by wealthy employers—among the white elite the British nanny and butler and the Irish maid were the standard. However, as the number of immigrant women dropped and those already in the US found opportunities to leave domestic service behind, Black women migrants in search of employment and an escape from the South increasingly filled positions as household workers.[39] Minnie, my grandmother Brunell, and hundreds of thousands of other Black women did the work that in the North had been done by Irish women just the generation before.[40]

Notably, this was a shift not only for Northern employers but also for many Black women. Like Minnie, who had grown up doing agricultural work, many Black women who took positions as maids, cooks, and mother's helpers had been farm laborers in the South. In 1890, the US Census revealed that there were just slightly more Black women doing domestic and personal service than agricultural work. A transition was underway, fueled by rural migrants moving to urban centers.

By 1930 the census revealed that more than two-thirds of working Black women were employed as domestics, a dramatic expansion of the number and proportion of Black women in household work. A report by the Women's Bureau noted: "The number of Negro women in domestic and personal service in 1930—1,150,000—represented a gain of nearly 50 percent from 1920 to 1930. Negro women in household employment increased by 81 percent."[41] Nationally, the ranks of domestic laborers had grown at such a dramatic rate that the economist George Stigler pointed out that although understudied and underserved by "social legislation," "domestic service is a . . . major field of employment" that in 1939 employed as many workers as "employees of the railroads, coal mines, and automobile industry combined."[42] Although Black women had always been laboring in white households, their growing numbers in these jobs reflected the reality that domestic employment was a phenomenon of the Migration. This was perhaps the largest change in Black people's labor since the advent of sharecropping.

Like white immigrant domestics before them, Black women were perceived by their employers as racially set apart, though now the distinction was driven not only by differences in skin color but also a set of crude stereotypes grounded in the history of enslavement. Frequently isolated from other workers, they suffered close and regular supervision from employers, dislocation from the places most familiar to them, and the ongoing threat of sexual assault from the men of the house. The assumptions of racial segregation and exclusion may have looked and sounded different in the North, but they had a very similar effect on Black women's daily lives. Switching the language of subservience from the Southern "ma'am" to the Northern "madam" must have been cold consolation.[43]

Even in spite of the dramatic improvements in labor laws in the Progressive Era—minimum wages for women workers, ten-hour workdays, and limitations on child labor in more than thirty states—reformers "often ignored the role of labor laws and their own reform agendas in creating, or at least allowing, exploitation of domestic workers. To them, the problem was that the occupation was inherently antimodern." The household worksites were thought to be part of the domestic sphere and wholly separate from other American workplaces.[44] So it came as a surprise to many that Black domestic workers began to organize, much like men and women in other lines of work.[45] They accommodated themselves to the lives set before them, building new networks that laid the groundwork for a new community, but one still grounded in love, empathy, and support for one another.

Southern-born women like Minnie and Brunell boarded the city streetcars bound crosstown either to work day by day or board week by week as domestics. It would be on the wooden slats of streetcar seats that they established new ties, speaking daily or weekly in quiet tones about what they were going through. They began to see the connections. They'd describe the women they worked for: the lonely ones, the angry ones, the ones who hit them, the ones who expected impossible work no matter the circumstances. They began to collectively envision what they wanted for themselves, a vision of mutual respect and fairness. Minnie recalled one domestic worker who said, "I hope I'll live to see a day when they will have to do the work that I'm doing. You know, do their own work, and then they'll know how to treat people."

These working women, many of whom initially felt distant from the rich kinship networks in their hometowns and home churches, made do. They bonded, not just based on the work that they did but on what they

"800 Block North Hancock Street." A community of Black migrants in Philadelphia.

COURTESY OF THE SPECIAL COLLECTIONS RESEARCH CENTER,
TEMPLE UNIVERSITY LIBRARIES, PHILADELPHIA, PA

believed the world should be like. They already knew how to treat people and support people in need. They knew to look out for the older woman who needed support the week she came down with a bad case of flu. They knew to look out for children like my mother, who might be journeying alone on a streetcar because their mothers could not leave their jobs. They knew to put some of their money in a penny savers club to prepare for the future. They knew how to meet and have a good time on a Thursday night, with uniforms off and their best outfits on, talking about life on the job and off. They knew to found new clubs based on the town or the region of their home, sharing news about what was happening there and connecting with distant relatives. These working women used their own resources to help one another, teaching one another about their new neighborhoods, commiserating about disappointments with a job, finding joy in the midst of sorrow while worshipping in church, relaxing in gossip and laughter across freshly swept marble stoops or over a drink and loud music in the "juice joint." They organized with one another to try to get ahead, both in good times and in bad. They sent money home to support families and children, maintaining the ties of community between the North and the South, both personally and politically. It would be these women who made the initial waves of migration successful, and who made further migration possible for future generations.[46]

These women were architects. They needed community, so they built it. They established informal childcare networks and raised money for annual picnics and reunions back home. They created the community institutions that would nurture the future, including new churches and social organizations. And determined that their new lives mean something, they founded unions to represent their collective will. Together, they laid the foundation for Black political organizing in their adopted cities, exercising the right of the franchise in the North that they had been unconstitutionally prevented from exercising in the South. Drawing on their love for one another, their faith that, despite evidence to the contrary, a broken America could be made better, they used what they had to craft a vision of what a better life could look like. Rising from their knees to construct that vision, the Black working-class women who migrated ended up creating new pathways for a more expansive American democracy.

———

BLACK WOMEN WORKING IN THE HOUSEHOLD OF A WHITE FAM-ily had to challenge longstanding clichés. Some of Americans' most beloved movies and television shows feature Black women happily cleaning, cooking, and doling out sage and sassy advice. The acclaimed 2011 movie *The Help*, based on a bestselling novel by the same name, was welcomed by many white (and many Black) moviegoers. It portrayed the challenges of domestic service historically with a feel-good sense of the possibility for sisterhood across racial boundaries. *The Help* perhaps resonated with many Americans because it soothed latent white guilt about participation in an exploitative labor market, and because it soothed a Black desire for recognition, but it fell well short of a realistic examination of the conditions of Black women household workers and erased the richness of the working-class community they founded.

Black women's degraded status as workers—in slavery and in freedom—was exacerbated by the gendered nature of household labor. Although it is easy to see continuity in the presence of Black women serving in white households across time—first as "house slaves" and then becoming "the help" in the decades that followed chattel slavery— broad cultural, political, and economic changes shaped and reshaped Black women's experience as laborers and domestic servants, so much so that any assumptions about their lives must be checked against an ever-changing context.

Enslaved Black women were some of this country's first working women, their unpaid labor extorted by force in the fields and households. Over time, slavery apologists developed pseudoscientific justifications to normalize the idea of Black women as laborers. As Black women worked as chattel for the benefit of their masters, white American culture turned Black women into objects of derision, promoting and propagating stereotypes about enslaved Black women as the hypersexual and violent Jezebel who could never be raped or violated by white men or the mammy—the fat, happy, masculine woman, naturally skilled in the kitchen, unintelligent but full of intuition, and willing to sacrifice her own family's well-being for the white family for whom she cared. No matter the specific stereotype, all enslaved Black people were painted as impervious to pain or exhaustion, lazy, and prone to stealing and trickery.[47] These stereotypes were created to paper over the degradations of slavery, the extreme pain that hard and often repetitive work inflicted on Black bodies, the violence and repeated sexual violation they suffered at the hands of slave drivers and slaveholders, and the fundamental theft of their freedom. Onto that papered-over reality the nation projected a grotesque distortion meant to distract. Minstrelsy—stage performances of skits, dancing, and songs mocking the enslaved and performed by white men in blackface—laughed away the unthinkable horrors of slavery. These depictions would popularize the Jezebel and mammy figures for the entertainment of white audiences throughout the nation, making minstrelsy the first truly American popular culture. The songs and stories of minstrelsy effectively taught American audiences that Black women were less than human and happiest when they were working hard for the benefit of others.

Post–Civil War cultural shifts changed how Black women's labor was remembered, mythologized, and imagined. In the South, Black women domestics were increasingly seen as a sign of prestige, par-

"Please Mammy, 1899." The mammy stereotype shaped American perceptions of Black women household workers.   *LIBRARY OF CONGRESS*

ticularly as mammy nostalgia, or what the cultural historian Cheryl Thurber called the "Mammy craze," swept the country in the decades after the turn of the twentieth century.[48] As a manifestation of a profound desire to silence Black dissent voiced by "new issue Negroes," who vigorously contested second-class citizenship, white southerners embraced the "old time Negroes"—the ex-slaves they considered their uncles and mammies, honoring them in songs and poems, and paying for their funerals when they passed away. These "mammy funerals" were elaborate undertakings put on by Southern segregationists trying to memorialize happy servitude. Accounts of the Onancock riot in 1907, to give another example, are peppered with stories of old and dutiful "good negroes" who supposedly lamented the protest of younger Black workers seeking fair wages and better treatment. The mammy craze may have reached its height in the 1920s when the United Daughters of the Confederacy organized a failed attempt to build a mammy memorial on the National Mall in Washington, DC. Southern white writers from William Faulkner to Margaret Mitchell recalled personal histories shaped by these mythical, almost magical Black women, whom they imagined served as their second mothers.[49] As mammy, the otherwise threatening presence of a Black woman becomes "more innocuous and benign."[50] Onto the body of a mammy Southern whites would project their desire for a more compliant, lumpen Black woman worker.

While not every white Southern household could afford the services of a live-in maid, middle- and lower-class women often employed "help" who cleaned once a week or assisted in the months after a new baby was born. The presence of Black women domestics in these poor households helped to demonstrate that even the lowliest white southerners weren't as low as African Americans in the segregated South. Black women servants provided white families with the opportunity to perform racial superiority and forge an imagined connection to elite slavery in the past.[51]

Although the mammy myth is almost always seen as primarily a Southern image, the mammy and the culture of minstrelsy were ubiquitous in national branding campaigns created in the American North. Aunt Jemima pancake mix might be the most famous of these. The mix faltered when it was first launched, but it became resoundingly successful when its makers relaunched the brand at the 1893 World's Fair in Chicago with Nancy Brown, a Black cook from the South Side of Chicago, dressed with a kerchief on her head and a distended grin on her face, playing the character of a former slave who loved to serve pancakes. The success of Aunt Jemima fueled a trend; brands from soap to cigarettes featured mammies to sell their products. Motion pictures brought the sights and sounds of minstrelsy to wider audiences. Blackface performances in Al Jolson's film *The Jazz Singer* in 1927, the critically acclaimed, first full-length sound film, and by America's sweetheart Shirley Temple, who was Hollywood's top box-office draw in the 1930s, helped normalize minstrelsy for the white moviegoing masses.

One of the most provocative cultural portrayals of a mammy as a domestic servant in the North is in 1934's *Imitation of Life*. The film, a box-office hit nominated for three Academy Awards, was remade in 1959 and selected by the National Film Board in 2005 for historic preservation. At the time of its release, it was considered progressive for its forthright depiction of the color line. The original film starred Claudette Colbert as the white mother, Bea, who hires Delilah, portrayed by Louise Beavers, a character actress who had by 1934 played the stereotyped, magically transformational Black maid in five major studio productions before *Imitation of Life*. Delilah is mother to a little girl, Peola, who grows into a young woman in the course of the film. Pale-skinned, with a dark-skinned mother, Peola grows frustrated with the stigma of being Black in a world where her skin color would allow her to pass for white. The director, John Stahl, pushed the realism of this storyline, casting a light-skinned black girl to play Peola as a child and the white-passing Black actress Fredi Washington to play Peola as an adult. Segregationists bristled at the presentation of a Black character who could pass for white and the implicit nod to the existence of miscegenation, or sexual relationships between Black and white people—liaisons that at the time were outlawed in more than thirty states.

Although the film is usually analyzed for its narrative of passing, it also offers a useful outline of the tropes of the Black maid. Even outside the South—the film is set in Atlantic City, New Jersey—Black women domestics were depicted as happy in their role as servants and always available to improve the lives of white women, providing ease without any racialized shame. After opening credits backed by a maudlin version of the Negro spiritual "Nobody Knows the Trouble I Seen," audiences were introduced to the overwhelmed white mother, Bea, whose husband has died recently. She's been drawn into the working world to maintain his maple syrup business. One day, at Bea's backdoor appears a smiling middle-aged Black woman named Delilah, speaking in a backwoods twang, saying, "I come in answer to your advertisement for a girl." Confused because she has misread the address on a help-wanted ad for a "cook, laundress, housemaid" who was also "colored" and "not afraid of hard work" for just "moderate pay," Delilah pushes her way into Bea's home, insisting that she can work for merely room and board and doesn't need a wage, essentially enslaving herself. In addition to the tasks listed in the ad, Delilah maintains that "taking care of children . . . comes natural" to her. This opening scene draws attention to her weight, with Delilah claiming that she won't be much trouble to her white employer: "I'se very deceiving as to proportion, I don't eat like I look." Emphasizing Delilah's size in comparison to the movie star playing Bea, the white child she will be caring for calls her a "horsie" over and over in their first encounter, to great laughs from both Bea and Delilah, foreshadowing how the maid will be dehumanized in service to this family.

Throughout the film this mammy come north serves Bea's family with little concern for herself. Delilah cares for the family proficiently, cleaning the house, watching the children, making delicious, timely meals, and offering insightful counsel as she rubs the "pretty feets" of her employer. However wise Delilah seems, the film never confuses her insights with intelligence, undercutting the possibility of seeing Black women's wisdom as intellect. As the title character Kitty Foyle, played by Ginger Rogers in the 1940 film, put it, "colored people don't have to stop and think in order to be wise; they just know about things naturally, it oozes out of them."[52]

One morning after enjoying Delilah's secret family recipe for pancakes, Bea decides to open a business marketing the pancakes without Delilah's permission. Marketing her new brand with an image of her open-mouthed, blank-eyed, grinning employee, Bea becomes a tremendous national success. All the while Delilah needs little in the way of praise or pay, and just before she dies an early and tragic death, she requests only an elaborate funeral reminiscent of the real-life "mammy funerals."

While the film offered a distorted depiction of the relationship between a domestic servant and her employer, it may have spoken to the desires of white viewers. In this time of turmoil in American homes in the midst of the Great Depression and with the growing threat of war, women who styled themselves as modern may have thought that, like Bea, they needed a sweet, smiling Southern Black servant to help them around the house. Perhaps they imagined that they would need a hand to hold theirs as they parented and managed their homes with husbands away at work or abroad at war. The maid could fill the gap, and help them face the challenges of a tumultuous time as a housewife and come out all the better for it. Bea and Delilah weren't depicted as being in a coercive relationship; theirs was more of an unequal friendship grounded in Black inferiority. The Delilah character demonstrated that working women did not require fair pay. There is no notion, in the film, of Black women as a class of workers deserving of protections extended to other working men and women. In *Imitation of Life*, white women saw a world in which Black domestics needed the chance to serve almost more than the employer needed their assistance.[53]

Working as a maid was much more challenging than Hollywood ever portrayed it. Ironically, as household technology improved, white women were acculturated to believe that even as housewives, they needed assistance "to keep up with the Joneses" and the increasingly detailed daily tasks of their households.[54] For example, homes with more than one bathroom, each with mass-produced porcelain flush toilets and built-in bathtubs and showers, required regular maintenance. Gas stoves required cleaning. Iceboxes and, by the mid-1940s, wildly popular refrigerators required stocking. Electric freezers required defrosting. Hoover vacuums weren't going to push themselves. A daily schedule for a "full-time housekeeper" featured in Charlotte Adams's 1942 guide for housewives, *The Run of the House*, included keeping a home impeccably clean and organized and stocked with modern hygiene products.

> Every day the bathroom was cleaned to best standards . . . the housekeeper was to "wipe tub, basin, and floor. Wash glasses. Clean toilet. Change or refold towels and washcloths. Check toilet paper, soap, and mouth wash for replacements." After cooking lunch and dinner, she was to brush kitchen floor, wipe working surfaces, and stove.

Weekly chores for the housekeeper included sorting and doing laundry in a household machine, ironing, shopping for groceries, vacuuming bedrooms, turning over mattresses so they wore evenly, cleaning lampshades, dusting and polishing woodwork, furniture, and moldings, cleaning out the icebox, and scrubbing wall and floor tile in bathrooms.[55]

The labor of household workers took place behind the scenes of everyday public life. The majority of these working women could not take comfort from collective workspaces; there was no factory floor, no shared field where they could organize. Their connections to one another—on public transportation, in parks, and back home in their neighborhoods—had to be intensively nurtured. Additionally, they lived a racial divide that marked their everyday experiences. The color line not only left them largely outside the bounds of an industrial world; it also ran through their workspaces, house by house, family by family.

They were intimate witnesses to the differences that race made in daily life; they knew exactly how the "other half" lived. They observed the conspicuous consumption of an increasingly consumerist white middle class. They cleaned the china, crystal, and silver and prepared the elaborate place settings in formal dining rooms. They saw the education the children they cared for enjoyed. They were paid meager wages while their employers donned extravagant clothing, jewelry, and furs. They had a front-row seat to white privilege. Their status also enabled them to know their employers very well, and be well equipped to organize to contest them.[56]

MINNIE FELL IN LOVE. FRED WAS FROM ACCOMACK, TOO, SO SHE felt a comfort and familiarity, a sense of being at home. He was the first real adult love Minnie had experienced, and it seemed to her as though he showed up just in time to make her feel better about the challenges of life in Philadelphia. Yes, she had family in the city, with whom she was staying, and yes, they looked out for her, even chaperoning her on dates, but having a big handsome guy by her side made her believe that she could finally make her own way. She could feel confident when she went out. The other girls would tease her less about being country; she could show them that she wasn't just a green country girl anymore, she was a woman.[57] The two dated for a few months before they married.

At first the relationship was good; he had a decent job with the city so he asked her to stop working. Soon after, they got pregnant and they returned to the Eastern Shore. Within a few short years Minnie had two children, a daughter and then a son. She had always thought this was the life she wanted—she had her own home and a family. But for Minnie life in Accomack was still a bad fit. She couldn't really be independent if all the limitations that had driven her away as a teen still existed.

After a few years, she amicably split from her husband and made plans to return to Philadelphia in order to better support her children. Leaving her youngest, Booker, to be cared for by her mother, Minnie was back in Philadelphia and doing domestic work in 1924, with a plan to work hard to send money home and visit as often as she could.

Minnie's new job was as the "upstairs girl" for a large household in the Wynnefield neighborhood. In the 1920s Wynnefield was an upscale Jewish American enclave for families who had not been welcomed by old-line white families in other parts of the city. Minnie worked for a wealthy woman with a reputation so bad that the agent at the employment service warned her that that she wouldn't make it through the week without quitting. Minnie proved the woman at the agency wrong. She stayed on for a few key reasons: the pay was good, a close friend and fellow migrant also worked in the household as the cook, and Minnie learned to tolerate the intolerable by setting strict boundaries on what she'd put up with and what she wouldn't. As Minnie explained, "She's mean, but I can be as mean as she is sometime."[58]

Minnie's employer was a taskmaster. Each day she would demand that Minnie clean things repeatedly, well before there was any chance that they were dirty again. The "lady of the house" cared nothing about her employees as individuals; she never bothered to consider that they needed breaks during the day and rest at night. Minnie remembered her employer as a "woman [who] had no sympathy for nobody but herself." For example, she demanded that Minnie climb onto the roof to wash the windows in every season. "Cold wintertime, she'd, you have to wash the windows. I don't care how cold it was. The rag would be sticking to the windows, just so long as you could get it off, you washed the windows." Minnie would assist her friend with cooking, particularly larger holiday meals, but then her employer would forbid them both to eat the meal. "Thanksgiving, she was going to have a turkey dinner, she would tell us . . . after we cooked it, 'You can't eat none of the turkey. You can have some of the giblet gravy.'" Her employer nit-picked her every movement. After Minnie accidently dropped a dish in the dining room, the lady of the house began to watch her every move, shouting, "Be careful, you'll drop that! Be careful, you'll drop that!" with every fragile object she touched. Minnie described her as "very nervous . . . and looked like everything bothered her." She had the atti-tude that Minnie "couldn't do nothing right."[59]

In a dramatic undermining of the mammy trope, Minnie learned to draw clear lines around what truly mattered to her. For example, after her mother wrote, worried about Booker's fever and asking Minnie to come home, she requested a Sunday off, promising to return first thing Monday morning. Her employer told Minnie that she couldn't leave and she would be fired if she left. Minnie left anyway, having settled in her

"San Augustine, Texas. Mrs. Thomas, the wife of a wholesale grocer, in her kitchen with her maid." Black women household workers were often closely supervised.

LIBRARY OF CONGRESS

own mind that her son was more important than any bathroom floor or dusty table. She fully expected to be fired as her employer had said, and returned that Monday just to collect her pay.[60]

When her employer's husband saw that she wasn't dressed in a uniform, he asked why. Minnie reported what his wife had said, but the husband insisted that Minnie continue to work, now reporting to him instead of his wife. In the end, Minnie had set boundaries and she was able to see her son, honor her mother's request, and increase her negotiating power in the household. Of course, the wife was angry; Minnie reported that they then "really had, [laughs] had a hard way to go."[61]

Things between Minnie and the lady of the house reached their lowest point one Sunday, when the woman told her to scrub a bathroom floor she had cleaned the day before. Minnie, who had always treasured her Sundays, believed firmly that she should not do heavy labor that day. Sunday to her was still a day of rest, and taking the day away from work was the best means of honoring her God. Like the pastor who was banished from Accomack County after the violence in 1907 for telling the women in his congregation not to do domestic work on Sundays, Minnie was making a principled decision. Again, her employer insisted that she would fire her, grabbing the bucket from the closet and slamming it down in front of Minnie. But Minnie kicked it over and walked away from the heated encounter, descending the back staircase of the large home and making her way into the kitchen. Her employer chased her, pushing Minnie in the back. Thankfully Minnie's friend was working in the kitchen and jumped between Minnie and the white woman before Minnie could swing to hit her, saving her from what would have surely been an arrest. Physical altercations between Black women workers and their white employers were not uncommon, but the Black women who defended themselves often ended up with harsh sentences for responding to workplace violence.[62]

When she later reflected on that day, Minnie connected the treatment by her employer with the coercion her grandmother had experienced when she was enslaved. Minnie insisted that "slavery's over, why should you still have to be pressured." She said that although she was a domestic worker, she was still the equal of the woman who paid her: "we all is one . . . only a difference in the skin." Doing heavy labor on a Sunday was out of the question: "I [have] never scrubbed a bathroom on Sunday in my life." We can't know if she ever saw *Imitation of Life*, but Minnie was no Delilah. Her continual spirit of resistance made a hard job more acceptable to her sense of self.

Minnie was far from unique in this respect. Black women set their schedules to accommodate their needs as mothers and wives as much as possible and quit jobs that demanded too much. Some might refuse to clean windows, a particularly arduous and often dangerous job that required balancing on second-story roofs and dormers to wipe grime from window glass. Others simply remained reluctant to serve in live-in positions where their private lives were essentially proscribed.[63] As one interviewee recounted, she was "always treated decently" and "no one ever tried to run over [her]" because she was "not the type you can run over."[64] The women who employed them might make unreasonable demands, but many maids felt empowered to call an employer's bluff, especially when there was high demand for domestic workers.

One hard line that many if not most household workers drew was taking jobs with working-class white families. They recalled an almost universal disdain for poor white employers. They paid less, paid less reliably, and were often cruel taskmasters. One interviewee warned friends, "Don't ever . . . go to work with one that's poor. They're going to be digging and digging all along because that poor Madam had [just] gotten to the place where she can sit down. . . . And, of course, she's going to work you to death."[65] Another woman with years of domestic service summarized the problem as one sitting at the intersection of class and race: "Because they've been poor all their lives, they want to make sure you don't get anything. Because, since you're Black, you don't have the right to anything."[66] Such judgments about the cruelty of poor whites as employers connected back to enslavement, when those in bondage thought of the working class as "mean whites" who were quick to exercise their racial entitlement by being cruel to Black people. Often employed as overseers and slave catchers, they made their living by enacting brutality on the enslaved. Arbitrary violence was part of their "psychological wage"; poor treatment of Black people was the very marker of their social status, which otherwise might have been difficult for outside observers to note.[67] As free workers, Black women continued to note all the ways in which poorer whites sought to overemphasize their power as a means of demonstrating their superiority. Simply put, the relative proximity in class standing made poor whites the least desirable employers.

The extraordinary burden of live-in employment, in which household workers were "on call" day and night, also made it undesirable long-term employment.[68] The poor living conditions and lack of personal space meant that they could not entertain family or friends; one woman reported sneaking her own children in so that she could see them while she was on duty. The profound encroachments that came with live-in domestic work were so corrosive, in fact, that over time it was almost universally rejected by the majority of Black women migrant workers. Black women who served as domestics tended to be older, often married with children of their own, in comparison to the younger European immigrant women who had previously served in these households. Their preferences for defined tasks and time away from the worksite shifted the market for houseworkers from primarily live-in to primarily live-out.[69] By the 1920s, most Black women domestics did daily or weekly work. Those who remained in live-in positions could therefore demand higher pay. Black domestic workers shifted the terms of the labor market simply through their refusal to be constrained or humiliated.

And, importantly, there were formal, collective efforts to organize among domestic workers. It was no surprise that the Black women of Harlem founded the most substantive union for domestic workers prior to the 1950s. Well known for its arts community in the age of the Great Migration, Harlem was also the heart of Black political organizing. Harlem became home not only for Black migrants from the South but also for tens of thousands of Caribbean immigrants. The intersection of these communities led Jamaican immigrant Marcus Garvey to found the Universal Negro Improvement Association, one of the largest Black nationalist organizations in the history in Harlem. Harlem was also home to the National Association for the Advancement of Colored People, as well as Black socialist and communist organizations like the African Blood Brotherhood and the Harlem Tenants League.[70]

One of the leading voices of the Tenants League, founded in January 1928, was Grace Campbell: a Southern migrant, the only woman leader in the African Blood Brotherhood, and the first Black American woman to join the Workers Party (later known as the Communist Party USA). The Tenants League became the voice of Black working-class women in Harlem. Highlighting the injustice of exorbitant rents for tiny kitchenette apartments, the Tenants League not only pushed for improved housing conditions through rent strikes, marches, and preventing unjust evictions, but also connected the struggle of the Black working class "to broader struggles against global white supremacy, capitalism, and imperialism." With almost five hundred mostly women household workers as members, the Harlem Tenants League was short-lived but it made an impact, not necessarily in growing the ranks of the Workers Party but in seeding a community-wide interest in organizing in more formal, confrontational ways.[71]

The desire for a unified voice for Black women workers continued. In response to the challenges of the Depression, the Domestic Workers' Union, affiliated with the American Federation of Labor (AFL), was launched in 1937. Both Black and white women were engaged in its work, but it quickly became an all-Black organization of women from the American South and the Caribbean. Led by a Black domestic worker named Dora Jones, it fought the brutalities of the "slave market" by providing spaces for women seeking work to congregate. In the union's offices, they could share time before or after work, cook a hot meal, and receive a political education. Formalizing much of what Black women had done informally for one another, it provided support for new migrants and immigrants to the city, connected women with resources and jobs, and provided space for women to share information about women employers who were unfair or brutal toward them on the job and male employers who were sexual predators.

The union turned women's concerns into policy advocacy. It fought for the inclusion of household workers in state minimum-wage laws, demanded coverage under unemployment insurance and Social Security, and contested punitive "health regulations that targeted black domestics as a potential source of disease." The Domestic Workers' Union became a place where women workers could seek assistance when they were attacked, overworked, or cheated out of their pay. The union also acted as an employment agency, placing domestic workers in new assignments but with workers' rights as their primary concern. Potential employers could call the union, which would negotiate fair pay and make sure that employers paid what they promised. If employers failed to provide the agreed wages, union members would picket their home. Although it was affiliated with the AFL, the union struggled to stay afloat on dues, given the low and irregular wages of its members. However, the union and others like it in the cities of the North serve as yet

THE MAIDS OF THE MIGRATION

another corrective to the notions that domestic work was somehow pre-modern, or that Black men were the only ones leading union efforts in this period.[72]

Even outside the unions, evidence of domestic workers' fight against indignity can be found throughout the historical record. Joseph D. Bibb, an African American lawyer, activist, and newspaper columnist, wrote an article for the *Pittsburgh Courier* in 1945 titled "Too Cocky," in which he complained that "those who have the least among us, now seem to be the most cocky and independent"—he was referring to domestic workers and manual laborers. Even though as a class they were not "protected by powerful unions," Bibb noted that they were "quitting their jobs, defying their employers, lording it over stakeholders and management." Bibb wrote that while during the Depression employers were empowered and could hire Black women workers at substandard rates, in the postwar period "the tables have been turned."[73]

His list of complaints against domestic workers reveals how working women were able to fight back when unemployment rates were low. He described them as "surly and precipitous," perhaps for refusing unrealistic work requests. He said many were "just itching for an argument and eager for a plausible excuse to quit and leave their hirers in a lurch." This was, of course, evidence that women were shopping for the best positions, controlling their time and work conditions by quitting. Indeed, one woman recounted that after a disagreement she told her employer to remember that she didn't "sign any contract" and warned her that she should never "feel that this is the only job."[74] A report on household employment backed up this woman's claim, finding that domestic workers quit because they "desire to have evenings free," because they "hope to get better job[s]," and because of "unreasonable demands" by their employers.[75]

Bibb noted that domestic workers could be "hired and fired with

impunity" but still felt that their supposed "cockiness and independence" would only serve to "stigmatize the colored workers." Instead,
he encouraged "tact, diplomacy, and sympathetic understanding." As
a leader in Chicago's local Republican Party, white patronage had
allowed him to become the first Black man appointed to statewide
office in Illinois. Perhaps he could no longer relate to the experience of
Black workers who were overwhelmingly not treated with any of the
"tact, diplomacy, and sympathetic understanding" he wanted them to
extend to white employers.[76]

———

IN THE END, MINNIE FINALLY FOUND A WAY TO MAKE PROG-
ress. She quit working for the family in Wynnefield when they were preparing to move to Europe for three years and asked Minnie to come with
them. This was metaphorically and physically too far for Minnie, who
intended to see her children regularly and reunite with them when she
finally had the resources to make a household of her own.

Hearing that there were opportunities in New York, Minnie hoped
for the real possibility of leaving private domestic work for good. With
a lead from a friend, she was able to get a job working in a city-run laundry facility. It was hours farther north from her family, and it was still
hard work; a seventy-two-hour week that required her to start before
dawn and work well into the evening, laundering, drying, starching,
and pressing uniforms and bedding for public facilities. However, Minnie was excited because the hours were set and clear. Most important of
all, there was opportunity for advancement. She was able to "go from
one step to another until [she] learned everything, and . . . could run a
business [herself]." Her boss was fair-minded and saw great potential in
Minnie because of her work ethic and her ambition. Eventually she was

promoted to serve as the manager of the unit, responsible for supervising twenty women and four men.

Minnie would join the laundry workers' union, which provided even greater freedom in her everyday work life. For the first time she got a mandated lunch break and an eight-hour day with overtime pay. Empowered, Minnie could see a way to make a better life for herself and for her family. She recalled at the end of her interview with oral historian Charles Hardy, III, in 1984, on which her story in this chapter relies: "So that's why I stayed all my life right here. I lived more in the cities, than I did at home, because I was only in, to my home 16-and-a-half-years. And when I was 16 and a half, I left. So, all the rest of my time has been right here in the city." The city, her own determination to survive, and the work of those who organized provided the pathway for Minnie to begin to feel free, to reunite with her children, and to have her work better reflect that freedom.[77]

In the 1950s, Brunell also found her way toward something better. After taking the civil service exam, a test required for federal employment, she landed a position working at the Philadelphia Navy Yard, among the first generation of Black women allowed to work there. She began in an entry-level position, typing and assisting with paperwork processing naval ships. It was a simple job, but for her it changed everything. Not only did it pay well, but now Brunell qualified for government benefits including medical insurance, and days off if she was sick. Getting away from what her husband called the "white folks' toilet" was a relief, too. Her hours and her limits were clearly set, and her free time was her own. It made all the difference—a difference that enabled her to build her savings and eventually purchase land for them to build a home for their family outside the city, in a circumstance that looked much more like what she had pictured when she first moved north. The change had not been easy; on the contrary, it was the result of her own labor and the labor of thousands of others who refused their employers' whims and who organized themselves, all to open doors. She was thankful for her new life, and for the connections that had kept her afloat when she feared she might drown. She kept working hard, but she had already helped make the world more like right.

CHAPTER SEVEN

Everything Sufficient for a Good Life

Hartford Boykin grew up in Wilmington, North Carolina, but his people came from nearby Sampson County. More specifically, from a few acres of land located in the coastal plains somewhere between the county seat of Clinton and the tiny town of Turkey. The latter was said to have been named for the birds that fed on the fruit of the land's bountiful forests and on the little insects and unharvested grain from nearby fields. To the original natives, turkeys were understood to be a sign of abundance, that this was good, fertile land, a fine place to settle. Escaping the violence of white settlers to the east who were trying to seize their ancestral territory, the people who eventually called themselves the Coharie Indians began living near the river that bears their name, many decades before the founding of the United States. There they fished, cultivated fields of sorghum, corn, and squash, and hunted for game in the forests, including the plentiful wild turkeys.[1]

So, community existed there long before Byus Boykin, a white settler

---

"African American postal employees sorting mail into cubby-holes."

WARREN K. LEFFLER, *LIBRARY OF CONGRESS*

traveling south through Sampson County, laid his eyes on its rich land. Said to have been on his way to claim lottery land in Georgia, his caravan of his family and the families he held in bondage, most likely including Hartford's ancestors, was held up by floods along the Coharie River. Stuck on the flooded banks, Byus decided to settle there, tasking the enslaved and skilled African bondsmen and women to build the infrastructure of a plantation. With handsaws and axes the enslaved clear-cut ancient forests of longleaf pines, drained swamps, and leveled wide acres to build a plantation out of the wilderness. Living on the prosperity created by the men and women they enslaved, the white Boykins became wealthy and powerful in the state of North Carolina, with three successive generations serving in the state legislature.[2]

Hartford's great-great-grandfather Boalam was born into bondage in 1810, shortly after the Boykins established their plantation. Within the community of those held in bondage, Boalam had a large family with his wife, Hannah, and among his many sons was a child named Isaac, born sometime in 1846. In 1863, during the Civil War, seventeen-year-old Isaac was sent to be a manservant and labor for the Confederacy at Fort Fisher, near Wilmington. Isaac was among the thousands of enslaved men and conscripted free people of color, including both Native Americans and African Americans, who were kidnapped at gunpoint and forced to labor to build an earthen fortification more than a mile long, essential to the defense of the city. These same men could not have had the opportunity to do that same labor for pay, given the Confederacy's insistence that all men of color were subhuman and unworthy of citizenship in any nation. Hundreds of the conscripted and enslaved died of injury, disease, and malnutrition at Fort Fisher. Hartford's ancestor Isaac survived.[3]

Finally freed at the end of the war, Isaac had spent years of his young life laboring for the benefit of the Boykin family and then the cause of the Confederacy. He now adopted the last name Boykin, a mark of the community in which he had lived as an enslaved person. As a free man he hoped to put what he knew about agriculture to work on his own land, for the benefit of his own family. Eventually, Hartford's great-grandfather was able to purchase fifty acres between Clinton and Turkey, not far from where he had been held in bondage.[4]

Most white residents in Sampson County had not substantively changed their attitudes toward men like Isaac. While all small family farms struggled in an economy that favored large landholders, and could suffer setbacks due to a bad crop or invasive insects, Black family farms were not only exposed to the vagaries of nature and the economy, but were also vulnerable when they did well. A prosperous Black farm too often signaled to local whites a disruption of the racial order, so much so that Black farmers avoided outward indications of success. Indeed, the hard work and market-based competition white Americans often say they value were a danger to Black people when they applied the same principles. To earn too much was thought to be too "uppity" or forgetful of their place in the racial hierarchy.[5]

Over the decades, white resentment compelled most of Hartford's ancestors to move away. Only his great-uncle Ed Boykin stayed, along with his wife and family and elderly parents, in Sampson County. Ed was pastor of a local church and he hoped to keep preaching and working the family land, somewhere between Clinton and Turkey.

When Hartford's father, Isaac—namesake of his own formerly enslaved grandfather—came of age, he was one of many in his generation who wanted to build a life away from Sampson County. After all, he was a high school graduate; though he was a skilled farmer, there wouldn't be much else he could do in rural North Carolina, so he hoped that migrating to Wilmington might provide more stability as well as safety within urban community life. In Wilmington, he first worked as a waiter at one of the big new hotels on the coast to which his family had supplied milk and vegetables, but it was seasonal work with short-term benefits that left him vulnerable to the unreliability of tips from patrons. Isaac looked for another field.

Eventually, Isaac found postal work on the railroad. He took the civil service exam, a test required for federal employment, and he did well, scoring highest in his pool of applicants. Mail work on the rails was skilled labor, requiring memorization of the complex routes, postal codes, and towns along the way. It had also historically been dangerous. Mail cars were on most trains that passed through small towns across the country, in many cases without stopping. Clerks had to drop off and pick up mail using a catcher arm while standing in the open door of the moving train car. Up until 1912, mail cars were constructed of wood, so if the train were to wreck, the cars could not stand up to the force of the crash. Given the hazards, railway postal work was a place where Black men had greater opportunities, as white men chose to avoid it.[6]

Isaac was hired after the adoption of steel mail cars, so outside of "throwing" and "catching" the mail at each station, the work was a bit safer. He was a quick study. He enjoyed the mobility, job security, and the stable hourly wage that the position afforded as a result of efforts by the union of Black railway mail workers, called the National Alliance of Postal Employees, which was founded in 1913, when the all-white Railway Mail Association union purged Black workers after the mail cars were upgraded to steel. In their charter, the Alliance included an echo of the French revolutionary dictum "liberty, equality, fraternity." Its members pledged to "grasp every opportunity that makes for the advancement of our welfare as a class and for the improvement of our condition in the service," ideals that were important to Isaac. In 1923 the Alliance expanded to welcome all postal employees and became the foremost Black postal labor union in the nation.[7]

For Isaac, it wasn't easy to be away from his young family for long stretches of time, so when an opportunity to be a local mail carrier opened in Wilmington, he applied, and due to his experience with the railway mail service he got the job. He was one of just a small cohort of Black postal workers in the 1920s. Wilmington's postmaster allowed Black men to be hired on a limited basis—hardly a progressive policy, but better odds than Black men could find in most other Southern and Northern communities.

From the start of his work on the railways, the stable and fair pay Isaac received changed his circumstances. Hartford remembered the profound impact his father's pay made on his family and by extension his community. He recalled that "if a black man was making five dollars a week he was living in high cotton. And oh . . . eight dollars, a week? Shucks, he could do a lot of things." Indeed, postal work was among the highest-paying jobs available to Black men, their earnings just below those of the small Black professional class of doctors, lawyers, and business owners. No longer dependent on the always changing price of crops or the fairness of white landholders or unreliable tips, Isaac had achieved a relative security rare for the Black working class. To Hartford, the third child of six, his father's position meant that "everything was . . . sufficient for a good life with his salary." His mother "never worked, never had to work and stayed home" to tend to the children. Hartford noted that they lived "a life above and away from the average run of [Black] people at that . . . time." Isaac purchased land and built his home in a middle-class, mixed neighborhood. He got the call to serve as a minister in the AME church, so he was respected not only for his stable employment at the post office but also for his position as a leader within the community.

Not satisfied with caring for his own family, Isaac used his relative prosperity to care for others. On payday he would purchase hundreds of pounds of meat, canned goods, fresh fruits, and vegetables to provide for the other Black families in Wilmington. Just as his forebears had done when they lived in Sampson County, in Wilmington Isaac taught his son to share what he had and that along with his pay came a responsibility to the community. This communal web of support allowed more prosperous families to share not only their resources, but their stability.

Though his father set an aspirational example of the success one could achieve through working at the post office, Hartford thought he would find another line of work. After graduating from high school in 1939, he worked at Camp Davis, a US Marines training facility in Onslow County, North Carolina, forty-six miles north of Wilmington, but Black men were severely limited in what jobs they could hold there. When the North Carolina Shipbuilding Company opened in 1941 on the east bank of the Cape Fear River as part of the government's emergency shipbuilding efforts, Hartford applied for a job. At first, he had better success there, working his way up to become a riveter, but then he was permanently injured on the job by a piece of steel that flew free at high speed and struck him in the spine between the shoulder blades. The white shipyard doctor dismissed his debilitating injury as minor. Hartford was Black; the doctor did not want him to receive appropriate compensation for his injury. Eventually, Hartford received adequate treatment from a doctor hired by his father. After recovering, he was drafted. Promoted to corporal and then staff sergeant at Fort Bragg in his first seven days, he served valiantly overseas in the segregated US Army. He returned home with a greater appreciation for the safety and stability the post office could offer, particularly to veterans, so he too took the civil service exam and waited to see if he would be hired.

Even with the comfort his father's income had provided, Hartford's mother, Alice, was haunted by all she had witnessed growing up in rural Georgia, seeing Black men, sometimes men she knew, arrested on false charges and sentenced to time on the chain gang. She never forgot the sounds the shackles made when men, chained at the ankles, were forced to shuffle from jailhouse to courthouse. She never forgot seeing men working in the hot sun at the point of a white man's gun. Alice feared that in spite of her family's success, there was no guarantee of their safety. The threats she had known growing up still loomed over the lives of her sons, despite everyone's best intentions and their hardest work. From his mother, Hartford learned that Black freedom was precarious. So even though his father's job at the post office often felt like "high cotton" relative to the lives of other working Black people, his mother's warnings about steering "clear of trouble" also rang in his head. He understood that no real trouble was required to put all their lives in jeopardy.

Hartford's great-uncle Ed, the one who had stayed back on the land somewhere between Clinton and Turkey, was doing well growing tobacco plus corn, tomatoes, and bell peppers. As children Hartford and his siblings loved to visit him, staying for months in the summer when school was out. Close to where their ancestors had been held in bondage, they would attend Ed's country church, learn about the land, and help their great-uncle with the hard work of tending to the crops. But doing well remained dangerous. The local whites hesitated to allow Ed to purchase supplies, suddenly curious neighbors posed questions, while other whites refused to let Ed ship produce to Northern markets on the railroads and suggested that he and his family watch before they forget their place. One summer, Hartford learned that he would not have the chance to visit with Great-Uncle Ed; he had been shot in the heart by a white man, murdered in a squabble over the land. Even as his father's good government job elevated his entire family, Hartford understood that no Black person could ever make a truly secure life.[8]

TODAY, POST OFFICE WORK IS CLOSELY ASSOCIATED WITH THE Black working class. The United States Postal Service reports that, currently, 21 percent of its employees are African American, almost twice the proportion of the country as a whole. In some cities, Black workers make up 75 to 80 percent of postal workers.[9]

In many ways the transformation of the post office mirrored the struggle for fair inclusion in the armed services. After the First World War, and especially after the Second World War, Black men and women who had served in the armed forces—which was segregated and whose officer corps was rife with Southern whites—gravitated toward postal work. A position with the post office could help ensure that their sacrifices in the military had counted for something—their veteran status made them favored for employment, and it was a route for those seeking to leave the vulnerability of their prewar agricultural work behind. In most urban communities in both the South and the North, most white-collar jobs, and the majority of blue-collar trades, were still closed to Black workers. The shift from exclusion to inclusion at the post office was not happenstance. Black postal union members organized, advocating for the rights of Black citizens to be fairly considered for positions. It would be their working-class advocacy that transformed postal work from whites-only employment to a growing opportunity for Black workers. Finally gaining access to stable, unionized salaries and benefits allowed generations of postal workers to become foundation stones for Black communities. A fair shot at a job in the post office changed the circumstances of Black working people across the country.

It was not an easy fight. Black postal workers would work to contest segregation, serving as postmasters despite the grave danger they faced, particularly in rural Southern communities. Deploying what anti-lynching advocate Ida B. Wells-Barnett called "the thread-bare lie" that Black men were regularly targeting and raping white women, white mobs organized to attack Black postal appointees on the pretext that they were protecting their wives and daughters. Many Black postal workers stayed on in the effort to contest white supremacy, while others fled their home communities in hopes of finding better opportunities elsewhere. Fighting both federal segregationist policies and extralegal violence, Black workers continued to push for their equal right to deliver the mail.

Even after gaining access to postal work, mail carriers used the mobility the job entailed as a tool for organizing. Walking their routes kept them connected with the families and institutions in the neighborhoods they served. Indeed, their workspaces were community spaces. The postal routes they walked daily, past the homes of family, friends, schoolmates, and church congregants, were often building blocks of interconnectivity and support.

Esteemed within Black communities, postal workers were union members, joining national unions and creating local organizations to support one another even as they were barred from joining whites-only postal unions. Their union work was not conceived solely to improve their own pay and conditions but also as a means of making sure others had equitable opportunities. Their work was yet another reminder, too, that the exclusion of Black workers from whites-only unionizing was a profound hindrance to the success of a national labor movement.

Much like the Pullman porters, within civil rights organizations postal workers pushed to center the fights of laboring men and women in broad calls for justice. The Black working class recognized that essential to the fight for equal rights would be equal access to employment. Black postal workers laid the groundwork for the integration of federal employees and the fight for civil rights unionism.[10] Most importantly, Black postal workers carried with them the traditions of the Black working class, above all a commitment to use the resources they earned and the things they learned to build pathways for their kith and kin. It reads as a triumphant story, in the end, but obscured by the currently high proportion of Black post office employees is a long history of struggle. It is a history of a battle against intimidation, racial violence, systematic exclusion, segregationist policy, and even anti-Communist purges—and of building a platform on which they might advocate for all.

———

YEARS AFTER THE CIVIL WAR, WILLIAM HARVEY CARNEY, JR., still had a limp, his step hindered not only by the cold shoreline air that made his bones ache and the weight of the sack of mail on his shoulder, but also by the lead remnants of the minié ball still embedded near his right hip bone.[11] However, when he considered the thousands of soldiers with similar injuries who were amputees or hadn't survived their wounds, he thought of himself as fortunate. Despite his impairment, he completed his postal route like clockwork each day, so reliable that the residents in New Bedford, Massachusetts, could set their watches by the time he slipped the mail in the slot on their front doors. His valor as a war veteran was followed by his groundbreaking efforts as one of the first Black men to be hired as a postal employee.

When the US Postal Office was established shortly after the nation's founding, by custom only white workers were hired to deliver the mail. Although slaveholders frequently used enslaved people to deliver letters, and mail carriers used enslaved people to assist them on their routes, as free laborers Black people were excluded. When news of the Haitian revolution reached the halls of Congress in 1802, legislators led efforts to formally declare that only "free white persons" could serve as mail carriers,[12] fearing that the mobility, literacy, and networks of communication that postal work naturally fostered would fuel Black resistance to enslavement. Congressmen imagined that Black postal workers might be ideal abolitionists, fostering insurrection as they traveled the highways and byways with the mail. Indeed, postmen would have had access to information in the letters of slaveholders, and as they followed their routes, they would have been able to decipher the notes scrawled on the backs of postcards. In the fear-filled imaginings of a nation upholding chattel slavery and suppressing rebellions, a Black postal worker had everything at hand needed to start a revolution to overthrow slavery. It is no surprise, then, that the 1802 law was reaffirmed in 1810 and 1825, once again restricting "mail conveying to free white persons only." So terrified were officials about the insurrectionary potential of postal work that in 1828 Postmaster General John McLean warned that if Black labor was required "to lift the mail from the stage[coach] into the post office" it had to be "performed in the presence and under the immediate direction of the white person who has it in custody."[13] Postal historian Philip Rubio notes that the exclusion of Black workers from the post office became "one of the first labor laws" in United States history.[14]

The ban on Black mail carriers was not lifted until 1865, after the close of the Civil War. The new legislation, penned by Massachusetts senator Charles Sumner—the anti-slavery stalwart who was brutally beaten with a metal-tipped cane for his speech voicing opposition to the admission of Kansas to the Union as a slave state in 1856—repealed the former laws in declaring that "no person, by reason of color, shall be disqualified from employment in carrying the mails." The bill, signed into law on the same day the Freedmen's Bureau was established, was a keen reminder that the rights of Black workers were intertwined with the future of Black freedom, Black citizenship, and the establishment of civil rights for Black Americans.[15]

Of course, Black people had demonstrated time and time again that they were more than worthy of citizenship and the opportunity for work and service. William Carney, Jr., was most likely the second Black postal worker in US history, hired just months after the first, James B. Christian, made international news.[16] A fugitive slave, William and his family had escaped bondage in Norfolk, Virginia, in the 1850s and sought refuge in the abolitionist stronghold of New Bedford, Massachusetts. Much like Frederick Douglass, though younger, William was educated clandestinely in the South, attending a "secret school" in Norfolk, where his talent for writing and speaking was revealed and where his desire to become a minister was sparked.[17] In New Bedford, he could be educated without fear of reprisal. But even that education did not afford him equal access to employment. Black men in the Northern city were limited to the poorest-paying, most dangerous jobs. William could find only entry-level employment at the same port where, decades earlier, white dockworkers had threatened to strike if Douglass was hired. While the North proved to be a respite from chattel slavery, it was no relief from discrimination and de facto segregation.

Though Black men had served in every war in American history, Abraham Lincoln had to be convinced to let Black soldiers volunteer to serve in the Union Army. William did not hesitate to volunteer when the president finally acceded to Black activists' demands, writing that he felt he "could best serve [his] God by serving [his] country and [his] oppressed brothers." Carney joined New Bedford's Morgan Guards, a local militia unit, which changed its name to the Toussaint Guards in honor of Toussaint Louverture, who led the slave revolt in Haiti in 1791. Carney and forty-five other Black men soon became part of the 54th Massachusetts Volunteer Infantry, an all-Black Union regiment. So many Black men volunteered, in fact, that the 55th Massachusetts Volunteer Infantry was formed to accommodate them. William was one of the more than 200,000 African Americans who would serve in the Union army during the Civil War.[18]

Serving valiantly, he was shot five times while carrying the flag across the battlefield at Fort Wagner in Charleston, South Carolina, on July 18, 1863, after the original color bearer was killed in the firefight. Despite injury after injury, he made his way to enemy lines with the flag intact. Even though the Union troops failed to capture Fort Wagner, the 54th had demonstrated the valor of Black Americans to the entire nation—and to the South. White claims that Black men wouldn't, or couldn't, fight were dispelled. Yet it would take almost forty years before Carney was fully recognized for his valor and awarded the Medal of Honor.[19]

Getting a job with the US Post Office was, however, a crucial recognition of his service and citizenship in its own right. Despite his accomplishments as a soldier, William's opportunities for employment in New Bedford remained tightly restricted by his race. The city that had once provided refuge for Frederick Douglass still held a limited view of what a Black man might accomplish. William was systematically blocked from most of the trades or factories in the city.

The post office was a new opportunity. Congress had just passed a law prioritizing the hire of disabled Union veterans wounded during the war as long as they were honorably discharged. Along with the passage of the Sumner-led legislation that opened the door for Black applicants, this suggested to William that he had a good chance. He applied to the post office and was appointed in 1869 to a position he would hold for more than thirty-two years. Carney's service in the Union army and his desire to serve as a mail carrier were intertwined, in that both positions were delineated in the Constitution and thus were opportunities for Black people to demonstrate the depths of their citizenship.

William's job as a mail carrier changed the circumstances of his young family. Postal records reflect that he earned $850 per year, equivalent to just over $22,000 a year in today's money. It was solid and steady working-class employment that came with regular pay, benefits, and job security. Yet William remained concerned about laying a pathway for other Black workers and became a founding member of the New Bedford Branch 18 of the National Association of Letter Carriers, serving as its first vice president. On the coldest of days walking his postal route, Carney wore his Union overcoat, a reminder to all who saw him that he was a veteran and a signal that he was part of a community of Black men who were more than worthy of the opportunity to serve, on and off the battlefield. Their service would stand as a bold correction to those who had systematically and legally barred Black men from service in any form.

———

CARNEY WAS ONE OF HUNDREDS OF BLACK MEN AND WOMEN hired by the US Post Office in the years after the Civil War. Although extant postal records from this era do not include the racial identity of employees, a study by the National Postal Museum estimates that almost five hundred African Americans were hired as postal workers during Reconstruction. For example, there were at least fifteen Black male letter carriers in the nation's capital. So respected were they within the African American community that ten of them were asked to serve as pallbearers for Frederick Douglass's casket in 1895.[20]

On paper, the possibilities for equitable access to federal employment were enhanced by the passage of the 1883 Civil Service Act, which did away with the appointment system for the post office. Indeed, one Northern newspaper reported that in Norfolk, Connecticut, "fitness, and not color" was the bar.[21] The post office offered Black employees the same steady pay as white letter carriers and the same pension at retirement. When white postmasters allowed Black men and women a fair shot at taking the civil service exam, as was required by law, they frequently scored well and qualified for employment. However, there was a loophole: officials could opt not to hire the top candidate and select one of the three highest-scoring candidates instead. If a postmaster did not want to employ Black workers, he could easily skip over an applicant if one of the other top-scoring candidates was white.[22]

Given this loophole, access to postal employment varied from community to community. While some cities welcomed Black mail carriers, in other places it was the practice to bar Black residents from holding positions in the post office well into the mid-twentieth century. Macon, Georgia, perhaps surprisingly, welcomed Black mail workers. A column written in 1919 in the *Macon Telegraph*, the city's white newspaper, fondly recalled seven Black mail carriers alongside white ones, naming them all.[23]

In contrast to the apparent ease with which some communities accepted Black mail carriers, in Trigg County, Kentucky, in 1907, protests against the hiring of an African American, William L. George, led to a situation in which "practically every white person entitled to the service removed his box" and "negro patrons were the only ones to whom George had mail to deliver." The post office was forced to discontinue the route "because of lack of sufficient patronage" and William lost his job. Although the newspaper insisted that no threats had been made, William must have perceived that he and his family were in danger, particularly in an age when Black men, women, and children lived under the threat of lynching, and threats against Black postal workers were common across the nation. William and his family moved away from Trigg County. William worked briefly as a teacher and then, later, obtained a position as a railway mail clerk in Owensboro, Kentucky. Eventually they left Kentucky altogether for Evansville, Indiana.[24]

William George must have known that postal employees Thomas Moss and Frazier Baker had been lynched. The salary that Moss earned as a mail carrier was what had enabled him to open the People's Grocery, and that financial independence was at the root of the anger that led to his murder. Just six years after she reported on the lynching of Moss and his two employees in Memphis, Ida B. Wells-Barnett would chronicle the 1898 lynching of Black postmaster Frazier Baker in Lake City, South Carolina. Outraged at Frazier's appointment by the McKinley administration, white residents declared Lake City to be a "white man's town" and had already responded violently, shooting at a Black postal clerk, burning down the first post office in the town, and making continual threats to lynch Frazier himself. Eventually they determined to kill him and his entire family rather than receive their mail from a Black man.

Armed with a veritable arsenal of guns, gasoline, and torches, the mob of three hundred white men and boys gathered outside the new post office, which was also the home of Frazier, his wife, Lavinia, and their six children. At 1 a.m., the mob set fire to the building and lay in wait to shoot as the family fled the flames and smoke. Firing a barrage of over one hundred shots, the marauders cut down Frazier in the doorway. Only two children, Sarah and Willie, escaped without physical injuries. Three of the children, Rosa, Cora, and Lincoln, were shot and seriously injured, as was Lavinia, who was shot through her hands while cradling their infant daughter, Julia, in her arms. The child was killed instantly. Local Black families who heard the gunfire and saw the flames light up the night sky came to aid the injured, pulling them away from the flames consuming the post office and the bodies of Frazier and Julia Baker.

After the Baker lynching, Wells-Barnett led a campaign to push the federal government to act. Hosting a meeting in Chicago with two thousand attendees, she noted the bitter irony that the mob that shot a child in her mother's arms claimed to be protecting women. Following national outrage over the attack on a federal employee, thirteen of the murderers were indicted by a federal grand jury. However, the trial was a farce; witnesses lied, and defense attorneys called on the all-white jury to defend white supremacy and acquit. The jury deadlocked and the judge declared a mistrial. No one ever served time for the heinous crime. The remaining members of the Baker family were taken to Boston by sympathetic white supporters, where four of the five surviving children contracted tuberculosis and died between 1908 and 1920.[25]

Although the lynchings of Moss and the Baker family were extraordinarily awful, violence targeting Black postal workers was common and frequent. In 1903, white residents near Gallatin, Tennessee, protested when the highest scorer on the civil service exam, Allen F. Dillard, was hired as a mail carrier.[26] Fearing backlash from white residents, Allen resigned, and the second highest-scoring candidate, John C. Allgood, who also happened to be African American, was hired. Days after beginning his appointment, John was stopped on a rural route four miles outside Gallatin "by two masked men with drawn guns." John, who had been the target of intimidation since his hire, was told by the vigilantes not to deliver the mail and to quit without telling the postmaster why. The men said he would be lynched if he reported the threat, gave him a dollar, and sent him back in the direction from which he had come.[27]

Reporting on the incident, the *Richmond Times–Dispatch* used the threat of rape to justify the attack, explaining "that the white men in the rural districts . . . were afraid to have a negro calling regularly at their homes on any errand when the women were there without protection." Dismissing "civil service rules and all that," the *Times–Dispatch* argued that "every negro man is more or less under suspicion" and called on President Theodore Roosevelt to "sympathize with" white "southerners in thinly settled communities," arguing that "the apprehension is notoriously warranted by much Southern experience."[28] Again in 1906, in response to the hire of a Black letter carrier named T. L. McKay, white postal customers in Raleigh, North Carolina, declared that they would rather not have mail delivery for fear that "while they are at work in the fields and away from their homes . . . their wives and daughters are the only ones to receive and deliver mail."[29]

Local authorities did little to protect John Allgood from the threat of being murdered on his mail route, so he and his wife and their three young children fled the town of his birth for Chicago, where he again found work as a mail carrier.[30] The move north was an unfortunate one for the Allgood family, however. John's wife died of tuberculosis at the age of thirty-three, in 1908; his eldest daughter died of the same illness at age fifteen, five years later; and John died the next year, in 1914, also of tuberculosis. His second wife—he had remarried—received his $1,200 death benefit from the US Post Office.[31]

In 1913 white federal employees organized the ironically named National Democratic Fair Play Association, which resolved that it was "mutually disagreeable" and "destructive to the moral welfare" to have Black people in positions that would allow them to supervise white employees. Calling integrated workspaces "UnDemocratic, UnAmerican, and UnChristian," the white supremacist organization called for the dismissal of Black supervisors, workspace segregation, and quotas limiting the number of Black employees to mirror Black voting strength, which was, in the age of voter disenfranchisement, artificially low. Dismissing Black workers as "greasy" and "ill smelling," the group sent letters to officials in the Woodrow Wilson administration and to the president himself.[32]

Wilson was a great boost for segregationists when he was elected in 1912. Some Black leaders, including W. E. B. Du Bois of the NAACP and William Monroe Trotter, a leading African American newspaperman and activist, had hoped that Wilson might be forward-thinking on questions of race, as they had grown frustrated with the inaction of the Taft administration and the Republican Party. However, Wilson quickly demonstrated his desire to institute racially divisive policies on every front, appointing three of the main voices of Southern segregation to head the agencies with the largest numbers of Black employees. William Gibbs McAdoo was named Secretary of the Treasury and Josephus Daniels Secretary of the Navy; Albert S. Burleson was appointed Postmaster General. Easily the most egregious appointment was Josephus Daniels, a newspaper publisher and the leading proponent of the purge of Black leadership in Wilmington, North Carolina, that led to a massacre of Black residents in 1898. Wilson systematically ignored the pleas of his Black supporters and, insisting that he had promised them nothing other than "justice," dismissed the thirty-one highest-ranking Black federal appointees, replacing only eight of them with Black Democrats.[33]

In what first appeared to be a concession to Black leaders who were voicing concerns, Wilson nominated A. E. Patterson, an African American lawyer from Oklahoma, to serve as the Register of the Treasury Department. The segregationist novelist Thomas Dixon, author of *The Clansman* and a close friend of the president, wrote Wilson to express his disgust at Patterson's nomination, insisting that "the establishment of Negro men over white women employees in the Treasury department has . . . long been a serious offense against the cleanliness of our social life." Wilson responded by clarifying that his appointment of Patterson, who had the support of Black Democrats, was just part of a "plan of concentration" to gather all the Black workers together in one department so that Patterson would have no real authority or the ability to supervise white people. Even then, senators from Mississippi, South Carolina, and Georgia—James Vardaman, Ben Tillman, and Hoke Smith, respectively—"violently opposed the appointment" and Patterson quickly withdrew himself from consideration for the job.

In 1913, following complaints from white workers about sharing bathrooms with Black men, Wilson's postmaster general, Albert S. Burleson, segregated the Railway Mail Service and the Washington, DC, Post Office Department. Several high-ranking Black postal employees were fired because they were no longer permitted to supervise white employees. The highest-ranking Black postal employees in the nation's capital who were allowed to keep their jobs were assigned to the dead letter office, where lost and untraceable letters were sent, and where they would not encounter the white public in any way. The lower-level Black workers who remained were forced to work in alcoves separated from white employees, behind demeaning screens, and were forbidden to eat in cafeterias, leaving them no choice but to eat lunch in segregated restrooms.[34] W. E. B. Du Bois wrote in horror about the degrading conditions in an open letter to Wilson in the NAACP's magazine, the *Crisis*:

> In the Treasury and Post Office Departments colored clerks have been herded to themselves as though they were not human beings. We are told that one colored clerk who could not actually be segregated on account of the nature of his work has consequently had a cage built around him to separate him from his white companions of many years. Mr. Wilson, do you know these things? Are you responsible for them? Did you advise them? Do you not know that no other group of American citizens has ever been treated in this way and that no President of the United States ever dared to propose such treatment? Here is a plain, flat, disgraceful spitting in the face of people whose darkened countenances are already dark with the slime of insult. Do you consent to this, President Wilson? Do you believe in it? Have you been

able to persuade yourself that national insult is best for a people struggling into self-respect?[35]

In fact, President Wilson believed wholeheartedly. Undeterred by a NAACP petition with 20,000 signatures protesting the segregation of federal employment, the Wilson Civil Service Commission began, in 1914, to require that all civil service applicants submit a photograph with their application. Although officials insisted that the requirement was to ensure applicants' identity and prevent fraud, in practice it was a powerful means of ensuring that postal officials would not make a mistake and choose high-scoring Black candidates.[36]

Among the most vocal Black supporters of Wilson prior to the election was William Monroe Trotter, the son of James Monroe Trotter, a member of the famed 55th Massachusetts Volunteer Infantry (sister regiment to Carney's 54th Massachusetts), one of the first Black commissioned second lieutenants to serve in the army, and the first Black man to be employed in the Boston post office. So, Trotter knew personally the impact that new federal segregationist policies would have on Black workers' rights. In a meeting with the president in November of 1914, he was insistent that given the history of Black and white federal employees working relatively peaceably in integrated workspaces, segregation was a stigmatizing step backward for the nation. In response, Wilson argued that "segregation is not humiliating but a benefit" and that Black leaders should encourage workers to think differently about the firings and cages his policies imposed. Trotter then asked if Wilson's goal was to create a "'new freedom' for white Americans and a new slavery for your African American fellow citizens?"[37] Offended by Trotter's tone of voice and his insistence on being heard, the president cut the meeting short. Although he was not as publicly vocal as some politicians, Wilson was just as adamant and effective a white supremacist as any race-baiting firebrand from the deep South. He believed that segregated workspaces reflected the natural order of racial hierarchy, and were more efficient, too—indeed, in his eyes, progressive. Of course, in reality Wilsonian segregation downgraded Black workers to a bottom tier no matter their performance records or achievements. Indeed, the firings and segregationist policies had a long-term deleterious effect on Black people: forcing them into lower-paid positions measurably increased the pay gap between white and Black employees, slowed their rates of homeownership, and stunted their ability to give their children a good start.[38]

Access to postal work for Black applicants had never been easy, even prior to Wilson's draconian policies, so Black postal workers continued to organize, encourage others to apply for jobs, and advocate for change. Their efforts to unite in the wake of exclusion and to fight systemic oppression would make them central to the broader push to secure better rights for all workers. They didn't have equal access, but they had a cause, and a tradition of coming together to support one another. Out of this labor a movement was born.

———

IF YOU SAW HIM IN THE LATE 1940S ON HIS POSTAL ROUTE, HIS work would have looked highly unremarkable—it involved delivering letters to mailboxes and leaving parcels on front porches—but you might have noticed his countenance. He was a proud man; he moved with the confident stride of a soldier in his gray-blue uniform. On cool days, when the wind carried a salty snap of the coast inland, he wore his uniform's zip-up jacket. On hot and sunny days in the port city, you would have seen him in his starched and pressed uniform shirt neatly tucked into his pants. No matter the weather, he sported Red Wing's Postman Oxfords. Given the miles he walked on his route through Wilmington's Black and white neighborhoods, the oxfords were almost perpetually worn, with soles made thin too quickly from daily use, but the shoes were still polished and buffed until the black leather gleamed in the sun. He was a fixture in the communities he moved through, walking the small streets and sidewalks, pleasantly greeting friends and neighbors with pride in spite of the weight of the heavy mail sack he toted on his tired back, worn from war and work.[39]

Hartford Boykin, son of Isaac Boykin and the land somewhere between Clinton and Turkey in Sampson County, North Carolina, was now a veteran of the Second World War and a mail carrier for the US Post Office in Wilmington. Though he was wearing a familiar uniform, his existence would have been notable to the Black workers who came before him, including those men who experienced the Wilson administration. Hartford Boykin represented a generational change. In 1920, with the segregationist policies started under Woodrow Wilson in full

"African American postmen loading bags of mail into U.S. mail truck." A tradition of organizing allowed Black postal workers to share their success with the community as a whole.   WARREN K. LEFFLER, *LIBRARY OF CONGRESS*

effect, there were fewer than 4,000 Black mail carriers and postmasters nationally; by 1950, after men like Hartford joined the ranks, there were more than 45,000. And they had proven more than deserving of the equal opportunity to serve.

Hartford had much in common with those earlier generations whose worn shoe leather tamped down the pathways that led to greater rights for Black workers. He was a veteran, the son of a postal employee, and a fifth-generation North Carolinian whose ancestors' labor was critical to the prosperity of his home state. Due to the Veterans' Preference Act of 1944, which granted returning soldiers special consideration for federal employment, by the second half of the 1940s most postal employees were veterans, and many of them were Black southerners. Additionally, many of the Black women who had taken on postal work when men were drafted kept their jobs after the war. There were more than 2,800 Black women in the postal ranks in 1950.[40]

Yet the war didn't change everything, particularly in the South. For example, Black mail carriers could not be found in every city in North Carolina. They still represented a small and exclusive group when Hartford was hired. A 1944 population study of North Carolina found that there were only fifty-three Black mail carriers in the entire state, "most of which are employed in Wilmington, Raleigh, Goldsboro, and Fayetteville." Durham did not hire its first Black postal worker until the spring of 1954. George Booth Smith was a student at Durham's North Carolina College for Negroes, and his professor, Elwood Boulware, encouraged all those in his classes to take the civil service exam, even providing time off for study. But the city's postmaster refused to hire Black workers. When George applied, he was told that postal jobs "weren't for niggers, these jobs were for white high school graduates." An official from the National Alliance for Postal Employees heard the story and arranged for George to meet the Postmaster General of the United States, Arthur

Summerfield. In response to the blatant discrimination, Summerfield called Durham's postmaster to explain that if he didn't give George a position, he should look for a new job himself. When George returned to Durham, he was told that a position had suddenly become available, and he became Durham's first Black mail carrier. He went on to become the founding member and president of Durham's Alliance chapter, which boasted thirty-five members by 1956.[41]

George's and Hartford's post–Second World War generation flooded into postal work, and made it into one of the quintessential Black jobs in America. While the majority of Black workers still suffered the injustices of sharecropping, the unfair wages of Jim Crow, or were relegated to dirty and dangerous work, in the 1940s and 1950s postal employees earned what Hartford called a "very decent living." Given the decades of systematic inequality Black workers had endured in every sector of society, the simple access to an equal shot became the groundwork for profound change.

Advocacy by the National Alliance of Postal Employees led to the overturning of the policy of requiring a photograph with a civil service application. With little national fanfare, President Franklin Delano Roosevelt changed the rule in November of 1940. To some outside observers this change may have seemed inconsequential, particularly in light of the sweeping reforms brought on by the New Deal, but for Black workers it was a turning point. Roosevelt not only banned the use of photographs but also "ordered that the rules governing civil service appointments be changed to prohibit discrimination." While this didn't immediately end discrimination in hiring, it did suggest that a fairer future was near.[42]

The Alliance provided a crucial organizing base for Black postal employees nationwide. Much like the Brotherhood of Sleeping Car Porters, it transcended the bounds of a traditional union. Drawing on varied traditions of Black fraternal societies, civil rights organizations, leftist organizing traditions, and the legacy of the Black church, the Alliance became influential not only for postal workers but in the fight to dismantle Jim Crow for Black laborers in particular and Black people in general. The workers of the Alliance helped organize a bus boycott in Harlem, New York, to promote the hiring of Black bus drivers in 1941. In 1943, they led the charge to end segregated cafeteria facilities at the St. Louis, Missouri, post office. When the US Supreme Court overturned the white primary—a form of disenfranchisement in place in seven Southern states that prevented Black voters from participating in state-held primary elections—with the 1944 *Smith v. Allwright* decision, the Alliance led Black voter registration drives. In Atlanta, Alliance member John Wesley Dobbs helped to found the Atlanta Negro Voters League, which registered 18,000 Black voters in Fulton County in just two months.[43]

Herman Marion Sweatt—letter carrier, leftist, Alliance member, and son of an Alliance founder—brought a suit against the University of Texas Law School with the assistance of the NAACP Legal Defense Fund for failing to admit him simply on the basis of his race. A highly qualified candidate, he had applied in 1946, but he was rejected outright because Texas state segregation statutes prevented Black students, no matter their qualifications, from being admitted. When, under the direction of famed Black civil rights attorney Thurgood Marshall, the NAACP petitioned the state courts, the state of Texas opened a second law school specifically for Black students, one that was separate and profoundly unequal. Herman was willing to serve as the test case for the Legal Defense Fund because he believed the time was right to challenge segregation head-on in the courts, rather than demanding that racially separated spaces actually be made equal. His vision that the end of segregation was possible dovetailed with the work of the Alliance.

When *Sweatt v. Painter* ended up at the US Supreme Court, the justices found in a unanimous decision that the hastily created law school for Black people was not an adequate replacement and that segregation was harming Black people. Insisting that the University of Texas Law School had an obligation to admit Herman Sweatt, the court handed the NAACP a major victory, and, in a way, handed the Alliance one, too. The case was a major stepping stone on the road toward *Brown v. Board of Education* (1954) and the legal end of school segregation.

Probably the most notable obstacle that the Alliance faced in their fight for civil rights was Joseph McCarthy. McCarthy, a Republican senator from Wisconsin from 1947 to 1957, rose to infamy in 1950 when he began to assert that the Communist Party had infiltrated all sectors of American society and government. His campaign started with the State Department, but eventually implicated Americans across the country and federal workers in every department. The work of Black postal workers and Alliance members in contesting Jim Crow segregation became a shorthand for so-called un-American activities. When the search for Communists started during the Truman administration in 1948, the NAACP and other liberal organizations kicked out suspected Communist Party members. In contrast, the Alliance defended union members who faced the 1948 purge. Protecting active Alliance members in Philadelphia, Pennsylvania; Cleveland, Ohio; Detroit, Michigan; Brooklyn, New York; Newark, New Jersey; and Santa Monica, California, the union successfully cleared its members' names of the false accusations and won their exoneration and back pay. When hundreds more postal workers were accused of affiliation with the Communist Party in 1952, the union fought back and won again. Alliance advocacy led to the creation of a Board of Appeals and Review for those pushed out by the post office. Alliance president Ashby Carter explained the union's stance:

Members of our organization in several cities have been cited to
show cause why they should not be separated from the postal service for alleged disloyalty to the government. We realize that Jim
Crow is a venerable old bird, but we insist that taking pot shots
at him is not disloyal to America.[44]

The Alliance's brave and vigorous defense of Black postal workers
accused of being Communists because of their work contesting segregation set it apart from the NAACP.[45] Its integrity in a terrible time made
members even more loyal to the cause.

When the modern civil rights movement began, the Black working class was at the ready, with postal workers in the vanguard. Rosa
Parks, the activist whose resistance spurred the Montgomery bus boycott in 1955, was a working-class seamstress and a quiet but fierce political powerhouse who had been active in the NAACP for more than a
decade. One of the architects of the Montgomery movement was E. D.
Nixon, a longtime member of the Brotherhood of Sleeping Car Porters and NAACP leader. Boycott participant, household worker, cook,
and organizer Georgia Gilmore founded the Club from Nowhere, an
"underground network of cooks [who] went door-to-door selling sand-
wiches, pies, and cakes, and collecting donations" to support the boycott.
Alliance-affiliated postal workers in Montgomery used their knowledge
of the city to draw detailed maps for the impromptu ride service that
enabled the city's Black workers to get to their jobs.[46] Black postal workers, including Alliance members and those who were not, drove cars for
the ride service, making a yearlong boycott not only possible but incred-
ibly effective.

One of the keys to Black postal workers' success in activism in
Montgomery and across the country was that they were federal employees. So, while working-class people who were sharecroppers, household

workers, or employed by state and local governments could be easily kicked off the land or fired in retribution for registering voters or contesting segregation, local postmasters were accountable to authorities in Washington, DC, for their decision-making. When postal workers were targeted and fired for civil rights activism, they had the means to appeal and be reinstated.

———

ONE OF THE SINGLE BEST EXAMPLES OF POSTAL-WORKER-AS-activist was civil rights trailblazer Amzie Moore. Amzie was the son of sharecroppers, born into hard circumstances in Grenada County, Mississippi, on September 23, 1911. His parents separated when he was young, and he was on his own after his mother died when he was just fourteen years old; his father returned to retrieve his younger siblings but left Amzie behind. Struggling to care for and feed himself, Amzie depended on a community already stretched thin by poverty. Though challenged by the loss of his mother, he prioritized his own education in a separate and unequal society. He moved to Greenwood, Mississippi, to attend Stone Street High School, where he completed tenth grade, the highest grade available to Black children in the county. After getting a perfect score on the civil service exam, he was appointed to a position at the Cleveland, Mississippi, post office as a postal custodian in 1935, at the age of twenty-four. He was politically active as well, joining a Black voters' organization, the Black and Tan Party, and registering to vote in 1936.[47]

Being drafted to serve in the Army Air Corps during the Second World War, in the 332nd Fighter Group—the famed Black Army pilots known then as the Red Tails, known now as the Tuskegee Airmen—changed Amzie's outlook. In the service his favorite assignment was teaching aircraft recognition. This sharecropper's son served in Europe, then in Burma and the Middle East, before being honorably discharged.

One of more than 83,000 Black Mississippians in a segregated military and trained at segregated bases across the South, Amzie's time abroad showed him that racial separation wasn't God's will, as he had been taught growing up, but man's creation.[48]

The man-made, white supremacist world he returned to was profoundly unfair, stacked against Black people. In 1940, 80 percent of Black Mississippians lived below the poverty line. The state led the nation in disenfranchisement; only 5 percent of eligible Black citizens were registered to vote, when the South-wide average was around 33 percent. In some counties only one or two Black residents were registered, while all the white residents were. In three Mississippi counties—Amite, Tallahatchie, and Walthall—there were no Black voters registered at all.[49]

Even before returning home from the war, Amzie joined the NAACP, exhibiting the same bravery he had shown as a soldier to build a life for himself and a better life for Black Mississippians. He would need it; Amzie recalled that Cleveland, Mississippi, had launched a "home guard" to protect white women from the supposed voracious sexual appetites of Black veterans who were said to prefer white women after their service in Europe. Several Black veterans were targeted and killed.[50]

From his earnings as a postal employee and using a federal GI loan of $6,000, he was able to buy land and build his own home. He was, in fact, the first Black veteran in Bolivar County, Mississippi, to receive a federal loan.[51] Amzie built the home with brick he purchased outside the county when local suppliers refused to sell to him. His choice of building material may have been strategic—it was harder for arsonists to torch a home made of bricks than one made of wood.

In Bolivar County, he threw himself into the fight to register voters, and made an immense difference. He would tour churches throughout the county with a gospel quartet, and then go on to share the good news of the need for Black Mississippians to register. Over 17,000 Black people in Bolivar registered to vote for the first time between 1940 and 1952, in large part owing to Amzie's actions. He was elected president of his NAACP chapter and expanded it to be the second-largest chapter in the state. In 1951, Amzie banded together with veteran activists across the state, including Medgar Evers and Aaron Henry, to co-found the Regional Council of Negro Leadership, which boycotted segregated gas stations, protested police violence, and continued to register voters.[52]

All the while, Amzie kept working at the post office. His job allowed him to open his own business in Cleveland along with his wife, Ruth: a gas station that featured a café and beauty shop. He refused to segregate the facility, despite the laws of the state, and never put up a "colored only" sign in the window. Local white business owners tried to undercut his enterprise, preventing him from receiving the credit he needed to run the station. He was regularly threatened, so he remained armed and vigilant.[53]

When Student Nonviolent Coordinating Committee member Bob Moses came south to organize in Mississippi in 1961, longtime activist Ella Baker sent him to Amzie Moore. Amzie found a kindred spirit in the young organizer, and they began the work that would one day lead to the Freedom Summer movement of 1964. It was Amzie's partnership with Bob Moses and SNCC that would see him fired from the post office on April 1, 1961. After he was told that he was dismissed because of his civil rights work, he called the Justice Department to demand his job back. Kennedy administration Justice Department officer John Doar brought Amzie to Washington, where he determined that there was no due cause for Amzie Moore's dismissal and ordered the local postmaster to reinstate him.

Amzie's brick house, described by movement historian Charles Payne as "well armed" and "at night the best-lit spot in Cleveland," became a touchstone for SNCC activists. Amzie originally assumed that the educated young activists wouldn't be open to learning from him. But he soon learned that the experiences he'd had—working at the post office, serving in the Second World War, organizing in Mississippi from home to home, singing with his rich tenor from church to church—were some of the bricks required to build a Black working-class movement.[54]

He would teach SNCC activists that trust was essential in a place as dangerous as Mississippi, and that they could only make gains if they were members of the community. So they walked house to house, talking and getting to know local people and their families. They laughed and played cards on front porches, they provided free lessons for the children, they attended church and joined in the songs and worship, they picked cotton, they helped with the cooking and cleaning along with the families that hosted them. They became tied into these local communities, and ended up making sure that the movement in Mississippi represented the people who needed it most.

———

ON MARCH 18, 1970, POSTAL WORKERS IN NEW YORK CITY BEGAN to walk out, forming picket lines outside the Grand Central Station Post office. Their strike was technically illegal; the Lloyd–La Follette Act gave federal employees the right to form unions but expressly forbade them to strike. The unions, and Black union organizers in particular, had made strides over the hundred-plus years that Black workers had been employed by the US Post Office, but by the 1970s the good pay postal workers received had not kept up with inflation. Dependent on Congress for raises, they had little power to negotiate salaries; astonishingly, there were no raises for postal workers between 1925 and 1943. Postal unions negotiated five raises between 1943 and 1953, but met mostly resistance for the next fifteen years. Postal work, which had once provided solid wages, now left employees in urban areas unable to afford homes near their jobs. At the very moment when larger numbers of Black workers joined the ranks, increases in pay dried up.

The scope and scale of postal work had also profoundly changed during the twentieth century, moving from mere letter carrying, to parcel delivery, and all the way to banking services. The amount of mail Americans were sending by the 1970s was enormous, so there was a serious need for more employees. Black postal workers, drawing on years of experience leveraging their positions within the post office to push for access and equity, led a new post-Vietnam generation of workers, including young veterans and women of all backgrounds—but particularly much larger cohorts of women of color—in a finally unified cross-racial coalition to fight for better work conditions, increased pay, and more union autonomy.

Starting in New York City, where 30 percent of the postal workers were Black, the wildcat strike of 1970 tapped into the experience that came from years of fighting white supremacy in the ranks of the postal service. In contrast to fields where tensions over civil rights victories had led to greater competition between Black and white workers, in the post office civil rights gains and bonds of solidarity forged through service in integrated armed services allowed Black and white workers to see each other as allies, fellow veterans, and fellow employees with aligned interests. As a result, there was more cross-racial unity among postal workers than there had ever been. That unity resulted in the first postal stoppage in American history, when 200,000 postal workers in more than thirty major cities and 671 local post offices decided to leave the mail behind to protest.

Stopping the mail created a national crisis. Sympathy came pouring in from the public, who wanted fair treatment for the men and women who delivered the nation's mail. When President Richard Nixon called in the National Guard, their failure to successfully restart the mail service, with its 270 million pieces of mail a day, demonstrated the knowledge and skills postal workers possessed. With the threat of draft notices not reaching the young men who were still being pulled in to fight in Vietnam, Nixon came to the bargaining table, and the talks resulted in a retroactive pay raise, with the promise of another after the US Post Office was reorganized to become the United States Postal Service, a public–private partnership. The postal unions achieved full autonomy for negotiating increases in pay, insurance, pensions, and working conditions. None of the striking workers were fired. If not for the legacy and leadership of Black unionists, no such strike would have been successful, or even thinkable in the first place.

REFLECTING BACK IN 1993, HARTFORD BOYKIN FELT THAT HE had built a truly good life as a postal worker, but he lamented the way his body had deteriorated. His shipyard accident, coupled with the wear and tear of his postal route, left him with disabling injuries by the 1970s. He quit the postal service, but by that time he had a home with his wife and children in Wilmington, and he could be rightly proud. He went on to serve as a magistrate for the city, pleased with his record of service to his country and community.

In the interview, his only lament was that his house had been taken by the government, through eminent domain, to make room for a highway. As in thousands of communities across the country, Black homes and businesses in Wilmington were carved up for the highways that facilitated white flight. For Hartford, it was too much to tolerate; he resettled in a decent neighborhood but never fully recovered from the shock of the dislocation. The forcible removal of a disabled veteran of the army and the post office, without any regard to his service, left Hartford with complex, contradictory feelings about his country.

Black postal workers today might well feel similarly. The post office has long been a site of Black struggle, and a gateway for Black and Brown postal workers to receive the fair and steady wages that finally allow for fuller access to the security of the middle class. So, it is no accident that over recent decades, the post office has been framed as a problem. Even as the shipment of packages only increases in importance in the American economy, the adoption of racially coded language that labels the post office as inefficient, wasteful, and outdated has allowed for the erosion of this critical institution. The George W. Bush era Postal Accountability and Enhancement Act, passed in 2006, made the US Postal Service financially unstable by introducing the mandate to prepay all retiree health care costs for the next seventy-five years. The change required $5.6 billion over a ten-year period and confused the public into thinking that inefficiency rather than bad policy was causing the post office to run in the red. Such a frame also puts a solidly Black employer in jeopardy.

Recent efforts to defund and dismantle the US Postal Service have attempted to undermine the cause of the Alliance and civil rights postal workers who follow in the footsteps of people like Amzie Moore. Conservative opponents have tried to privatize the post office, to suppress Black access to the vote during the coronavirus crisis of 2020–21, and to weaken one of the few remaining unionized spaces for the Black working class today. The post office is thus a reminder that the Black working class is a bellwether of the health of democratic citizenship in America—and that any gains left unprotected are fragile, though more than worthy of the fight.

Brunell

Her grip on my hand was unshakable. My grandmother Brunell Raeford Duncan would hold my tiny palm so tightly whenever we went out that I used to imagine that her grasp was preventing me from flying away in a strong gust of wind or keeping me from sinking into some unseen hole in the ground. Even if it was not strong enough to save me from some terrible calamity, it was certainly quite efficient at stopping the blood from circulating properly from my palm to my narrow, little-girl fingers. At first, I would try to wiggle my hand away from her, to mark my displeasure, but soon I learned that would only make her hold even tighter. Eventually, I grew comfortable with it, particularly the way she would occasionally knead the surface of my palm, like she was pressing lard, flour, and water into dough. Her handhold soothed her worry and kept my young mind and thin body from roaming away. I learned that her tight clasp was protective, confirmation that I was right there. Over time, I came to understand her tight grip as love.

Grammy and me.

On her land around her home in Atco, New Jersey, behind what felt like miles of chain-link fence, she would let me run free, away from her hands, up the long driveway to water the golden-faced marigolds, up and down the rows of her tomatoes, okra, strawberries, turnip greens, and string beans. In her garden she grew the food her family had grown in rural South Carolina. She taught me how to recognize when the shining green corn stalks that towered over my head held a mature cob in their golden silks, and that both the root and leaf of the turnip were delicious. She let me taste the cool, tiny grapes that grew on her vine in the shade even as I feared their seeds. In her garden, her strong hands were gentle and quick, picking beans without breaking the plant, or plucking golden pears and blushing crabapples from her trees without harming the branches.

In her small, warm kitchen, she turned her garden's bounty into stews of corn, tomatoes, and okra to store in her deep freezer for eating all winter, while the pears and crabapples were the base for the thickest, sweetest preserves tucked away in Mason jars sealed with wax for safekeeping in the pantry. I loved standing close to her hip while she tossed dumplings into a steaming pot of chicken stock, her fast hands tearing the pieces from the ribbons of raw dough draped and balanced over her arms, the way her mother and grandmother taught her. She told me stories about growing up Geechee in a place I had never seen for myself, but she said I was Geechee too even all the way away in New Jersey because of how much I loved her cooked rice.

I remember so much about her: the smell of her kitchen, the feel of the soil, the sounds of the birds and crickets, the laughter that punctuated the intense fussing between my grandparents. But my primary memory, the very first thing I think of when I think of her, is that haptic memory of her strong hand wrapped around my tiny one. Learning more about my family over the years has helped me understand the grief that made her handhold so tight.

Blair is a family name. My mother named me after her maternal grandmother, Julia Blair Raeford. Julia Blair was the child of Preston Blair and Jemima McCracken. Both of Julia's parents were born in bondage in Newberry County, in the rural midlands of South Carolina, a place where my maternal grandmother's family can be traced as far as slave records will allow. Newberry was at the center of a state where in the decades after slavery Black life was regularly threatened by attacks by white men, both extralegal lynchings and legal ones: quick and arbitrary executions of Black residents accused of crimes by the state.

I cannot know the very last thing that pushed them all to leave, but leave they did, between 1922 and 1924. Mothers and fathers, grandparents, brothers and sisters, cousins—all seemingly evacuated the place where they and their forebears had once been considered property. My grandmother would be the last one born in South Carolina in her branch of the family. Together, the Blairs, the Raefords, and the McCrackens would build their families away from the place where they had been enslaved and the climate of violence that surrounded them. Most moved, as a story in this book recounted, first to the small town of Thomasville, North Carolina, seeking opportunities for skilled work in the furniture industry. Instead, they lived on its margins, blocked from opportunities for success or advancement in the famed factories whose white bosses would not allow Black people to work the good jobs. So they swept the floors and assembled the boxes in the dusty factories, cleaned the homes and did the laundry of the white factory managers.

They hoped for an escape, but Thomasville ended up being the place where many of them would die. Although Thomasville now reads as a sleepy, small Southern town, its relative industrial density in comparison to rural Newberry must have made it dangerous to my family's health. Evidently, growing up in rural Newberry left them with no built-up childhood immunity to tuberculosis, so in Thomasville they were sickened by this incurable disease, just as Frazier Baker's surviving family fell ill in Boston and the Allgoods contracted TB in Chicago. Tuberculosis preyed on the bodies of the working poor, particularly Black people in densely populated urban areas.

Contracting the disease one by one, they began to suffer from and eventually succumb to the myriad painful and debilitating conditions the respiratory illness caused. I never heard my grandmother talk about her own grandparents' deaths, but Preston Blair and Jemima McCracken Blair would be the first to die in Thomasville, both in 1933 just a few months apart, when my grandmother was thirteen, taking with them the last living vestiges of the experience of the enslaved. Although her stories about her family always came in bits and pieces, my grandmother never failed to smile when she told me that her father, Earnest Raeford, had small hands and small feet, just a little bit bigger than his wife's feet. He would pass away as a victim of tuberculosis in 1935, at the age of forty-one. He left behind five children who had survived early childhood and his wife, Julia. My Grammy was the oldest; at the time of her father's death, she had just turned fifteen. Her youngest sibling, my great-uncle Billy, was just nine months old at the time.

After Earnest passed, my great-grandmother Julia was left to support her children with just her wages as a washerwoman, but that work allowed her to both bring in money and care for her kids. Said to be a hard and beautiful woman with rich jet-black hair and little time for traditional affection, her love was evidenced by her determination not to let my grandmother drop out of high school. My grandmother was proud that she completed her high school education; she was, as I mentioned earlier, an avid reader and loved to follow politics. Her mother lived to see her finish school, marry, and give birth to her first child, my mother, but not much longer than that. Julia worked hard despite the presence of tuberculosis in her lungs, but pressing forward soon became too much for her, too, and in 1941, at the age of forty-four, she died from complications of tuberculosis as well.

That wasn't the last time death would come to call on the family. Although I never remember her saying her name, my grandmother had a younger sister, nearest to her in age, named Cordie Mae. The two must have been close; my grandmother had stood as a witness when Cordie Mae married her sweetheart, Willie Morrison, in September of 1940. Cordie Mae and her young husband would be the next to die. Five years after they married, both Cordie Mae and Willie would pass, one day apart, on September 10 and 11, in the Negro wing of the segregated North Carolina sanatorium. The couple's two small children, Andera and Willie, died from complications from tuberculosis, too. So, by the age of twenty-five, my grandmother had lived through the passing of her grandparents, parents, her sister closest in age, her brother-in law, and her infant niece and nephew in a twelve-year period. I learned the depth of what she suffered not in her kitchen as a child, but in archival records as an adult. No one likes to recall that they survived while others didn't. Why I never heard my grandmother say Cordie Mae's name became clear.

Although she tried for a brief time, my grandmother was too young and poor to manage raising her younger brothers and sisters. They were taken in by her maternal aunts, raised separately in various communities on the East Coast, but they kept in touch. My grandmother moved with her own young family—my grandfather and mother—to Philadelphia to see if they could start again. And they did, even after disease and its accompanying shame and destruction ravaged her family. The experience made my grandmother anxious for the rest of her life, teaching her to hold tight and to worry. Thirty years later, without knowing where that handhold came from, I would feel that generational pain in her grip of my hand, which she would occasionally knead like dough.

OTHER THAN THAT THEY BOTH SPREAD THROUGH AIRBORNE transmission, the disease that took my relatives and Covid-19 are not epidemiologically similar. Tuberculosis is an ancient bacterial disease that has killed an unfathomable number of people over the centuries; Covid-19 is a never-before-seen viral infection. While not a parallel disease, it offered a comparable lesson about the tremendous vulnerability of Black Americans, and the particular burden borne by the Black working class.[1] Covid-19 causes sickness that is amplified by the unequal circumstances created by racial discrimination. In 2020 and 2021, the rate of death was almost three times higher for Black people than for white people; once again, whole families were decimated by the unequal burden of disease and death.[2] Thousands of Black people have died, and somehow amid all this suffering and loss they were blamed for their own demise, stigmatized for the circumstances of their lives and labors. The so-called comorbidities that Black people disproportionately suffered from were said to be their fault. It is as if there is an implicit question: Why can't Black people stop suffering from higher rates of diabetes, heart disease, cancer, and asthma? There was no mention that the higher rates of diabetes, heart disease, cancer, and asthma arose from the deeper diseases of segregation, redlining, employment discrimination, lack of access to health care, and unequal treatment by doctors—the unique set of circumstances under which Black Americans suffer.

Contemporary scholars characterize these unequal health outcomes as the "racial health gap." You can find the root of this health gap in the subjugation of slavery, and in the fact that in its afterlives the hard, body-breaking labor of Black people was viewed by whites as having hardly any value in a free market. You can see the disproportionate impact when you look at the segregation of not only land and labor, but also access to care—the policies of segregation or exclusion from hospitals and medical care, a system that wrought unthinkable violence on the bodies of ailing Black people during the age of Jim Crow. You see how Covid-19 traced the paths of black migrations to the urban South and North, etched into the rural landscape and urban redlining that put heavy industry—which has poisoned and still poisons the land—in close proximity to the bodies of Black working-class people. You can find the roots of the racialized pandemic in the rapid deindustrialization that turned the industrial Black working class into the dispossessed, people who only had access to service jobs while workers in the information economy could work from the safety of home.

More than 28 percent of 42 million Black people in America today—the majority of the Black working class—are "essential workers."[3] During the height of the pandemic, they were not allowed to shelter in place; instead, they would be the people who made quarantine possible for the white middle class and the wealthy. They would process the food, stock the shelves, drive the buses, box the Amazon Prime purchases, deliver the packages, Instacart the groceries, bring the mail, nurse the elderly, clean the hospitals, gather the dead. Any appreciation they received did not come in the form of hazard pay, paid sick leave, or medical care. After all, their deaths were largely their fault—they were responsible, the nation effectively told them, for their unhealthy diets while living in food deserts, the poison already coursing through their veins due to tainted groundwater, the smoke already choking their lungs. This current story is an old one. As the Black working class continues the fight for justice, fair pay, union representation, secure housing, and equal citizenship, the Covid-19 crisis is a reminder that this fight is not incidental to everyday life. It is fundamental.

This country often speaks of Black resilience, and indeed, Black folks have survived generation after generation of profound oppression and violence. But it is important to remember that not everyone survived. When we plumb the histories of the Black working class, we can recall how we arrived in this moment, and remember the costs borne.

———

IT IS EASY TO FORGET NOW, BUT IN THE EYES OF WHITE SUPREM-acist lawmakers at the turn of the twentieth century, segregation was a progressive policy, a good way to organize an increasingly urban society full of free Black people who challenged white authority. As Black folks fled the rural areas where their ancestors had been enslaved, they first moved toward growing Southern cities, then later, during the Great Migration of the 1920s, to the cities of the North and West. Racial segregation and exclusion replaced the personalized brute force of landowners. Segregation or exclusion governed every aspect of public life, including employment. Both segregationist Southern progressives and Northern industrialists believed in Black inferiority, but needed both Black and white workers to build infrastructure and industry. They invested in both de jure and de facto segregation in the hope that it would teach Blacks their proper place in the racial hierarchy and win the support of dispossessed whites.

In the South, employment segregation was coupled with disenfranchisement and the looming threat of lynching to try to keep working-class white people content with their place above Black southerners and distracted from noticing the white elite. In the North, while there were fewer laws restricting Black life, de facto segregation kept Black people at the margins of freedom, and the white working class enjoying the "wages of whiteness." The overwhelming majority of Black people in both the North and the South were limited in what jobs they could secure, no matter their education, skills, or interests.

Most Americans assume that citizenship is the domain of the middle class, reverting to a portrait of people debating over comfortable dinner tables about policies and candidates, using their spare time on weekends to attend forums or knock on doors. We tend to believe, whether we realize it or not, that the people with the best educational background and the most leisure time and social capital are model citizens. But in the wake of Donald Trump's election in 2016, the sudden vocal engagement of the white working class in national politics caught the professional political class off guard. Although the average Trump voter was actually white and middle-class, self-described working-class voters have been his most passionate supporters, filling his rallies even as many of his policies gave little beyond lip service to the challenges working people face. Trump's rhetoric stoked old fires, fueling the idea that the white working class should be the elite among the working class, elevating themselves by standing on the necks of Black and Brown others. National political leaders and pundits were ill-equipped to talk about race and the reactionary language animating the white working class's fervor and its support of Trump's racialized pseudo-populism. Democrats and progressives wondered how candidates could win over some portion of the white working class, especially the many first-time voters in 2016, and have helped put the real crises that the white working poor now face—tenuous employment, drug addiction, a housing crisis, and more—at the center of our political discourse. Some pundits insisted that people from other groups be nicer to the white working class: stop associating them with racism, or quit mentioning the xenophobia, white nationalism, and conspiracy theories. They argued that uncritical empathy is the best means of winning these voters over.

The Trump-caused obsession with the white working class, however, has obscured the reality that the most active, most engaged, most informed, and most impassioned working class in America is the Black working class. All along, Black working-class folk have been the canary in the coal mine, suffering first from deindustrialization, a housing collapse, and an epidemic drug crisis. Nevertheless, the Black working class—particularly working Black women—consistently has some of the highest voter participation rates, even in the face of gerrymandering and voter suppression. Without the benefit of middle-class resources, they organize, they get out the vote, they rally behind candidates, they fight suppression tactics, they organize in their churches and in their neighborhoods. Though they are at the bottom of American capitalism's economic ladder, they are a political force. Their engagement is grounded in their history.

Black working-class people are not marginal within the larger Black community. In fact, the Black working class is central to the heart of the Black experience. Members of the Black working class aren't stigmatized as trash; rather, they are often lionized as leaders. And they are helping lead a new multiracial working-class movement today. While race has been used by generation after generation of politicians seeking to divide and distract American workers from challenging the structural barriers that make it hard for the working class to get ahead, history and the present day are rich with promise. Indeed, if we better understand all the paths Black workers have taken, we can see what might be possible.

———

I THINK OFTEN ABOUT WHAT BRUNELL WOULD WANT TO SAY about these questions, about what lessons John Dee might leave with me. She had cancer twice, surviving a life-threatening bout of kidney cancer in 1960, then succumbing to a terrible stomach cancer in 1989.

Family reunion, 1980s.

My grandmother Brunell Duncan and her younger siblings at the reunion.

My grandfather John Dee Duncan, his siblings, and their spouses at the reunion.

John Dee died of lung cancer, emphysema, and a broken heart the next year. But they lived full lives. They split up and reunited years later. They were together when their children graduated not only from high school but from college. Together, they built the home that they had always wanted on a big plot of land, just around the corner from John Dee's big brother, Obbie. They retired from working-class jobs, but not from their roles in their church or neighborhood or in our family.

On that land they hosted big family reunions, where all sides of the family came together and celebrated. The descendants of Solicitor and Preston, and even folks from my father's side representing Bruce, met in the summer for food and fellowship. I recently inherited a photo album with images of one of the last reunions in New Jersey, faded photos of pitchers of sweet tea next to platters of sliced pound cake. Folks seated in folding chairs pulled up to picnic tables covered in flowered tablecloths, heads tilted over plates or back in laughter. Big straw hats shielding grandmothers from the sun, along with blue tarps strung across the wide yard. Cadillacs of every color parked on the grass out front. Folks leaning over in conversation, in postures of "Remember when?" framed by tall oaks and pines in the yard. Sips of the adult drinks that I wasn't allowed to taste dipped out of buckets into paper cups. All the men, then all the women posing together. My grandmother and her siblings in their white and yellow, smiling so hard that you can't see their eyes. My mother, head turned away from the camera, looking just like me. My grandfather sitting with his three surviving siblings, all of whom escaped on a wagon in the dark that night, then more than fifty years later captured in that bright light. With an inheritance all their own.

ACKNOWLEDGMENTS

Although I've only been formally engaged in the work of this book since 2018, the questions, sources, and voices that undergird this project have been part of me since I was a girl. The stories told by my mother, father, grandmother, grandfather, aunts, and uncles were imprinted on my consciousness at an early age. They are how I first understood what a past was; they are the beginnings of my study of history. So, I would need to begin any acknowledgment by thanking my ancestors, those I know on this side and those gone before I was born. Their lives are the fertile ground that nurtured the seed of *Black Folk*.

Thank you to my extended family, the descendants of the Duncan, the Raeford, the Murphy, and the Burris lines. Your prayers, laughter, and remembrances of love animate this work. Thank you for always being supportive of my goals. Grateful thanks to Craig and Toni Murphy for the time spent in their beautiful home where I completed the final set of edits for the project. Particular thanks to my father, Leroy Murphy, and my uncle, Nathaniel Murphy, for their insights into their father, grandfather, and great-grandfather. Thanks also to my informants on the other side: my mother, the late Frances Geraldine Duncan

Murphy, and my maternal grandparents, the late Brunell Raeford Duncan and the late John Dee Duncan. I now know that their storytelling, often the same stories again and again, were given to me for a purpose. I am thankful for being the vessel to carry their words forward.

I can't imagine this project without my agent, Tanya McKinnon. Our conversations about what this book could mean and what it could strive to capture are reflected here. I am thankful to have her as a fierce advocate, mentor, visionary, and loyal friend. There are none better.

Thank you to my editor, Dan Gerstle, for the idea at the heart of *Black Folk* and the faith that I could write such a project. His keen questions, excellent sense of what is needed, and the space to speak in my own voice were a gift. How fortunate I am to have him as an editor and the team at Liveright to support this work.

The research and writing of this book would not have been completed without generous financial support. During a bleak pandemic year, being awarded a 2020 Creative Nonfiction Grant from the Whiting Foundation was an unexpected joy that gave needed space to retreat, travel, write, and reflect. I am grateful to the foundation for nurturing my work and my spirit in a hard time.

I am also tremendously thankful and honored to have been awarded the 2022–2023 John Hope Franklin Fellowship at the National Humanities Center supported by the Center and the National Endowment for the Humanities. The solitude alongside community, and intellectual and physical sustenance offered by the Center are unparalleled. Thanks in particular to Matthew Booker, Vice President for Scholarly Programs at the Humanities Center and Professor at North Carolina State, who encouraged me to dream big about this project and myself as a scholar.

To my North Carolina State administrative team, I am thankful for your support for me as a scholar and leader. I'd like to thank Dean Jeff Branden and Dean Deanna Dannels, who provided time away from my administrative role to research and write, supported summer appointments at the National Humanities Center, my sabbatical year, and gave me the chance to participate in the Faculty Success Program of the National Center for Faculty Development and Diversity. Thanks to retired assistant dean Betty Byrum not only for her willingness to guide and mentor me, but for the friendship, advice, and camaraderie. Her listening ear and strategic mind helped me harness the time and the resources to get things done. Her belief in me always pushed me to see what might be possible.

Portions of what would become chapters of this book were presented virtually during 2020 and 2021. Thank you to David Zonderman for inviting me to present a chapter to the Triangle Labor History Colloquium; thanks to Julia Jordan-Zachery for inviting me to present the conclusion of *Black Folk* for my keynote talk at the Nation in Peril: Race, Health, and Democracy Symposium in the Department of Africana Studies at University of North Carolina–Charlotte; thanks to Camilo Lund-Montaño for nominating me to present *Black Folk* for the Skotheim Lecture in the Department of History at Whitman College; thank you to Vanessa Valdés for having me join the New Student Experience— Creativity, Community, and Change course at the City College of New York–CUNY to present my scholarship on Black postal workers; and thanks to Laurent Dubois for the invitation to share this work with the Scholars Happy Hour, Duke University Forum for Scholars & Publics, hosted by Vert and Vogue. Thanks go to my dear friends Melissa Harris-Perry and Dorian Warren for the opportunity to talk about the ancestral portions of this project on their *Nation* podcast *System Check*.

A number of colleagues and friends have taken time to read all or part of the manuscript. Thanks to my NC State faculty colleagues who participated in the works-in-progress seminar, particularly Susanna Lee and Kat Mellon Charron, for their willingness to read, critique, and share. Thanks to Brittney Cooper, Robin D. G. Kelley, Tera Hunter, Eric Arneson, Martha Jones, James Manigault-Bryant, Imani Perry, Michael Eric Dyson, and Tiya Miles for their support of the project. The feedback, critiques, encouragement, and generous letters of support made a tremendous impact.

I've benefited greatly from phenomenal students and scholars who helped with research and assistance. Thanks go to Cheryl Dong, Kawan Allen, and Graham Pitts, who put their formidable research skills to work to make *Black Folk* rich and substantive. Thanks to Melody Hunter Pillion, Hannah Scruggs, Jasmine Cannon, and Lisa Withers, who went above and beyond to find and organize the sources I needed to always keep my lab open, even as a busy administrator. Thanks also to my newest students, Ari Green and Brittany Hutchinson, for their support. I am proud to say that as a collective, my students are my finest legacy.

I am lucky to have Cara Smelter and Phillip MacDonald in my life. Cara served tirelessly as my program associate with grace and love; I constantly benefited from her skill as a historian, writer, editor, and problem-solver. Her excellence gave me the space to achieve what appeared to be impossible. And I am grateful to Phillip for his work as my photographer, folklorist, and library professional, for taking on the task of photo editing with me, and always making headshots that I love.

Karla Holloway handed me a note that said "intentionality" at a brunch one morning. I thought I knew what it meant at the time, but the word became a mantra and a tremendous guide to me as I did this work. I am thankful to her; her support in many hard times has served as a blessed force for good in my life.

My godmothers, Ruby Thompkins and Peggy Hester, provided support, spiritually holding me up as I did this work. Their mentorship and models of service are reminders of the legacy of Black folk. I am thankful for their willingness to love me up to such a high standard. Thanks to

ACKNOWLEDGMENTS

my church family at Peace Missionary Baptist Church for the constant prayer, encouragement, and community.

Particular thanks go to my dear sister-friend Rhon Manigault-Bryant. Her reading, criticisms, and strategic vision helped me push the project forward even during a pandemic. Her love, encouragement, scholarly insight, and firm counsel made all the difference.

Candis Watts-Smith has read every word of *Black Folk*, some a few times, so I probably owe her a free pass on reading everything she writes that needs review for at least the next two years. Her rigor, honesty, and insight honed and polished my words. Her belief in me pushed the project forward. There would be no *Black Folk* without Candis as my most faithful and brilliant interlocutor. I am thankful she took this journey with me.

Gratitude goes to Kelly Richmond Pope, my steady phone-a-friend in a world full of texts, my ride or die, and my biggest cheerleader. I am thankful for all the ways she models excellence to me every day. Thanks for being such a faithful sister-friend, pushing me when I felt too tired to try.

Thank you to my children, Demi and Brooks, for being patient with my diverted eyes and occupied mind when I was deep in this project. Their words of love, feedback, hugs, and willingness to listen to pages read aloud were a phenomenal gift.

Finally, to Patrick Kelley, my best, my rock and protector; I could do nothing without him as my partner for life. He was always listening, even in the middle of the night, to every passage of this book. I am in awe of his love and laughter, and his deep belief in us.

NOTES

In researching *Black Folk,* I used Ancestry.com to consult census and other public documents, such as wills. As a digital search tool, I found it to be an indispensable research aid. Given that Ancestry.com requires a membership and these documents are available through multiple sources, I have structured my Census Bureau citations to include whatever locator record is available in order to promote accessibility.

There are various types of US Census documents: the manuscript census is what was recorded by enumerators; slave schedules are distinct population schedules recording the enslaved without their names; demographic volumes are digests of the information collected.

EPIGRAPHS

1. Vince Brown, "Social Death and Political Life," *American Historical Review* 114, no. 5 (December 2009): 1249.
2. Richard Wright, "12 Million Black Voices: A Folk History of the Negro in the U.S.," in *Richard Wright Reader,* edited by Ellen Wright and Michel Fabre (New York: Harper and Row, 1978), 184–85.

INTRODUCTION: SOLICITOR

1. W. E. McLendon, "Soil Survey of Franklin County, Georgia," US Department of Agriculture, *Field Operations of the Bureau of Soils, 1909,* 541.
2. "Classroom Segregation: History and Current Impact on Student Education,"

American University, School of Education, August 19, 2020, https://soeonline
.american.edu/blog/classroom-segregation/.

3. Valerie Wilson, "People of Color Will Be a Majority of the American Working
Class in 2032," Economic Policy Institute, June 9, 2016, https://www.epi.org/
publication/the-changing-demographics-of-americas-working-class/.

CHAPTER ONE: HENRY, A BLACKSMITH

1. US Census Bureau, Ninth Census of the United States, 1870, Ruckersville, Elbert,
Georgia, Roll M593_148, National Archives, Washington, DC.

2. The removal of native families from their homes at gunpoint cleared the way for a
boom in white settlement. See James C. Cobb, *Georgia Odyssey: A Short History of
the State* (Athens, GA: University of Georgia Press, 2008), 11; Georgia Land Lottery Records Research Guide, https://raogk.org/georgia/ga-land-lottery/, accessed
October 7, 2020.

3. For more on the domestic trade, see Steven Deyle, *Carry Me Back: The Domestic
Slave Trade in American Life* (New York: Oxford University Press, 2005).

4. Charles Ball, *Slavery in the United States: A Narrative of the Life and Adventures of
Charles Ball* (New York: John S. Taylor Brick Church Chapel, 1837), 80; Sharyn
Kane and Richard Keeton, *In Those Days: African American Life Near the Savannah River* (Atlanta: National Park Service, Southeast Region, 1994), 11. For a more
detailed account of the domestic slave trade, see Deyle, *Carry Me Back*.

5. Kane and Keeton, *In Those Days*, 11; Cobb, *Georgia Odyssey*, 13.

6. Ball, *Slavery in the United States*, 211–12, 217.

7. Ball, *Slavery in the United States*, 80.

8. There were just over 30,000 enslaved people in Georgia in the 1790s; by 1810 there
were over 100,000 people held in bondage in the state. The population grew dramatically, to almost half a million enslaved by 1860, through both the domestic
slave trade and natural reproduction. That power was concentrated in the hands
of a minority of white Georgians; just over 30 percent of white Georgians held
slaves, and among them only 15 percent of slaveholders held fifteen or more people
in bondage. Cobb, *Georgia Odyssey*, 13.

9. William H. Heard, *From Slavery to the Bishopric in the A.M.E. Church: An Autobiography* (Philadelphia: A.M.E. Book Concern, 1928), 25.

10. While according to the law the enslaved might have been marked as "socially dead,"
to use Orlando Patterson's framework, in their own lived experience they contested
this kind of totalizing dislocation by making community, kin, family, and new
practices of faith and mourning. Vince Brown explains that "social connections

and communities of memory had to be created in struggle, and alienation had to be overcome by political action." As Vince Brown highlights, even Patterson himself "recognize[d]: 'Because [a slave's] kin relations were illegitimate, they were all the more cherished. Because he was considered degraded, he was all the more infused with the yearning for dignity. Because of his formal isolation and liminality, he was acutely sensitive to the realities of community.'" Brown, "Social Death and Political Life," 1248.

11. W. E. B. Du Bois was the originator of this language, writing in *Black Reconstruction* that the "theory of race was supplemented by a carefully planned and slowly evolved method, which drove such a wedge between the white and black workers that there probably are not today in the world two groups of workers with practically identical interests who hate and fear each other so deeply and persistently and who are kept so far apart that neither sees anything of common interest. It must be remembered that the white group of laborers, while they received a low wage, were compensated in part by a sort of *public and psychological wage.* They were given public deference and titles of courtesy because they were white. They were admitted freely with all classes of white people to public functions, public parks, and the best schools. The police were drawn from their ranks, and the courts, dependent on their votes, treated them with such leniency as to encourage lawlessness. Their vote selected public officials, and while this had small effect upon the economic situation, it had great effect upon their personal treatment and the deference shown them." (Emphasis mine.) W. E. B. Du Bois, *Black Reconstruction: Toward a History of the Part Which Black Folk Played in the Attempt to Reconstruct Democracy in America, 1860–1880* (1935; Piscataway, NJ: Transaction, 2002), 626. David Roediger's groundbreaking historical study *The Wages of Whiteness: Race and the Making of the American Working Class* (1991; New York: Verso, 2007) built on Du Bois's framework to explore the origins of white working-class racism.

12. Ball, *Slavery in the United States*, 146.

13. Rev. William H. Heard was born enslaved in Elbert County, Georgia, in 1850, the same rural county where this branch of my family was enslaved. He was owned by John A. Trenchard, who was listed as a teacher and was also listed as holding eight people in bondage. William H. Heard was probably the nine- or eleven-year-old "mulatto boy" listed in 1860. US Census Bureau, Eighth Census of the United States, 1860, "John A. Trenchard—Slave Schedules," M653. Census records indicate that after gaining freedom, Heard lived in the town of Moss in Elbert County, the same town where most of my family resided. US Census Bureau, Tenth Census of the United States, 1880, Microfilm T9, 29; Heard, *From Slavery to the Bishopric*, 21–22.

14. Ball, *Slavery in the United States*, 163; Heard, *From Slavery to the Bishopric*, 20–

21; "Plantation Life as Viewed by Ex-Slave Alice Green, Athens, Georgia," Federal Writers' Project: Slave Narrative Project, vol. 4 (Georgia, Part 2), 3.

15. Heard, *From Slavery to the Bishopric*, 26–27.

16. Jennifer Morgan's *Reckoning with Slavery* explores the tension between commodification and kinship in the lives of enslaved women. Reflecting on Angela Davis's exploration of the traumatic relationship of women who lived at the intersection of their childbearing and commodity, Morgan reminds us that "enslaved women were positioned to 'attain practical awareness' of both the slave owner's power and the slave owner's dependence on her productive and reproductive body." This enslaved woman in Elbert County was aware of the power she had to mutilate her own hand in order to devalue her body and preserve her relationship to her own children. She perceived her children and herself as much more than a commodity for trade. Jennifer Morgan, *Reckoning with Slavery: Gender, Kinship, and Capitalism in the Early Black Atlantic* (Durham, NC: Duke University Press, 2021), 7.

17. Acts of mutilation, suicide, and infanticide were common among the enslaved who were threatened with sale and separation. See Herbert G. Gutman, *The Black Family in Slavery and Freedom: 1750–1925* (New York: Vintage, 1976), 349; Heard, *From Slavery to the Bishopric*, 26–27; Kane and Keeton, *In Those Days*, 13; "An Opinion of Slavery by Isaiah Green, Ex-Slave," Federal Writers' Project: Slave Narrative Project, vol. 4 (Georgia, Part 2), 6.

18. To examine the question of the meanings and ramifications of the culture of the enslaved, we must begin with scholars of the Atlantic, the Middle Passage, and the colonial period. The work of historians of enslavement, particularly John Thornton, Vince Brown, Jennifer Morgan, Stephanie Smallwood, and Walter Rucker, reminds us of the constant contest for meaning that can be traced when we consider enslavement from the perspective of the enslaved themselves. Here I am hewing closely to the assessment of Vince Brown, who called for a shift from "seeing slavery as a condition to viewing slavery as a predicament, in which enslaved Africans and their descendants never ceased to pursue a politics of belonging, mourning, accounting and regeneration." Brown, "Social Death and Political Life," 1248.

19. Charles Ball chronicled one of these days of celebration and Black community on the plantation: "A man cannot well be miserable, when he sees every one about him immersed in pleasure; and though our fare of to-day, was not of a quality to yield me much gratification, yet such was the impulse given to my feelings, by the universal hilarity and contentment, which prevailed amongst my fellows that I forgot for the time, all the subjects of grief that were stored in my memory, all the acts of wrong that had been perpetrated against me, and entered with the most sincere and earnest sentiments, in the participation of the felicity of our community." A

rich testimony about the community the enslaved built, his narrative also contains accounts of the earliest worship of the enslaved and the blend of African faiths with Christianity. Although Ball, a Christian, was highly critical of African forms of worship, his narrative demonstrates that the practice continued well into the nineteenth century. Ball, *Slavery in the United States*, 203.

20. University of Virginia, President's Commission on Slavery and the University, https://slavery.virginia.edu/a-brief-history-of-free-people-of-color-and-uva/, accessed October 19, 2020. The work of the enslaved artisans who built UVA was not unusual; a majority of the architecture the South is known for was constructed by enslaved people. In describing his memories of the building of Wilmington, North Carolina's city hall, John H. Jackson wrote: "I remember all the bricklayers; they was all colored. The man that plastered the City Hall was named George Price, he plastered it inside. The men that plastered the City Hall outside and put those columns up in the front, their names was Robert Finey and William Finey, they both was colored . . . most all the fine work around Wilmington was done by slaves. They called them artisans. None of them could read, but give them any plan and they could follow it to the last line." John H. Jackson, Federal Writers' Project: Slave Narrative Project, vol. 11 (North Carolina, Part 2, Jackson–Yellerday), 1936, 1.

21. Joyce M. Davis, *Elbert County* (Charleston, SC: Arcadia, 2011), 35–37.

22. "Elbert County, Georgia: Largest Slaveholders from 1860 Slave Census Schedules and Surname Matches for African Americans on 1870 Census," transcribed by Tom Blake, February 2002, https://sites.rootsweb.com/~ajac/gaelbert.htm. John H. McIntosh, *The Official History of Elbert County, 1790–1935* (Washington, DC: Daughters of the American Revolution, Stephen Heard Chapter, 1940), 96–97. US Census Bureau, Eighth Census of the United States, 1860, "Population Schedule, Elbert, Georgia," 865FHL microfilm: 803120. Value calculated using Measuring Worth.com.

23. Cobb, *Georgia Odyssey*, 19.

24. In her history of Black women's lives during the Civil War, Thavolia Glymph chronicled the ties maintained by a community of men and women from the same plantation as they escaped to Union lines and then later settled in Vicksburg, Mississippi, as free people after the war. She notes that "black women carried the reconstituted networks of family, kin, and community into the postwar era." Thavolia Glymph, *The Women's Fight: The Civil War's Battles for Home, Freedom, and Nation* (Chapel Hill: University of North Carolina Press, 2022), 230–32.

25. The work of Marisa Fuentes reminds us of the violence embedded in the various archives of slavery, masking what we can ask and know, and hiding the violence behind charts, graphs, and schedules. For more on the problems of enslavement

and archives, see Brian Connolly and Marisa Fuentes, "From Archives of Slavery to Liberated Futures?," *History of the Present* 6, no. 2 (Fall 2016): 105–16.

26. According to the Pew Research Center, "'mulatto' was a category [in the US Census] from 1850 to 1890 and in 1910 and 1920. 'Octoroon' and 'quadroon' were categories in 1890. Definitions for these groups varied from census to census. In 1870, 'mulatto' was defined as including 'quadroons, octoroons and all persons having any perceptible trace of African blood.' The instructions to census takers said that 'important scientific results' depended on their including people in the right categories. In 1890, a mulatto was defined as someone with 'three-eighths to five-eighths black blood,' a quadroon had 'one-fourth black blood' and an octoroon had 'one-eighth or any trace of black blood'": Kim Parker, Juliana Menasce Horowitz, Rich Morin, and Mark Hugo Lopez, "Race and Multiracial Americans in the U.S. Census," Pew Research Center, June 11, 2015, https://www.pewsocialtrends.org/2015/06/11/chapter-1-race-and-multiracial-americans-in-the-u-s-census/.

27. The story about Rucker and the value of his slave is recounted in McIntosh, *Official History of Elbert County*, 96–97. As James C. Cobb says, "the mania for slaveholding resulted in as much as half of Georgia's total wealth being invested in slaves. At approximately $416 million, the estimated aggregate value of slave property in 1860 was nearly forty times that of the state's total investment in manufacturing." Cobb, *Georgia Odyssey*, 1.

28. W. E. B. Du Bois asserted in his magisterial text *Black Reconstruction* that the Union could not have won the Civil War without the resistance of the Black enslaved. His "general strike" thesis is the root of a stream of historiography that considers all the ways in which Black resistance—running toward Union troops, escapes, work slowdowns, thefts of Confederate supplies, etc.—made the success of the Union a possibility. See the fourth chapter of Du Bois, *Black Reconstruction*, "The General Strike," 49–75.

29. Ball, *Slavery in the United States*, 166–67, 187, 190. The quote and an extended description of the "internal economy" described by Ball are discussed in Steven Hahn, *A Nation Under Our Feet: Black Political Struggles in the Rural South from Slavery to the Great Migration* (Cambridge, MA: Belknap Press of Harvard University Press, 2003), 22–33.

30. Ball, *Slavery in the United States*, 164–65.

31. The story of the making of Black Christian theology through struggle and suffering has been well chronicled by Black theologians and religious studies scholars. For more on this intersection, see Albert J. Raboteau, "'The Blood of the Martyrs Is the Seed of Faith': Suffering in the Christianity of American Slaves," in *The Courage*

to Hope: From Black Suffering to Human Redemption, edited by Quinton Hosford Dixie and Cornel West (Boston: Beacon Press, 1999), 22–39; Frederick Douglass, "Slaveholding Religion and the Christianity of Christ," excerpted from *The Narrative of the Life of Frederick Douglass: A Slave,* in *African American Religious History: A Documentary Witness,* edited by Milton C. Sernett (Durham, NC: Duke University Press, 1999), 106.

32. Peter Randolph, "Plantation Churches: Visible and Invisible," excerpted from *Slave Cabin to Pulpit: The Autobiography of Reverend Peter Randolph: The Southern Question Illustrated and Sketches of Slave Life,* in Sernett, *African American Religious History,* 64.

33. Howard Thurman, *Deep River: Reflections on the Religious Insight of Certain of the Negro Spirituals* (New York: Harper & Brothers, 1955), 36.

34. The foundational text for examining the faith of the enslaved is Albert J. Raboteau, *Slave Religion: The Invisible Institution in the Antebellum South,* updated edition (New York: Oxford University Press, 2004).

35. Joseph Rucker and Clarinda Pendleton Lamar Papers, 1792–1936, Hargrett Manuscripts Division, University of Georgia Libraries.

36. Adam Hochschild, *Bury the Chains: Prophets and Rebels in the Fight to Free an Empire's Slaves* (New York: Houghton Mifflin Harcourt, 2004), 50; Harry J. Bennett, "The Problem of Slave Labor Supply at the Codrington Plantations," *Journal of Negro History* 36, no. 4 (1951): 412–16.

37. Charles Colcock Jones included a long review of earlier theologians' take on the question of Christian education and the responsibility of masters to minister to the enslaved that included Richard Baxter, *A Christian Directory* (London: Nevill Simmons, 1673). Charles Colcock Jones, *The Religious Instruction of the Negroes in the United States* (Savannah: Thomas Purse, 1842), 7.

38. Hochschild, *Bury the Chains,* 53.

39. Bennett, "The Problem of Slave Labor Supply"; Hochschild, *Bury the Chains,* 57.

40. Harry J. Bennett, "The S.P.G. and Barbadian Politics, 1710–1720," *Historical Magazine of the Protestant Episcopal Church* 20, no. 2 (1951): 190–206.

41. As arguments about slavery and reparations were reignited in the twenty-first century, the Anglican Church apologized in 2006 but provided for no reparations for the profits made from the plantation or the funds received from the Compensation Act. The retelling of this history in Adam Hochschild's *Bury the Chains* was said to have led to the apology. Stephen Bates, "Church Apologises for Benefiting from Slave Trade," *Guardian,* February 9, 2006, https://www.theguardian.com/uk/2006/feb/09/religion.world; Ben Fenton, "Church's Slavery Apology 'Is Not Enough,'" *Telegraph,* February 11, 2006, https://www.telegraph.co.uk/news

/worldnews/centralamericaandthecaribbean/barbados/1510213/Churchs-slavery
-apology-is-not-enough.html.

42. Herbert Wilcox, "Old Dan Tucker Was a Grand Old Man, and He Really Lived in Elbert County in the Good Old Days," *Georgia* magazine, February–March 1965.

43. Heard, *From Slavery to the Bishopric*, 31–32.

44. Jones, *Religious Instruction*.

45. For more on James Colcock Jones, see Erskine Clark, *A Dwelling Place: A Plantation Epic* (New Haven: Yale University Press, 2005).

46. Randolph, "Plantation Churches," 66.

47. "An Opinion of Slavery by Isaiah Green, Ex-Slave"; Douglass, "Slaveholding Religion," 106.

48. Sister Kelly, "Proud of That 'Ole Time' Religion," excerpted from *Unwritten History of Slavery: Autobiographical Accounts of Negro Ex-Slaves*, in Sernett, *African American Religious History*, 70; and Douglass, "Slaveholding Religion," 105; Raboteau, *Slave Religion*, 372; "Plantation Life as Viewed by Ex-Slave Alice Green," 2–3; Heard, *From Slavery to the Bishopric*, 31–32.

49. Ball, *Slavery in the United States*, 221–22.

50. Kane and Keeton, *In Those Days*; "Plantation Life—Rachel Adam, Athens, Georgia," Federal Writers' Project: Slave Narrative Project, vol. 4 (Georgia, Part 2), 5.

51. Stephanie M. H. Camp, *Closer to Freedom: Enslaved Women and Everyday Resistance in the Plantation South* (Chapel Hill: University of North Carolina Press, 2004), 7.

52. Randolph, "Plantation Churches," 67.

53. State of Georgia, Returns of Qualified Voters and Reconstruction Oath Books, 1867–69, Ancestry.com Operations, 2012.

54. "Rural freed people did not need tutors or outside agitators to nurture their desire for, or sense of entitlement to, the land. They neither had to be apprised of the advantages that proprietorship would hold nor reminded that their long-endured and uncompensated toil and suffering built both the South's great fortunes and the nation's prosperity." Hahn, *A Nation Under Our Feet*, 135.

55. Forty acres and a mule was a promise remembered in Elbert County for generations. See Kane and Keeton, *In Those Days*.

56. "Freedpeople needed to innovate new family economies to cope with conditions of starvation and want; they sought a balance between their ties to specific communities and plantation lands and their need for cash, or food and basic goods." Leslie A. Schwalm, "'Sweet Dreams of Freedom': Freedwomen's Reconstruction of Life and Labor in Lowcountry South Carolina," in *The Black Worker: A Reader*, edited by Eric Arnesen (Urbana: University of Illinois Press, 2007), 20.

57. "By 1866 the Bureau's definition of 'free labor' had been significantly transformed. Instead of carrying out a two-pronged labor policy, in which some blacks farmed independently, while others worked as hired laborers for white employers, the Bureau found itself with no alternative but to encourage virtually all freedmen to sign annual contracts to work on the plantations." Eric Foner, *Reconstruction: America's Unfinished Revolution, 1863–1877* (New York: Harper Perennial, 2014); State of Georgia, Office of the Governor, "Returns of Qualified Voters Under the Reconstruction Act, 1867," Georgia State Archives, Morrow, GA.

58. Cobb, *Georgia Odyssey*, 27; Foner, *Reconstruction*, 243, 278.

59. Foner, *Reconstruction*, 282.

60. Kane and Keeton, *In Those Days*, 19.

61. Heard, *From Slavery to the Bishopric*, 89.

62. Heard, *From Slavery to the Bishopric*, 89.

63. "Report of Outrages Committed by Whites Against Freedmen in Abbeville County So. CA. during the Month of November 1868," Records of the Assistant Commissioner for the State of South Carolina, Bureau of Refugees, Freedmen and Abandoned Lands, 1865–1870, National Archives microfilm publication M 869, roll 34; Kane and Keeton, *In Those Days*, 21.

64. Henry McNeal Turner, "Celebration January 13, 1866," quoted in Andre E. Johnson, *The Forgotten Prophet: Bishop Henry McNeal Turner and the African American Prophetic Tradition* (Lanham, MD: Lexington Books, 2012), 1

65. Rev. Henry McNeal Turner, "I Claim the Rights of a Man," 1868, uploaded to Black Past, January 28, 2007, https://www.blackpast.org/african-american -history/1868-reverend-henry-mcneal-turner-i-claim-rights-man/.

66. Lee W. Formwalt, "Camilla Massacre," *New Georgia Encyclopedia*, https://www .georgiaencyclopedia.org/articles/history-archaeology/camilla-massacre/, accessed June 29, 2022.

67. Cobb, *Georgia Odyssey*, 27.

68. Here I am invoking Thulani Davis's text *The Emancipation Circuit*, which points to the existence of a network of Black political organizations fueling the circulation of ideas that created a "geography of the ideas of freedom." Even in the wake of the formal defeat of Reconstruction, Davis argues that these efforts laid the groundwork for freedom work for the following generations. Thulani Davis, *The Emancipation Circuit: Black Activism Forging a Culture of Freedom* (Durham, NC: Duke University Press, 2022), 7.

69. Heard, *From Slavery to the Bishopric*, 90–91.

70. Glymph, *The Women's Fight*, 175.

71. Kane and Keeton, *In Those Days*, 19.

NOTES TO PAGES 65–66

CHAPTER TWO: SARAH AT HOME, WORKING ON HER OWN ACCOUNT

1. "I made my way to the back yard, jumping a mud hole in the walk, walking in the grass that mired down every step I took." Sadie B. Hornsby and Sarah Hill, "Bea, the Washwoman," Athens, GA, February 1, 1939; Federal Writers' Project, Folklore Project, Life Histories, 1936–39.

2. "In the back yard two negro girls were bending over old fashion wash tubs washing. There were four lines filled with clothes drying in the sun. Sarah was sitting on the porch talking to another Negro woman, I heard her say: 'It's too bad he had to get in jail.'" Hornsby and Hill, "Bea, the Washwoman."

3. "She called to one of her daughters who was washing. 'Ca'Line git that clean pot rag hanging on that chair, and come here and wipe mistessess shoes off for her.' I told her that was quite all right I didn't mind a little mud. 'Well, that's all right than, but come here and git the lady a chair.'" Hornsby and Hill, "Bea, the Washwoman."

4. There aren't many historical interviews with Black women who did laundry for a living, so the story of Sarah Hill contains valuable insights about her life and the collective nature of her work. But the interview is limited by the biases of the WPA interviewer, Sadie Hornsby. When she met Sarah Hill that cold morning, she brought with her little understanding of what informed the lives of Black working women like Hill and her daughters. Hornsby had been working as an accountant before the Depression, but like hundreds of others in her hometown she was unemployed. The opportunity to work for the Federal Writers' Project must have come along just in time for the widowed mother of two. The work interviewing ex-slaves and Black workers was a good opportunity for her to support her family in a time of crisis. However, it would be wrong to think that her vulnerabilities as a single mother in the midst of the Great Depression made her more empathetic to interviewees like Sarah Hill. To Hornsby and the majority of white southerners, the perceived barriers of race were so ineradicable that the human similarities and economic problems that could have bound white and Black people together, created solidarity, and led to cross-racial political organizing were imperceptible to her. The 1940 Federal Census listed thirty-nine-year-old Sadie B. Hornsby as a white female, born in North Carolina and residing in Athens, Georgia. Her marital status was "widowed" and she was head of household. Her occupation was listed as accountant, and she had been unemployed at one time but listed her status as an employed government worker. US Census Bureau, Sixteenth Census of the United States, 1940, T627.

5. "A Bundle of Rags," Collection of the Smithsonian National Museum of African American History and Culture.

6. Bookmark for Higgins Soap, Ephemera Collection, EP001.01.021.02.04.026, Historic New England Collection, Boston, MA, https://www.historicnewengland.org/explore/collections-access/gusn/243972.

7. Monday Higgins Soap, advertising card owned by the author. Saturday Higgins Soap, advertising card, Box 3, Folder 9, Series Soap, Warshaw Collection of Business Americana, 1838–1953, Archives Center, National Museum of American History, Washington, DC.

8. Heather Biola, "The Black Washerwoman in Southern Tradition," in *Black Women in United States History: Theory and Practice*, vol. 1, edited by Darlene Clark Hine et al. (Brooklyn, NY: Carlson, 1990), 72–73.

9. Historian Catherine Stewart says of the work of Hornsby and other FWP interviewers in Georgia: "Georgia writers were clearly in thrall to a long-standing tradition of literary minstrelsy that used broad misspellings to authenticate their representations of black speech as a racial, rather than regional, characteristic." Catherine A. Stewart, *Long Past Slavery: Representing Race in the Federal Writers' Project* (Chapel Hill: University of North Carolina Press, 2016), 208.

10. Although here Catherine Stewart is describing Federal Writers' Project interviews with former slaves, the same interests and principles undergirded the Folklore Project life histories as well: "Southern white women's representations of 'faithful slaves,' predicated on notions of white paternalism, black dependency, and racial inferiority, and rendered through depictions of black southern speech, folk customs, and quaint mannerisms and dress, converged with FWP[. . .]'s emphasis on capturing those same elements to lend authority and authenticity to the . . . narratives." Stewart, *Long Past Slavery*, 207.

11. "I has been sick in bed with the flues, this is the first day I has been up, and I is power'ful weak. But I couldn't stay in no longer 'cause I had to see that the children was wash them clothes clean." Hornsby and Hill, "Bea, the Washwoman." The 1930 US Census recorded Sarah living with her husband, Whitman, and four of her children. US Census Bureau, Fifteenth Census of the United States, 1930, Clarke, Georgia, Family History Library Microfilm: 2340081.

12. "Mistess, I use to git good money for washing. I have made about ten dollars heap of weeks way back yonder. I [?] had a heap of washings than, now – don't git near as much for them as I use to. And folks are lots harder to please." Hornsby and Hill, "Bea, the Washwoman."

13. "The lady sont me word one of the little boy's shirts was not in the laundry I had

sent home. I reckon sister lost it 'cause she was working for the lady and knowed the shirt was in the wash when the lady got 'em up. So sister had to take her money what the lady paid her for working and buy the little boy a new shirt." Hornsby and Hill, "Bea, the Washwoman."

14. "Lawdy Mistess, if I had knowed it was a white lady I would have let you come through the house so you wouldn't git your shoes muddy." Hornsby and Hill, "Bea, the Washwoman."

15. " 'Now, Mistess, what in the name of the Lord do you want to know that for?' I stated my mission, she laughed. 'Well, if you want a history of my life I can tell you what I knows. Yet and still, I am sho' you can find somebody else what had a better story than me to tell. 'Cause what I knows ain't no 'count you know cullud folks don't have money to do things like white folks does, leastwise us don't.'" Hornsby and Hill, "Bea, the Washwoman."

16. As the introduction to the first chapter of *Remembering Jim Crow* states: "Jim Crow was not merely about the physical separation of blacks and whites. Nor was segregation strictly about laws, despite historians' tendency to fix upon such legal landmarks as *Plessy v. Ferguson* (1896), *Brown v. Board of Education* (1954), and the Civil Rights Act of 1964. In order to maintain dominance, whites needed more than the statutes and signs that specified 'whites' and 'blacks' only; they had to assert and reiterate black inferiority with every word and gesture, in every aspect of both public and private life." *Remembering Jim Crow: African Americans Tell About Life in the Segregated South,* edited by William H. Chafe, Raymond Gavins, Robert Korstad, and the staff of the Behind the Veil Project (New York: The New Press, 2001), 1.

17. Hornsby and Hill, "Bea, the Washwoman."

18. As psychologist John Dollard's 1937 sociological study of Indianola, Mississippi, revealed, "The Negro must maintain a position of continuous affirmation of the white [people's] wishes." Racial deference was an imperative, enforced by the threat of violence. "When we see how severely Negroes may be punished for omitting these signs of deference, we realize that they are anything but petrified customs." John Dollard, *Caste and Class in a Southern Town,* 3rd ed. (New York: Doubleday Anchor, 1957), 179–80.

19. "I did want to have a supper for the church but its been too bad for that. I buy the food and cook it then I let the folks know about it and they come and buy their supper. Sometimes I has a fish-fry, than again I has a oyster supper. I gets 25¢ for every plate sold. After I pay for the food I buy, I turn the rest over to the church. If I don't git to washing I will have to have a supper to git some money for ourselves it looks like." Hornsby and Hill, "Bea, the Washwoman."

20. "If you know of anybody that wants carpenter work done, I wish you would pint

them out to me. And sent the old lady a washing. Times is might tight. I got to go down to Arnoldsville and get some of my good . . . friends to sign a paper for me so's I can git the old age pension. I reckon they is living, yet and still I ain't been back there in 40 years." Hornsby and Hill, "Bea, the Washwoman."

21. Zora Neale Hurston—also one of a handful of Black interviewers who participated in the Federal Writers' Project—taught us what these intrusive interviews were like for Black informants. She wrote: "You see we are a polite people and we do not say to our questioner, 'Get out of here!' We smile and tell him or her something that satisfies the white person because, knowing so little about us, he doesn't know what he is missing." While Hornsby's status as a white government employee gave her entrée into the Hill household and the women's racialized deference, it didn't give much of the true character of what they felt, or, as Hurston would have said of Hill, she remained "reluctant . . . to reveal that which the soul lives by." The niceties the Hill family extended were part of the dance, a way to fill the time and cover the discomfort. As Hurston said, "The Negro offers a feather-bed resistance. . . . It gets smothered under a lot of laughter and pleasantries." Zora Neale Hurston, *Mules and Men* (New York: Harper and Row, 1990), 2.

22. Hornsby and Hill, "Bea, the Washwoman."

23. Sadie Hornsby and millions of others had been raised in an environment where laws and daily customs dehumanized Black people, so much so that the obvious parallels between them were obscured. Both Hill and Hornsby were working women, mothers in the same small Southern town, managing households ravaged by the same national economic crisis. And yet Hornsby's account shows little connection, sympathy, or empathy toward the working-class woman who opened her home and shared hours of her time away from her own work in order to assist a stranger with her assignment. For more on the racial dynamics of the Federal Writers' Project interviews, see Stewart, *Long Past Slavery*.

24. "The majority of black wage-earning women, especially, mothers and wives, usually did not believe that their presence or their position in the labor force was an accurate reflection of who they were." Sharon Harley, "When Your Work Is Not Who You Are: The Development of Working-Class Consciousness Among Afro-American Women," in *We Specialize in the Wholly Impossible: A Reader in Black Women's History*, edited by Darlene Clark Hine, Wilma King, and Linda Reed (Brooklyn, NY: Carlson, 1995), 25.

25. Glymph, *The Women's Fight*, 181.

26. For more on the viewpoints of Washington and Burroughs, see Biola, "The Black Washerwoman in Southern Tradition," 66–68.

27. Langston Hughes, "A song to a Negro wash woman" (1927), in *The Collected*

Poems of Langston Hughes, edited by Arnold Rampersad (New York: Vintage Classics, 1994).

28. Carter G. Woodson, "The Negro Washerwoman, a Vanishing Figure," *Journal of Negro History* 15, no. 3 (July 1930): 269–77.

29. Deborah G. Plant, *Zora Neale Hurston: A Biography of the Spirit* (Westport, CT: Praeger, 2007), 37.

30. Laundry done by hand was women's work. By 1900 almost 87 percent of all laundry in the United States was done by women, but Black women dominated the field. "The negro race, representing only 11 per cent of the total number of women, compromised 64.5 percent of all the laundresses and found this occupation the third in importance in their choice of employments"; "If the race and nativity distribution of the laundresses is compared with that of the women engaged in each of the other 46 occupations employing at least 5,000 women, it will be found that in no occupation was a smaller percentage formed by native whites of native parentage and that in only two was a larger percentage formed by negroes"; "the negroes practically monopolize the laundry work of the Southern states, forming 94.4 per cent of the number of laundresses in the South Atlantic division and 90.2 per cent of those in the South Central division. This is a natural result of the fact that they constituted about one-third of the entire population of these sections, but even in the other divisions where they formed less than 2.5 per cent of the inhabitants, they comprised from 13.2 to 39.7 per cent of the total number of laundresses." US Census Bureau, "Statistics of Women at Work: Based on Unpublished Information Derived from the Schedules of the Twelfth Census, 1900" (Washington, DC: Government Printing Office, 1907), 57.

31. Cedric Robinson, "A Critique of W. E. B. Du Bois's *Black Reconstruction*," *Black Scholar* 8, no. 7 (1977): 44–50.

32. Oral historians Anne Valk and Leslie Brown noted that "African American women recalled learning [as children] to farm or to do household chores as contributions both to the family's daily survival and as wage work. They assisted ... mothers, older sisters, and other female relatives, transferring skills acquired through chores into paid jobs in private households and on farms. Domestic burdens fell especially heavy on oldest daughters ... doing food preparation, laundry, and cleaning." Anne Valk and Leslie Brown, *Living with Jim Crow: African American Women and Memories of the Segregated South* (New York: Palgrave Macmillan, 2010), 18; Hornsby and Hill, "Bea, the Washwoman."

33. "Slave women also benefited by acquiring skills [during slavery] that enhanced their status and labor value in the closing decades of the 19th century. While black men ultimately faced dwindling employment opportunities during these decades,

black women saw their employment potential enhanced well into the 20th century." Christopher E. Linsin, "Skilled Slave Labor in Florida, 1850–1860," *Florida Historian Quarterly* 75, no. 2 (Fall 1996): 191; Hornsby and Hill, "Bea, the Washwoman."

34. "Large numbers worked in their own homes in a relatively autonomous craft as laundresses, which had the advantage of accommodating family and community obligations." Tera W. Hunter, *To 'Joy My Freedom* (Cambridge, MA: Harvard University Press, 1997), 26.

35. Hornsby and Hill, "Bea, the Washwoman."

36. "The Negroes of Athens, Georgia," Phelps–Stokes Fellowship Studies, no. 1, Schomburg Center for Research in Black Culture, Jean Blackwell Hutson Research and Reference Division, New York Public Library, http://digitalcollections.nypl.org/items/510d47df-9d97-a3d9-e040-e00a18064a99.

37. US Census Bureau, "1890 Census: Volume 1. Report on Population of the United States" (Washington, DC: Government Printing Office, 1895).

38. Whitman Hill and Sarah Hyram: Georgia, Marriage Records from Select Counties, 1828–1978, Ancestry.com; Almanac for Athens Area, GA, June 5, 1907, NOAA Weather Online Data, iWeathernet.com, https://www.iweathernet.com/atlanta-weather-records; "Colored Churches," *Advertiser's Special Directory*, Athens, GA, 1928; Ebenezer Baptist Church West, church history, https://ebcw.org/site/index.php/about-ebcw/church-history, accessed October 15, 2019.

39. Although Sarah Hill did not tell Sadie Hornsby that her firstborn son had died, the boy is listed in her household shortly after his birth in 1910 and then not listed in 1920. While my research has not turned up a death certificate, a family tree on Ancestry.com that includes the Hill family lists him as dying at age ten. Hornsby and Hill, "Bea, the Washwoman"; US Census Bureau, Thirteenth Census of the United States, 1910, "Athens, Clarke, Georgia," T624_180, FHL microfilm: 1374193; It Takes a Village Family Tree, https://www.ancestry.com/family-tree/tree/49145258/family, accessed September 21, 2019; US Census Bureau, Fifteenth Census of the United States, 1930, Clarke, Georgia, FHL microfilm: 2340081.

40. Both the statistic and the quote are drawn from https://dlg.usg.edu/record/dlg_zlgb_gb1001, uploaded October 25, 2022.

41. US Census Bureau, "Statistics of Women at Work: Based on Unpublished Information Derived from the Schedules of the Twelfth Census, 1900," Table 21, "Distribution by Marital Condition, of Female Breadwinners 16 Years of Age and Over, Classified by Race, Nativity, and Occupation, for the United States" (Washington, DC: Government Printing Office, 1907), 174.

42. Blanche Davis interview, "Behind the Veil" Oral History Project, David M.

Rubenstein Rare Book and Manuscript Library, Duke University, https://library
.duke.edu/digitalcollections/behindtheveil_btvct02022/; Valk and Brown, *Living
with Jim Crow*, 84.

43. "Plantation Life as Viewed by Ex-Slave Carrie Hudson," interview by Sadie B.
Hornsby, Federal Writers' Project: Slave Narrative Project, vol. 4 (Georgia, Part 2,
Garey–Jones), 1936.

CHAPTER THREE: RESISTANT WASHERWOMEN

1. *Daily Clarion and Standard* (Jackson, MS), June 24, 1866.
2. "Washing," *Vicksburg Herald*, March, 18, 1870, 1.
3. A full account of Callie House's work as an advocate for reparations can be found
in Mary Frances Berry, *My Face Is Black Is True: Callie House and the Struggle for
Ex-Slave Reparations* (New York: Alfred A. Knopf, 2005).
4. Virgil E. Statom, "Callie House," *Tennessee Encyclopedia*, https://tennesseeencyclo
pedia.net/entries/callie-house/, accessed July 28, 2022.
5. Berry, *My Face Is Black Is True*, 37.
6. Berry, *My Face Is Black Is True*, 37.
7. Hunter, *To 'Joy My Freedom*, 56.
8. "Wants a Co-Operative Laundry in Salem," *Independent* (Elizabeth City, NC),
May 2, 1919, 1.
9. Thavolia Glymph, *Out of the House of Bondage: The Transformation of the Plantation Household* (New York: Cambridge University Press, 2008), 120.
10. Glymph, *Out of the House of Bondage*, 140.
11. Testimony of Mrs. George Ward, Report of the Committee of the Senate Upon
the Relations Between Labor and Capital and Testimony Taken by the Committee
(Washington, DC: Government Printing Office, 1885), 4:345–46.
12. Testimony of Mrs. George Ward, 4:318.
13. Glymph, *Out of the House of Bondage*, 151.
14. Glymph, *Out of the House of Bondage*, 151.
15. Anne Valk and Leslie Brown, *Living with Jim Crow: African American Women
and Memories of the Segregated South* (New York: Palgrave Macmillan, 2010), 8.
Tera Hunter describes the ways that Black women's desire to "distance themselves
physically from erstwhile masters ranked high in their priorities" after the Civil
War. Their desires set the tone for decades to come: "One important advantage of
laundry work was that whites were not employers of laundresses as much as they
were clients." Hunter, *To 'Joy My Freedom*, 58.
16. Elsa Barkley Brown notes that washerwomen "had the skills and they had long

before dreamed the dreams and laid the plans together. And when they moved from there to organize a bank and a department store, and then to dream of beginning a factory, it was with the assurance and the skills that came from already having been entrepreneurs." Elsa Barkley Brown, "Mothers of Mind," *Sage: A Scholarly Journal on Black Women* 6 (Summer 1989).

17. "Once free, black women who had labored in planters' homes . . . drew on a long tradition of struggle and negotiation. In some ways, the particularity of the struggle within the plantation household gave former household slaves an advantage over field hands in postwar negotiation and over their former mistresses as well. Women slaves employed in the household had already begun the process of rationalizing their labor, sometimes largely unknown to their mistresses." Glymph, *Out of the House of Bondage*, 150.

18. Testimony of Mrs. George Ward, 4:344.

19. Testimony of Mrs. George Ward, 4:327–28.

20. Testimony of Mrs. George Ward, 4:327–28.

21. "Washerwoman Will Be Good," *News* (Frederick, MD), February 3, 1910, 1.

22. "The white people stopped her in the street to ask where she got it; they thought maybe she was a laundress and stole it from some white woman." Mamie Garvin Fields with Karen Fields, *Lemon Swamp and Other Places: A Carolina Memoir* (New York: Free Press, 1983), 9.

23. "How White Caps Work," *Tennessean* (Nashville), August 30, 1888, 8.

24. Hunter, *To 'Joy My Freedom*, 31.

25. Hunter, *To 'Joy My Freedom*, 88–97.

26. Hunter, *To 'Joy My Freedom*, 75–76; Ken Lawrence, "Mississippi's First Labor Union," Libcom.org, https://libcom.org/history/mississippis-first-labour-union -ken-lawrence, submitted September 10, 2016, accessed July 17, 2020.

27. "Items of Interest," *Athens Weekly Post* (Athens, AL), July 7, 1866, 1.

28. "False Reports," *Charlotte Observer*, May 14, 1881, 3.

29. "That Steam Laundry Again," *Charlotte Observer*, August 9, 1881, 3.

30. "Wants a Co-Operative Laundry in Salem," 1.

31. "House Servants," *Daily Arkansas Gazette* (Little Rock), June 9, 1870, 4.

32. "A New Project," *Paducah Sun*, February 3, 1904, 1.

33. "Gossip of State Capital," *Charlotte Observer*, November 16, 1908, 9.

34. "It May Be a Washerwomen's Trust," *Charlotte Observer*, May 18, 1889, 2.

35. "Engineers at Morganton," *Charlotte Observer*, August 9, 1901, 8.

36. "Brewton," Alabama Communities of Excellence, https://www.alabama communitiesofexcellence.org/ace-town/brewton/, accessed August 1, 2020.

37. Editorial note, *Laborer's Banner*, June 2, 1900, 2.

NOTES TO PAGES 105–110

38. "Washwomen of the City Refuse to Work During Christmas," *Atlanta Constitution*, December 24, 1905, 3.

39. "The Strike in Raleigh," *Raleigh News*, May 21, 1873, 2; "State News," *Southern Home* (Charlotte, NC), May 26, 1873, 3.

40. Philip S. Foner and Ronald L. Lewis, eds., *The Black Worker: A Documentary History from Colonial Times to the Present*, 8 vols. (Philadelphia: Temple University Press, 1978–84), 3:251–52.

41. Foner and Lewis, *The Black Worker*, 3:251–52; Harley E. Jolley, "The Labor Movement in North Carolina, 1880–1922," *North Carolina Historical Review* 30, no. 3 (July 1953): 358–59.

42. "Notes and Comments," *Florence Herald* (Florence, AL), June 23, 1904, 3.

43. For more on the origins of the segregated streetcars, see Blair L. M. Kelley, *Right to Ride: Streetcar Boycotts and African American Citizenship in the Era of Plessy v. Ferguson* (Chapel Hill: University of North Carolina Press, 2010).

44. "Negroes Boycott White Man," *New York Times*, March 18, 1904, 1.

45. "Boycott on 'Jim Crow' Cars," *Baltimore Sun*, November 11, 1903, 9.

46. "Let us examine what is going on here, right under our noses in Richmond City in the Capitol Square. The 'jim crow' car, once confined alone to our steam cars and long distanced travel, is now upon every steam and electric line in the state.... The Negro in traveling pays first class price, for second and third class accommodation." Maggie Lena Walker, "An Address for Men Only," Maggie Lena Walker Papers, Maggie Lena Walker Historic Site, Richmond, VA.

47. Walker, "An Address for Men Only."

48. Maggie Lena Walker, speech at the Negro Young People's Christian and Educational Congress, Convention Hall, Washington, DC, August 5, 1906, Maggie Lena Walker Papers, Maggie Lena Walker Historic Site, Richmond, VA.

49. In a speech that seemed to hearken back to her childhood, Walker preached to her audience: "Whatever I have done in this life has been because I love women. Love to be surrounded by them. Love to hear them all talk at once. Love to listen to their trials and troubles." Maggie Lena Walker, "Nothing but Leaves," 1909, cited in Gertrude Woodruff Marlowe, *A Right Worthy Grand Mission: Maggie Lena Walker and the Quest for Black Economic Empowerment* (Washington, DC: Howard University Press, 2003), 56.

50. Walker, "Nothing but Leaves"; Elsa Barkley Brown, "Womanist Consciousness: Maggie Lena Walker and the Independent Order of Saint Luke," *Signs: Journal of Women in Culture and Society* 14, no. 3 (1989): 616–17.

51. See Elsa Barkley Brown, "Constructing a Life and a Community: A Partial Story of Maggie Lena Walker," *OAH Magazine of History* 7, no. 4 (Summer 1993): 28–31.

52. Walker, "Nothing but Leaves."

53. Elsa Barkley Brown theorized about the organizing that took place among these working women: "It was not merely the economic resources that the washerwomen wielded; I came to realize that those mornings spent scrubbing were also spent organizing." Barkley Brown, "Mothers of Mind."

54. US Census Bureau, *Twelfth Census of the United States, 1900, Special Reports*, vol. 13, *Occupations* (Washington, DC: Government Printing Office, 1904), 480–763; Elsa Barkley Brown and Gregg D. Kimball, "Mapping the Terrain of Black Richmond," *Journal of Urban History* 21 (March 1995): 296–346.

55. "Who Are the Lynchers?" and "Editorial Notes," *St. Luke Herald* (Richmond, VA), September 3, 1904.

56. Kelley, *Right to Ride*, 199–200.

57. "Washerwomen Threaten Strike," *News and Observer* (Raleigh, NC), September 20, 1917, 7.

58. "Negroes Organize," *Charlotte Observer*, September 12, 1906, 3.

CHAPTER FOUR: THE JEREMIAD OF THE PORTER

1. "Loot, Arson, Murder!," *Black Dispatch* (Oklahoma City), June 10, 1921, 1.

2. An excellent firsthand account of the Tulsa Massacre is Mary E. Jones Parrish, *Events of the Tulsa Disaster* (Tulsa, 1922), Beinecke Rare Book and Manuscript Library, Yale University.

3. "Loot, Arson, Murder!"

4. "I went to Tulsa, Oklahoma. My brother, William, lived in Tulsa at the time of the riot, and we couldn't get any information as to whether or not he survived the riot, and I finally went to Tulsa myself to try to locate him." C. L. Dellums interviewed by Joyce Henderson, December 15, 1970, January 13 and 26, April 14, and May 12, 1971, Earl Warren Oral History Project, Bancroft Library, University of California, Berkeley; "Loot, Arson, Murder!"

5. Three remaining survivors of the massacre testified in a congressional hearing on the centennial of the 1921 Tulsa Race Massacre on May 19, 2021, addressing not only the violent attack they witnessed but also the intergenerational economic loss they experienced due to the attack. See C-SPAN, https://www.c-span.org/video/?511795-1/hearing-centennial-1921-tulsa-race-massacre.

6. "In an act of self-invention, young Dellums gave himself the middle name Laurence, likely chosen for Paul Laurence Dunbar, a popular African American poet": Robert L. Allen, *Brotherhood of Sleeping Car Porters: C. L. Dellums and the Fight for Fair Treatment and Civil Rights* (New York: Routledge, 2016); "Young Del-

lums began to sign his name 'C. Laurence Dellums.' Soon after he began his public career, he became known simply by the initials of his given names. Few of C.L.'s associates know what his full name is": Introduction, C. L. Dellums interviewed by Joyce Henderson.

7. W. H. Dellums, Standard Certificate of Death, September 24, 1922, Texas Department of State Health Services, Death Certificates, 1903–1982, Ancestry.com; Allen, *Brotherhood of Sleeping Car Porters*, 23.

8. "I bought a ticket to San Francisco because I had chosen San Francisco as the most ideal place for a Negro to live in 1923; and secondly, I wanted to be a lawyer and I learned that the University of California had the best law school. So everything I wanted was right there.... In 1923 nobody knew anything about Oakland. Everything you could study or read was [about] San Francisco, and otherwise when you said California, people thought that you meant Los Angeles because that is all you heard about. When you said you were going to San Francisco, people would look at you, 'What do you mean San Francisco?' Everybody went to Los Angeles, another reason why I wouldn't go": C. L. Dellums interviewed by Joyce Henderson.

9. "The porter on the train saw that I was excited or nervous, and would sit and talk with me.... He found out I was going to San Francisco and he asked, 'Where are you going to stay?' I said I was going to ask the taxi driver to take me to a rooming house. So, he explained that there was no such thing out here as a rooming house. They have hotels": C. L. Dellums interviewed by Joyce Henderson.

10. "Finally, after he got the information, he said, 'Let me give you some advice, young man. Get off in Oakland. There are not enough Negroes in San Francisco for you to find in order to make some connections over there. Worst of all,' he said, 'you will never find a job.' ... Then he said, 'I know a very fine lady and I'm almost positive she's got a spare room that she'll rent to you. You'll get a room for about $3 a week, and it is here in West Oakland'": C. L. Dellums interviewed by Joyce Henderson; Google maps, Eleventh Street and Wood Street, Oakland, CA, accessed April 29, 2021; City of Oakland Planning Department, "Rehab Right: How to Rehabilitate Your Oakland House Without Sacrificing Architectural Assets," June 1978, http://www2.oaklandnet.com/oakca1/groups/ceda/documents/agenda/oak039424.pdf.

11. C. L. Dellums interviewed by Joyce Henderson.

12. Emmett J. Scott, "Letters of Negro Migrants of 1916–1918," *Journal of Negro History* 4, no. 3 (July 1919): 294, 295, 298.

13. In his memoir, Pullman porter Johnnie F. Kirvin imagined that one day he would retort with "Don't call me George! And I'm not your boy!" but he knew that it was dangerous to respond that way. He recalled that when passengers "called you boy or George, it was the ultimate in disrespect. He was saying you were George Pull-

man's boy . . . and not your own man." Johnnie F. Kirvin, *Hey Boy! Hey George: The Pullman Porter, A Memoir* (Carla S. Kirvin, 2009), 1.

14. Oscar Singleton described the insult of being called a boy. "Oh, yes. They can call me boy anytime. . . . 'Come here, boy.' . . . You hear boy from St. Louis to Tampa. You hear boy from Cincinnati to Jackson. And when I get on the other side of Cincinnati coming this way, they calls me porter. [Other people] couldn't call you porter. . . . 'Boy, I want so and so.' And then . . . they say it two or three times, say that to me, I make out like I don't hear. Keep on walking into the next car and sit down for a while. Come back and put the bell up. And I sit in the next car." Oscar Singleton interviewed by Leslie Kelen, July 14, 1983, Interviews with African Americans in Utah Collection, University of Utah.

15. Oscar Singleton's experience was not unusual. As one anonymous porter wrote, "To handle the traveling public is one of the hardest jobs that can be found today." "The Passing of Uncle Toms," *Cayton's Weekly* (Seattle), June 14, 1919, 4. Indeed, after union demands, in 1926 the Pullman Company changed policy so that a man could not be fired for not responding to a passenger who called him "boy" or "George." Melinda Chateauvert, *Marching Together: Women of the Brotherhood of Sleeping Car Porters* (Urbana: University of Illinois Press, 1998), 28–29.

16. Oscar Singleton remarked that there were limits to his tolerance with passengers. "Well, you know, it's a way to handle people. But sometime . . . you say so what. But if it overflow, you can't take any more of that and I have been there." Oscar Singleton interviewed by Leslie Kelen.

17. Indeed, the challenge of not responding in kind to rude passengers was a common one. The *California Eagle*, which closely followed news of the Pullman porters in that state, reported that "Joe Holmes, one of the most talked of Pullman porters in the Los Angeles District, was discharged from the Pullman Company last week over a disagreement with a passenger, and a long-standing grudge held against him by a well-known Pullman conductor." "Joe Holmes Let Out of Service," *California Eagle*, January 2, 1931, 11; "The Passing of Uncle Toms."

18. C. L. Dellums interviewed by Joyce Henderson.

19. C. F. Anderson, *Freemen Yet Slaves Under "Abe" Lincoln's Son or Service and Wages of Pullman Porters* (Chicago: Enterprise Printing House, 1904), 3.

20. Anderson, *Freemen Yet Slaves*, 37.

21. Anderson, *Freemen Yet Slaves*, 26.

22. Anderson, *Freemen Yet Slaves*, 4, 42–43.

23. For more on the impact of the transcontinental railroad on Indigenous lands, see Manu Karuka, *Empire's Tracks: Indigenous Nations, Chinese Workers, and the Transcontinental Railroad* (Oakland: University of California Press, 2019).

24. Stanley Buder, *Pullman: An Experiment in Industrial Order and Community Planning, 1880–1930* (New York: Oxford University Press, 1967), xi.

25. Buder, *Pullman*, xi.

26. Beth Tompkins Bates, *Pullman Porters and the Rise of Protest Politics in Black America, 1925–1945* (Chapel Hill: University of North Carolina Press, 2001), 5; Larry Tye, *Rising from the Rails: Pullman Porters and the Making of the Black Middle Class* (New York: Picador, 2004), 17.

27. "The work culture for porters, nurtured by the Pullman Company, was inherited from slavery": Tompkins Bates, *Pullman Porters*, 5.

28. Buder, *Pullman*, 17; Tompkins Bates, *Pullman Porters*, 5; Tye, *Rising from the Rails*, 2–3.

29. Tompkins Bates, *Pullman Porters*, 5.

30. Tompkins Bates, *Pullman Porters*, 5; Tye, *Rising from the Rails*, 18.

31. Chateauvert, *Marching Together*, 21–22.

32. Buder, *Pullman*, 17.

33. Chateauvert, *Marching Together*, 23.

34. The Passing of Uncle Toms."

35. Chateauvert, *Marching Together*, 22–23, 30.

36. Blair L. M. Kelley, *Right to Ride: Streetcar Boycotts and African American Citizenship in the Era of* Plessy v. Ferguson (Chapel Hill: University of North Carolina Press, 2010), 42.

37. Chateauvert, *Marching Together*, 31.

38. "Will the Porters Win?," *California Eagle*, August 26, 1927, 3.

39. Eric Arnesen, *Brotherhoods of Color: Black Railroad Workers and the Struggle for Equality* (Cambridge, MA: Harvard University Press, 2001), 56.

40. "Pullman Employees Win Recognition," *New York Age*, September 14, 1918, 1.

41. "Will the Porters Win?"

42. Philip S. Foner, *Organized Labor and the Black Worker, 1619–1981* (Chicago: Haymarket, 2017), 177.

43. Tye, *Rising from the Rails*, 106; As Beth Tompkins Bates details, the Association "was known to have a deposit of over $10,000 in Jesse Binga's bank." Tompkins Bates, *Pullman Porters*, 23, 53.

44. Program of the quinquennial celebration of the Brotherhood of Sleeping Car Porters, Dellums (Cottrell Laurence) Papers, MS 014, B02, F16, 001, Oakland Public Library; Foner, *Organized Labor and the Black Worker*, 178; Chateauvert, *Marching Together*, 27.

45. The Passing of Uncle Toms."

46. Foner, *Organized Labor and the Black Worker*, 178; "John Gilmer Speed," Find

NOTES TO PAGES 141–150

a Grave, https://www.findagrave.com/memorial/9294629/john-gilmer-speed, accessed February 14, 2021; John Gilmer Speed, "Tips and Commissions," *Lippincott's Magazine* 69 (January–June 1902): 748. For more on the practice of tipping and labor exploitation, see Saru Jayaraman, *Forked: A New Standard of American Dining* (New York: Oxford University Press, 2016), and Michelle Alexander, "Abolish the Racist, Sexist Subminimum Wage," *New York Times*, February 9, 2021, A2.

47. As Eric Arnesen noted, "low salaries . . . required blacks to work extremely hard for supplementary tips, often forcing them to assume a persona that was at once cautious, cheerful, even obsequious before their white patrons. To a considerable extent, the financially successful porter or waiter had to be both a keen student of human behavior (assessing his customer accurately) and an actor (playing the required part properly)." Arnesen, *Brotherhoods of Color*, 18.

48. "Will the Porters Win?"

49. Jervis Anderson, *A. Philip Randolph: A Biographical Portrait* (New York: Harcourt Brace Jovanovich, 1972), 32–33, 35–38; Andrew E. Kersten and David Lucander, *For Jobs and Freedom: Selected Speeches and Writings of A. Philip Randolph* (Amherst: University of Massachusetts Press, 2014), 3.

50. Kersten and Lucander, *For Jobs and Freedom*, 6.

51. Kersten and Lucander, *For Jobs and Freedom*, 9–10.

52. Kersten and Lucander, *For Jobs and Freedom*, 134.

53. A. Philip Randolph, "The Case of the Pullman Porters," *American Federationist*, November 1926, 1334–39, reprinted in Kersten and Lucander, *For Jobs and Freedom*, 43–47.

54. Foner, *Organized Labor and the Black Worker*, 180.

55. Tompkins Bates, *Pullman Porters*, 71–73.

56. Foner, *Organized Labor and the Black Worker*, 179.

57. "The Pullman Porter and the Brotherhood," *New York Age*, January 28, 1928, 4; Chateauvert, *Marching Together*, 43. For more on Mary Church Terrell's activism, see Martha S. Jones, *Vanguard: How Black Women Broke Barriers, Won the Vote, and Insisted on Equality for All* (New York: Basic Books, 2020), 153–74, and Alison M. Parker, *Unceasing Militant: The Life of Mary Church Terrell* (Chapel Hill: University of North Carolina Press, 2020).

58. Tompkins Bates, *Pullman Porters*, 52.

59. "The Pullman Porter and the Brotherhood."

60. C. L. Dellums interviewed by Joyce Henderson.

61. "Well, I didn't want the men to panic. I knew that my dismissal was just a beginning. The Pullman Company was going to use it to try to frighten the men and

break up the organization. So we started rounding up the men for a meeting. We had a pretty good grapevine; we could get the message out pretty quick. So we rounded up the men every day for the next three or four days in our little office that we had down there on Wood Street, and had meetings at which I talked to the men. I told them not to panic, stay together, that these things were to be expected": C. L. Dellums interviewed by Joyce Henderson.

62. C. L. Dellums interviewed by Joyce Henderson.

63. C. L. Dellums interviewed by Joyce Henderson.

64. "The tactics which the officials of the Pullman company used in the attempt to defeat this movement were ruthless and cool, faithless and immoral . . . men were intimidated, penalized, and fired, for daring to belong to the union. Black newspapers were purchased, and are still being purchased and deliberate lies were being published in these newspapers, designed to discourage the porters . . . journals carried false reports . . . calculated to have the same effect. Stool pigeons were active in framing and spying upon the union men and even now when the union is more than two years old, and has more than 75% of the Porters as its members, the membership rolls still has to be kept a secret. It is still dangerous for any Porter to be known as a member of the Brotherhood for it is almost certain that if he is known he will either be fired or discriminated against in some way": "Will the Porters Win?"

65. Tompkins Bates, *Pullman Porters*, 74–75; A. Philip Randolph, "To the *Chicago 'Surrender,'" Messenger* (October 1927): 304, 313–14.

66. Foner, *Organized Labor and the Black Worker*, 181.

67. Foner, *Organized Labor and the Black Worker*, 183.

68. Foner, *Organized Labor and the Black Worker*, 183–84.

69. Foner, *Organized Labor and the Black Worker*, 185, 198, 211.

70. Foner, *Organized Labor and the Black Worker*, 200–202.

71. Foner, *Organized Labor and the Black Worker*, 202.

72. "Will the Porters Win?"

73. Tompkins Bates, *Pullman Porters*, 152.

74. Foner, *Organized Labor and the Black Worker*, 240–41; Tompkins Bates, *Pullman Porters*, 150–62. For a broad history of the long March on Washington movement, see William P. Jones, *The March on Washington: Jobs, Freedom, and the Forgotten History of Civil Rights* (New York: W. W. Norton, 2013).

75. A. Philip Randolph interviewed by Thomas H. Baker, October 29, 1969, Lyndon Baines Johnson Oral History Collection, Lyndon Baines Johnson Presidential Library, Austin, TX.

76. Thomas J. Sugrue, *Sweet Land of Liberty: The Forgotten Struggle for Civil Rights in the North* (New York: Random House, 2008), 77.

CHAPTER FIVE: MINNIE AND BRUCE

1. James Weldon Johnson describes a cakewalk: "A half-dozen guests . . . took seats on the stage to act as judges, and twelve or fourteen couples began to walk for a 'sure enough' highly decorated cake. . . . The couples did not walk around in a circle, but in a square, with the men on the inside. The fine points to be considered were the bearing of the men, the precision with which they turned the corners, the grace of the women, and the ease with which they swung around the pivots. The men walked with stately and soldierly step, and the women with considerable grace. The judges arrived at their decision by a process of elimination. . . . This was the cake-walk in its original form." James Weldon Johnson, *The Autobiography of an Ex-Colored Man* (1916; Digireads.com, 2016).

2. "So in May one night, my father and I, we were going to church, and I was playing for a cake walk . . . so I told my uncle to tell my father that I had gone back home because I had a headache." Minnie (Savage) Whitney's vivid account of her migration was captured in two wonderful interviews by Charles Hardy III and became part of the oral history collection titled "Goin' North: Tales of the Great Migration," Louie B. Nunn Center for Oral History, University of Kentucky Libraries. This is from the March 6, 1984, interview.

3. When asked about her fondest memories of her rural home in Virginia, Minnie Savage Whitney replied, "When Sunday come . . . we knowed we was going to church and was going to be something different, we knowed we was going to eat something different that we didn't eat the whole week. And it was just like, and then people would get together and they'd have a little picnic and we'd do things like that. That was my fondest thing that I enjoyed when I was growing up." Oral historian Elizabeth Clark-Lewis also found that among the women she interviewed for her foundational study of the migration to Washington, DC, the majority of young women saw their Southern "home church" as "the only work-free haven they ever knew." Minnie (Savage) Whitney interviewed by Charles Hardy III; Elizabeth Clark-Lewis, *Living In, Living Out: African American Domestics and the Great Migration* (New York: Kodansha International, 1996), 36.

4. Although her father didn't want her to leave, Minnie still used her family networks to run north. "And my cousin, he helped get one of the fellas that had a fast horse to take me to the station." Minnie (Savage) Whitney interviewed by Charles Hardy III.

5. Almost seventy years later, Minnie was still emotional about having to sneak away. "Tell you the truth? I ran away. My parents never let me . . . you know like, it was very hard for me to get away . . . I got tired." Minnie (Savage) Whitney interviewed by Charles Hardy III.

6. Minnie's story of escape was unusual in some ways. Elizabeth Clark-Lewis found that the majority of young women who migrated moved with the consent of their families, their journeys carefully planned and undertaken to support families back home. In other ways Minnie's move was indicative of larger trends. Darlene Clark Hine's scholarship on women's migration shows that Minnie's story fits the larger pattern: "Single black women . . . traveled the entire distance in one trip [rather than stopping to work]. They usually had a specific relative . . . waiting for them at their destination, someone who may have advanced them the fare and who assisted with temporary lodging and advice on securing a job." Clark-Lewis, *Living In, Living Out*; Darlene Clark Hine, *Hine Sight: Black Women and the Re-construction of American History* (Bloomington: Indiana University Press, 1994), 91.

7. US Census Bureau, Fourteenth Census of the United States, 1920, "Pungoteague, Accomack, Virginia," M00152640.

8. "Onancock Wharf," AfroVirginia, http://places.afrovirginia.org/items/show/321, accessed February 19, 2021.

9. "New York, Philadelphia and Norfolk Railroad (NYP&N)," Norfolk, Virginia History, http://www.norfolkhistory.com/ngnypnrrhist.htm, accessed February 1, 2019; William G. Thomas III, Brooks Miles Barnes, and Tom Szuba, "The Countryside Transformed: The Eastern Shore of Virginia, the Pennsylvania Railroad, and the Creation of a Modern Landscape," *Southern Spaces*, July 31, 2007, https://southernspaces.org/2007/countryside-transformed-eastern-shore-virginia -pennsylvania-railroad-and-creation-modern-landscape/.

10. "Last Will and Testament of William Burton of Accomack County Made January 5, 1695, Probated March 17, 1695," Ghotes of Virginia, February 9, 2004, http:// www.esva.net/ghotes/wills/wmburtonwill.htm; US Census Bureau, Eighth Census of the United States, 1860, "St. Georges Parish, Accomack, Virginia," Family History Library Film 805330; "Big Dividends for Farmers: How Agriculturists of the Eastern Shore Combined for Self-Protection and How Their Combination Works," *Baltimore Sun*, December 7, 1902, 10; Ayres B. Drummond, "William A. Burton of Virginia," *Peninsula Enterprise*, March 31, 1939, reprinted in "The Countryside Transformed: The Railroad and the Eastern Shore of Virginia, 1870– 1935, Digital Archive," http://eshore.iath.virginia.edu/node/1893, accessed February 22, 2021.

11. Thomas et al., "The Countryside Transformed."

12. Leroy Murphy interviewed by the author, April 5, 2021, Durham, NC.

13. *Peninsula Enterprise*, January 6, 1906, 2.

14. "Resolutions of Colored People," *Peninsula Enterprise*, July 14, 1906, 3.

15. "Negroes' Oath of Idleness," *New York Times*, January 23, 1907, 1.

16. *Peninsula Enterprise*, September 8, 1906, 2.

17. US Census Bureau, Tenth Census of the United States, 1880, "Accomack, Virginia," Roll 1351; US Census Bureau, Ninth Census of the United States, 1870, "Eastville, Northampton, Virginia," Roll: M593_1668, Family History Library Film: 553167.

18. "Those Onancock Convictions," *Richmond Planet*, September 21, 1907, 4.

19. "The Colored Fair at Tasley, Virginia," *Richmond Planet*, August 3, 1901, 8. Also, ". . . must have been between three and four thousand, all negroes": Thomas Nottingham to Chas. J. Anderson, August 15, 1907, *Report of the Adjutant General of the Commonwealth of Virginia for the Year Ending 20th October, 1907* (Richmond, VA: Davis Bottom, Superintendent Public Printing, 1907), 93.

20. US Census Bureau, Ninth Census of the United States, 1870, "Eastville, Northampton, Virginia," Roll: M593_1668; Page: 667A, Family History Library Film: 553167; US Census Bureau, Tenth Census of the United States, 1880, "Accomack, Virginia," Roll: 1351; US Census Bureau, Twelfth Census of the United States, 1900, "Lee, Accomack, Virginia," FHL microfilm: 1241697; US Census Bureau, Thirteenth Census of the United States, 1910, "Baltimore Ward 14, Baltimore (Independent City), Maryland," Roll: T624_557; FHL microfilm: 1374570.

21. "The Mob's Work," *Memphis Appeal–Avalanche*, March 10, 1892, 5.

22. At a mass meeting, the all-white town council demanded that the governor supply them with weapons to fight Black residents and asked for "an injunction to prevent the colored people from holding their agricultural fair at Tasley, Va. on the ground that Uzzle and Burton are office-holders in the fair and both outlaws." "50 Colored Families Ordered to Leave," *Richmond Planet*, August 17, 1907, 1.

23. US Census Bureau, Twelfth Census of the United States, 1900, T623.

24. "50 Colored Families Ordered to Leave"; "Race War Is Over," *Baltimore Sun*, August 16, 1907, 11. A commander of the state militia reported that "every night there is firing by the whites upon the colored residents . . . and to-day three colored women appealed . . . for their protection, claiming that they have been molested and had to leave their houses every night": Thomas Nottingham to Chas. J. Anderson, August 15, 1907, *Report*, 89.

25. "Use the Torch in Race War," *News* (Frederick, MD), August 13, 1907, 3; "50 Colored Families Ordered to Leave"; "Race War Is Over"; Brooks Miles Barnes, "The Onancock Race Riot of 1907," *Virginia Magazine of History and Biography* 92, no. 3 (July 1984): 343. Barnes's account of the riot has a sympathetic bent toward local whites who led the charge against Black resistance. For a more critical take, see the *Richmond Planet*'s account of the case.

26. "Troops Now Patrolling Streets of Onancock; Town Council Orders Negroes to Leave; Governor's Plea," *Times–Dispatch* (Richmond, VA), August 13, 1907, 1.

27. An account of the governor's efforts to end the riot can be found in the *Report of the Adjutant General of the Commonwealth of Virginia for the Year Ending 20th October, 1907.*

28. "Those Onancock Convictions."

29. US Census Bureau, Thirteenth Census of the United States, 1910, Baltimore Ward 14, Baltimore (Independent City), Maryland, Roll: T624_557; FHL microfilm: 1374570. Conquest died in Philadelphia at a young age after suffering from Addison's disease; see "Sylvanus Conquest," Pennsylvania (State) Death Certificates, 1906–1967, Pennsylvania Historic and Museum Commission, Harrisburg.

30. "Editor Mitchell Travels," *Richmond Planet*, March 27, 1915, 6.

31. "Race Riot Negro Sues for $100,000," *Richmond Planet*, September 17, 1910, 8.

32. "Courts," *The Crisis* 5, no. 5 (March 1913): 222; "Industry," *The Crisis* 21, no. 3 (January 1921): 131.

33. "I worked in the farm with my father.... If when he got up in the morning at 6:00 and started in the field at 6:00, I was right with him ... we work until it was so dark that we could, just could see out each one of us in the field ... I started doing that when I was about seven years old.... So when I became ten my father hired me like a boy to work for him": Minnie (Savage) Whitney interviewed by Charles Hardy III.

34. 1910 US Census, Lee, Accomack, Virginia; Roll T624_1619, FHL microfilm 1375632; "Onancock and Accomack County," *Accomack News*, October 30, 1909.

35. Minnie (Savage) Whitney interviewed by Charles Hardy III. For a rich description of the historic land, crops, and foodways of the Eastern Shore, see Bernard L. Herman, *A South You Never Ate: Savoring Flavors and Stories from the Eastern Shore of Virginia* (Chapel Hill: University of North Carolina Press, 2019).

36. "I didn't have too much time in school. I had to go to school in the first of November ... then they had for the holiday Thanksgiving. Then ... that was always a week Christmas vacation. I'd start back ... in January and the last day of January, if it was a warm day, my father would take me out of school and I'd have to break the ground for planting potatoes": Minnie (Savage) Whitney interviewed by Charles Hardy III. The first high school for Black students in Accomack County, Mary Nottingham Smith High School, was not constructed until 1932. "Mary Nottingham Smith High School," Afro Virginia, http://places.afrovirginia.org/items/show/269, accessed February 22, 2021.

37. "And I couldn't stand this, you go in the store, and you'd be standing up there, and if some white person come this way, you had to stand and wait until they get waited on": Minnie (Savage) Whitney interviewed by Charles Hardy III.

38. Minnie (Savage) Whitney interviewed by Charles Hardy III.

39. Leroy Murphy interviewed by the author.
40. "You see, my father, his mother and father both were slaves. And my mother's father and mother both were slaves": Minnie (Savage) Whitney interviewed by Charles Hardy III.
41. Minnie (Savage) Whitney interviewed by Charles Hardy III.
42. "Well I say, if they come there, they wouldn't have found me anyway because when the train pull into Parksley, I went into the ladies' room and stayed there until the train pulled off": Minnie (Savage) Whitney interviewed by Charles Hardy III.

CHAPTER SIX: THE MAIDS OF THE MIGRATION

1. Emmett J. Scott, "More Letters of Negro Migrants of 1916–1918," *Journal of Negro History* 4, no. 4 (October 1919): 461.
2. "Although World War II has been known as the era in which women gained access to higher-paying factory work, most of the faces of the much-mythologized Rosie the Riveters were white." Lisa Krissoff Boehm, *Making a Way out of No Way: African American Women and the Second Great Migration* (Jackson: University Press of Mississippi, 2010), 144.
3. For more on Black women domestic laborers, see Tera W. Hunter, "'The "Brotherly Love" for Which This City Is Proverbial Should Extend to All': The Everyday Lives of Working-Class Women in Philadelphia and Atlanta in the 1890s," in *W. E. B. Du Bois, Race, and the City: The Philadelphia Negro and Its Legacy*, edited by Michael B. Katz and Thomas Sugrue (Philadelphia: University of Pennsylvania Press, 1998), 127; Krissoff Boehm, *Making a Way out of No Way*, 144.
4. Another Black woman who migrated recalled: "You was put down on that floor quick, too. They didn't ever offer you no mop. Why? You wasn't like a person, to get respect or nothing." Darethia Handy quoted in Clark-Lewis, *Living In, Living Out*; Clark Hine, *Hine Sight*, 161.
5. "After a while, my father and mother seen that I wasn't coming back. I started sending them money. All you do is send them money, then you can buy them off! So I started sending them little money, like couple dollars every week. I was making eight and I'd give them two": Minnie (Savage) Whitney interviewed by Charles Hardy III.
6. Ella Lee interviewed by Diane Turner, June 15, 1984, in "Goin' North: Tales of the Great Migration" oral history collection, Louie B. Nunn Center for Oral History, University of Kentucky Libraries.
7. Bonnie Thornton Dill, *Across the Boundaries of Race and Class: An Exploration of Work and Family Among Black Female Domestic Servants* (New York: Garland, 1994), 97.

8. Thornton Dill, *Across the Boundaries of Race and Class*, 98; "Working-class American women generally considered domestic service to be an occupation of last resort. In factory work, even poorly paid women enjoyed defined hours and tasks. Domestic service, in contrast, required isolation, endless chores, and constant employer surveillance." Vanessa H. May, *Unprotected Labor: Household Workers, Politics, and Middle-Class Reform in New York, 1870–1940* (Chapel Hill: University of North Carolina Press, 2011), 20.

9. "Household workers worked longer hours with fewer predictable tasks." May, *Unprotected Labor*, 39.

10. Jean Collier Brown, "The Negro Woman Worker," *Bulletin of the Women's Bureau*, no. 165, Department of Labor (Washington, DC: Government Printing Office, 1938), 3.

11. Amey Watson, "Household Employment in Philadelphia," *Bulletin of the Women's Bureau*, no. 93, Department of Labor (Washington, DC: Government Printing Office, 1932), 7.

12. Thornton Dill, *Across the Boundaries of Race and Class*, 57.

13. Watson, "Household Employment in Philadelphia," 8, 33.

14. "Unidentified Maid Dies on New Job," *Philadelphia Tribune*, December 9, 1945, 3.

15. Thornton Dill, *Across the Boundaries of Race and Class*, 83.

16. Kellie Carter Jackson, "'She Was a Member of the Family': Ethel Phillips, Domestic Labor, and Employers' Perceptions," *Women's Studies Quarterly* 45, no. 3–4 (Fall/Winter 2017): 164–66.

17. Thornton Dill, *Across the Boundaries of Race and Class*, 67.

18. Collier Brown, "The Negro Woman Worker," 4.

19. Thornton Dill, *Across the Boundaries of Race and Class*, 56, 71.

20. Collier Brown, "The Negro Woman Worker," 13.

21. Thornton Dill, *Across the Boundaries of Race and Class*, 100; "Progress of New Domestic Worker's Union Reviewed," *Pittsburgh Courier*, June 22, 1935, 12.

22. Ella Baker and Marvel Cooke, "The Slave Market," *The Crisis* 42, no. 3 (November 1935).

23. Thornton Dill, *Across the Boundaries of Race and Class*, 101; May, *Unprotected Labor*, 123.

24. Baker and Cooke, "The Slave Market." An excellent assessment of the migration and sex work can be found in LaShawn Harris, *Sex Workers, Psychics, and Numbers Runners: Black Women in New York City's Underground Economy* (Urbana: University of Illinois Press, 2016).

25. Collier Brown, "The Negro Woman Worker," 14.

26. Collier Brown, "The Negro Woman Worker," 14.

27. "We Who Cook, Clean and Wash," *Pittsburgh Courier*, September 30, 1933, 10.

28. "The roots of domestic workers' exclusion from labor laws, however, stretch back to the nineteenth century, when labor reformers began to create separate reform agendas for domestics and other working women. Then, in the 1930s, household workers lost a two-year battle for state-level legislation in New York": May, *Unprotected Labor*, 3–4.

29. Watson, "Household Employment in Philadelphia," 33.

30. "Housewives had found government allies for a system that supported white women's entitlement as mistress of a comfortable, well-ordered home, while other women found their futures defined by low-wage, unregulated jobs that rarely paid enough to support their own homes and families": Phyllis Palmer, "Black Domestics During the Depression: Workers, Organizers, Social Commentators," *Federal Records and African American History* 29, no. 2 (Summer 1997): 2. See also May, *Unprotected Labor*, 22.

31. Kathryn Blood, "Negro Women War Workers," Bulletin no. 205, Women's Bureau, US Department of Labor (Washington, DC: Government Printing Office, 1945), 17–18.

32. Thornton Dill, *Across the Boundaries of Race and Class*, 56.

33. Blood, "Negro Women War Workers," 1–7. For more on this postwar backward shift experienced by Black women, see Joe William Trotter, Jr., *Workers on Arrival: Black Labor in the Making of America* (Oakland: University of California Press, 2019), 141.

34. "To be called a 'race leader,' race man, or race woman by the black community was not a sign of insult or disapproval, not did such titles refer to any and every black person. Quite to the contrary, they were conferred on . . . men and women who devoted their lives to the advancement of their people." Evelyn Brooks Higginbotham, "African-American Women's History and the Metalanguage of Race," in *We Specialize in the Wholly Impossible: A Reader in Black Women's History*, edited by Darlene Clark Hine, Wilma King, and Linda Reed (Brooklyn, NY: Carlson, 1995), 13–14.

35. In the classic text *Black Milwaukee*, historian Joe Trotter reminds us that "wherever the work was hot, dirty, low-paying, and heavy, black men could usually be found." Joe William Trotter, Jr., *Black Milwaukee: The Making of an Industrial Proletariat, 1915–1945*, 2nd ed. (Urbana: University of Illinois Press, 2007), 12.

36. In the cities of the North there was "a great influx or western European immigrants who worked in domestic service between 1870 and 1915": May, *Unprotected Labor*, 4.

37. May, *Unprotected Labor*, 41.

38. May, *Unprotected Labor*, 7–8.

39. Thornton Dill, *Across the Boundaries of Race and Class*, 14.

40. May, *Unprotected Labor*, 8; Watson, "Household Employment in Philadelphia," 2.

41. Collier Brown, "The Negro Woman Worker," 2.

42. George J. Stigler, *Domestic Servants in the United States, 1900–1940* (New York: National Bureau of Economic Research, 1946).

43. Vertamae Grosvenor, "Diamonds in the Sewers: Corrine Sykes Remembered," *All Things Considered*, National Public Radio, April 3, 1998.

44. May, *Unprotected Labor*, 13.

45. As historian Vanessa May argues, "domestic service was not a static occupation, but instead changed in response to the same demographic forces that shaped industry, from mass immigration and migration to the shifting agendas of Progressive and New Deal reform organizations." May, *Unprotected Labor*, 14.

46. Penny savers clubs were common among the early generations of migrants, particularly those who did live-in domestic work; Clark-Lewis, *Living In*, 135–40. In her sociological study of Black domestic workers in New York and Philadelphia, Bonnie Thornton Dill centers the words of the workers themselves; one woman recalled that "in the late '40s . . . domestic girls used to get together and have clubs, social clubs. We would put money away all year and then at the end of the year we would have a big dance someplace . . . the girls working domestic had their own clubs. We would meet every Thursday night. Sometime[s] girls would be looking for a job and you discuss why they would want to leave." Thornton Dill, *Across the Boundaries of Race and Class*, 87.

47. Jacqueline Jones, *Labor of Love, Labor of Sorrow: Black Women, Work, and the Family from Slavery to the Present* (New York: Vintage, 1986). For more on the Jezebel and mammy stereotype, see the first chapter of Deborah Gray White, *Ar'n't I a Woman: Female Slaves in the Plantation South* (New York: W. W. Norton, 1985), 27–61. Two excellent interdisciplinary explorations of the mammy figure in American culture are Kimberly Wallace-Sanders, *Mammy: A Century of Race, Gender and Southern Memory* (Ann Arbor: University of Michigan Press, 2008), and Melissa Harris Perry, *Sister Citizen: Shame, Stereotypes, and Black Women in America* (New Haven: Yale University Press, 2011).

48. Cheryl Thurber, "The Development of the Mammy Image and Mythology," in *Southern Women: Histories and Identities*, edited by Virginia Bernard (Columbia: University of Missouri Press, 1992), 87–108. For more on the mammy movement, see Micki McElya, *Clinging to Mammy: The Faithful Slave in Twentieth-Century America* (Cambridge, MA: Harvard University Press, 2007).

49. For more on mammy remembrances and the making of white culture in segrega-

NOTES TO PAGES 208–219

tion, see Grace Elizabeth Hale, *Making Whiteness: The Culture of Segregation in the South, 1890–1940* (New York: Pantheon, 1998), 97–114.

50. Wallace-Sanders, *Mammy*, 5.

51. Grace Hale explains it thus: "Being white meant having black help." Hale, *Making Whiteness*, 103. For more on mammy remembrances and the making of white culture in segregation, see 97–114.

52. Phyllis Palmer, *Domesticity and Dirt: Housewives and Domestic Servants, 1920–1945* (Philadelphia: Temple University Press, 1989), 40.

53. As historian Phyllis Palmer summarized: "In novel, movies, and advice books, women got images of the [middle-class housewife] as a woman . . . whose manifold tasks 'deserved' help": Palmer, *Domesticity and Dirt*, 40.

54. "Keeping up with the Joneses became an American cliché in the 1920's. For middle-class wives, it was an imperative": Palmer, *Domesticity and Dirt*, 42.

55. Palmer, *Domesticity and Dirt*, 5, 25, 47.

56. Premilla Nadasen, *Household Workers Unite: The Untold Story of African American Women Who Built a Movement* (Boston: Beacon Press, 2015), 31.

57. "So when I would go out, after I'd met Fred, I would go out because I knew he was gonna be with me all the time. And I'd meet the other people there and after they seen that I had a friend, then they all think, Well she's not as green as we thought she is": Minnie (Savage) Whitney interviewed by Charles Hardy III.

58. Minnie (Savage) Whitney interviewed by Charles Hardy III.

59. Minnie (Savage) Whitney interviewed by Charles Hardy III.

60. Minnie (Savage) Whitney interviewed by Charles Hardy III.

61. Minnie (Savage) Whitney interviewed by Charles Hardy III.

62. Minnie (Savage) Whitney interviewed by Charles Hardy III.

63. Thornton Dill, *Across the Boundaries of Race and Class*, 15.

64. Thornton Dill, *Across the Boundaries of Race and Class*, 77.

65. Thornton Dill, *Across the Boundaries of Race and Class*, 104.

66. Thornton Dill, *Across the Boundaries of Race and Class*, 105.

67. For more on the history of class perceptions and the enslaved, see William L. Andrews, *Slavery and Class in the American South: A Generation of Slave Narrative Testimony* (New York: Oxford University Press, 2019), 168–247.

68. May, *Unprotected Labor*, 39.

69. May, *Unprotected Labor*, 115.

70. For more on the NAACP, see Patricia Sullivan, *Lift Every Voice: The NAACP and the Making of the Civil Rights Movement* (New York: The New Press, 2010). For more on the African Blood Brotherhood, see Minkah Makalani, *In the Cause of*

315

Freedom: Radical Black Internationalism from Harlem to London, 1917–1939 (Chapel Hill: University of North Carolina Press, 2011).

71. Erik S. McDuffie, *Sojourning for Freedom: Black Women, American Communism, and the Making of Black Left Feminism* (Durham, NC: Duke University Press), 30, 32–35, 37–39, 44–48 (quote is on 45).

72. Richard Wright, "Notes and Interviews, n.d.," Box 21, Folder 331–32, JWJ MSS 3, Series I, Richard Wright Papers, Yale Collection of American Literature, Beinecke Rare Book and Manuscript Library; Carl Offord, "Slave Markets in the Bronx," *Nation*, June 29, 1940, 780–81; May, *Unprotected Labor*, 9.

73. Joseph D. Bibb, "Too Cocky," *Pittsburgh Courier*, April 14, 1945, 7; Descriptive inventory for Joseph D. Bibb papers, 1919–66, Research Center, Chicago History Museum.

74. Thornton Dill, *Across the Boundaries of Race and Class*, 92.

75. Watson, "Household Employment in Philadelphia," 55.

76. Bibb, "Too Cocky"; Descriptive inventory for Joseph D. Bibb papers.

77. Minnie (Savage) Whitney interviewed by Charles Hardy III.

CHAPTER SEVEN: EVERYTHING SUFFICIENT FOR A GOOD LIFE

1. "Great Coharie River Initiative," Coharie Tribe, https://coharietribe.org/programs/great-coharie-river-initiative/, accessed March 17, 2022; "Keeping Traditions Alive," *Sampson [NC] Independent*, August 3, 2017.

2. Hartford Boykin interviewed by Karen Ferguson, "Behind the Veil" Oral History Project, David M. Rubenstein Rare Book and Manuscript Library, Duke University, July 16, 1993, https://repository.duke.edu/dc/behindtheveil/btvnc07004; Thomas Butchko and Jim Sumner, "General Thomas Boykin House," National Register of Historic Places—Nomination and Inventory, North Carolina State Historic Preservation Office, June 1985, https://files.nc.gov/ncdcr/nr/SP0014 .pdf; Isaac Boykin, North Carolina, Confederate Soldiers and Widows Pension Applications, 1885–1953, North Carolina Digital Collections, https://digital .ncdcr.gov/digital/collection/p16062coll21/id/19628/rec/1.

3. For more on conscription, see Jamie Martinez, *Confederate Slave Impressment in the Upper South* (Chapel Hill: University of North Carolina Press, 2013), and Nancy Fields, "Walking Through History Tour: Lumbee Conscription Tour at Ft. Fisher State Historic Site," Lumbee Tribe, https://www.youtube.com/watch?v=n64_ iHkA-Uo, accessed May 11, 2022. For more on enslaved men who were made to work for the Confederacy, see Kevin M. Levin, *Searching for Black Confederates: The Civil War's Most Persistent Myth* (Chapel Hill: University of North Carolina Press, 2019).

4. Hartford Boykin interviewed by Karen Ferguson; US Census Bureau, Ninth Census of the United States, 1870, "Clinton, Sampson, North Carolina," Roll: M593_1159; Page: 199A.

5. Agricultural historian Adrienne Petty found that outward shows of prosperity were risky to Black farmers, so much so that "black landowners kept their homes unpainted for fear of retaliation from white people who resented their property holdings." Adrienne Petty, "The Jim Crow Section of Agricultural History," in *Beyond Forty Acres and a Mule: African American Landowning Families Since Reconstruction,* edited by Debra A. Reid and Evan P. Bennett (Gainesville: University Press of Florida, 2012), 27.

6. US Selective Service System, World War I Draft Registration Cards, "New Hanover, North Carolina," M1509; US Census Bureau, Fourteenth Census of the United States, 1920, "Wilmington, New Hanover, North Carolina," Roll: T625 1313; Page 13B. "History of NAPFE," National Alliance of Postal and Federal Employees, https://www.napfe.com/about-napfe/history-of-napfe.html, accessed May 17, 2022; Philip F. Rubio, *There's Always Work at the Post Office: African American Postal Workers and the Fight for Jobs, Justice, and Equality* (Chapel Hill: University of North Carolina Press), 30–31.

7. Rubio, *There's Always Work at the Post Office,* 32.

8. "When it came to shipping your vegetables . . . to the North the allotment on the railroad cars was always used up and the blacks couldn't get his produce to the North . . . black farms fizzled": Hartford Boykin interviewed by Karen Ferguson; Butchko and Sumner, "General Thomas Boykin House." Boykin's uncle's death certificate listed the cause of death as gunshot wounds to the heart and ruled it a homicide. Edward Boykin, Death Certificate, August 31, 1932, North Carolina State Board of Health, Bureau of Vital Statistics, Microfilm S.123.

9. Mary Wisniewski, "U.S. Post Office Cuts Threaten Source of Black Jobs," Reuters, January 21, 2013, https://www.reuters.com/article/us-usa-jobs-africanamericans/u-s-post-office-cuts-threaten-source-of-black-jobs-idUSBRE90K0PR20130121.

10. Robert Rodgers Korstad, *Civil Rights Unionism: Tobacco Workers and the Struggle for Democracy in the Mid-Twentieth-Century South* (Chapel Hill: University of North Carolina Press, 2003).

11. Carney's story is highlighted in Philip F. Rubio's excellent monograph *There's Always Work at the Post Office,* 16–18.

12. "Colonial to Antebellum: The Beginning of Discrimination," History and Experience of African Americans in America's Postal Service, Smithsonian National Postal Museum online, https://postalmuseum.si.edu/research-articles/the-history-and-experience-of-african-americans-in-america%E2%80%99s-postal-service-0, accessed May 13, 2022.

13. Leon Litwack, "The Federal Government and the Free Negro, 1790–1860," *Journal of Negro History* 43, no. 4 (October 1958): 270.

14. Rubio, *There's Always Work at the Post Office*, 19.

15. Rubio, *There's Always Work at the Post Office*, 21.

16. "From Virginia it is reported that the first negro mail carrier ever employed by the United States has been awarded the contract for a route near Leesburg on the Upper Potomac": *The Times* (London), September 26, 1865, 20.

17. *Liberator* (Boston, MA), November 6, 1863, 4; Thomas M. Hammond, "William H. Carney: 54th Massachusetts Soldier and First Black U.S. Medal of Honor Recipient," January 29, 2007, HistoryNet, https://www.historynet.com/william -h-carney-54th-massachusetts-soldier-and-first-black-us-medal-of-honor-recipient .htm, accessed October 1, 2020.

18. "William H. Carney," Boston African American National Historic Site, National Park Service, https://www.nps.gov/articles/william-h-carney.htm, accessed August 6, 2022; Hammond, "William H. Carney"; Noralee Frankel, "Breaking the Chains, 1860–1880," in *To Make Our World Anew: A History of African Americans*, edited by Robin D. G. Kelley and Earl Lewis (New York: Oxford University Press 1994), 227.

19. "A Colored Man Proved His Bravery on the Battlefield," *Butte [MT] Daily Post*, January 21, 1898, 7; "Bravest Negro Soldier," *Lancaster [PA] Examiner*, June 29, 1904, 6.

20. "Reconstruction: Successes and Challenges," History and Experience of African Americans in America's Postal Service, Smithsonian National Postal Museum online, https://postalmuseum.si.edu/research-articles/the-history-and-experience -of-african-americans-in-america%E2%80%99s-postal-service-1, accessed May 14, 2022.

21. "Editorial note," *Fall River [MA] Daily Evening News*, September 15, 1883, 3.

22. Rubio, *There's Always Work at the Post Office*, 28.

23. Bridges Smith, "Just 'Twixt Us," *Macon Telegraph*, August 9, 1919, 6; Charles H. Holley, 1900 United States Federal Census, "Macon, Bibb, Georgia"; US Census Bureau, Twelfth Census of the United States, 1900. Washington, DC: National Archives and Records Administration, 1900. T623, 1854 rolls.

24. "Color Line Drawn: Kentucky Farmers Object to Negro Mail Carrier," *New Orleans Times–Democrat*, January 10, 1907, 9; US Census Bureau, Thirteenth Census of the United States, 1910, "Magisterial District 4, Trigg, Kentucky," Roll: T624_501, FHL microfilm: 1374514; US Census Bureau, Fourteenth Census of the United States, 1920, "Owensboro Ward 3, Daviess, Kentucky," Roll: T625_567.

25. For more on the Baker lynchings, see Philip Dray, *At the Hands of Persons Unknown: The Lynching of Black America* (New York: Modern Library, 2002), 116; David C.

Carter, "'No Painted Apache Ever Did Anything Half So Wanton, or Cannibal in Darkest Africa Ever Acted Upon a More Fiendish Impulse': Newspaper Reactions to the 1898 Lynching of Postmaster Frazier Baker in Lake City, South Carolina, on the Eve of the Spanish American War," paper presented at Media and Civil Rights History Symposium, University of South Carolina, Columbia, 2012; "Charged with Murder," *New York Times*, July 2, 1898, 4; "The Lake City Lynching," *New York Times*, April 8, 1899.

26. "Views Changed as to Negro Carrier," *Inter Ocean* (Chicago), May 11, 1903, 5.

27. "Cut Off Is Rural Free Delivery at Gallatin, Tenn.," *Courier-Journal* (Louisville, KY), May 8, 1903, 1.

28. "A Contemporary's Dilemma," *Times-Dispatch* (Richmond, VA), May 16, 1903, 4; "Fairness from the North," *Times-Dispatch* (Richmond, VA), May 24, 1903, 4.

29. "Negro Carriers Are Not Wanted," *North Carolinian*, May 17, 1906, 3.

30. "Rural Delivery Service Restored," *Chattanooga Daily Times*, May 23, 1903, 1; US Census Bureau, Thirteenth Census of the United States, 1910, "Chicago Ward 30, Cook, Illinois," Roll: T624_276.

31. US Census Bureau, Thirteenth Census of the United States, 1910, "Chicago Ward 30, Cook, Illinois," Roll: T624_276; John C. Allgood, Cook County, Illinois, U.S., Deaths Index, 1878–1922, Ancestry.com; Cook County, Illinois, U.S., Marriages Index, 1871–1920, Ancestry.com; John C. Allgood, Cook County, Illinois U.S., Wills and Probate Records, Administrators bonds and letters, 1877–1931, Ancestry.com; Illinois, Select Deaths Index, 1877–1916, Illinois Statewide Death Index, Pre–1916, Illinois State Archive, Ancestry.com.

32. "Democrats Forget and Learn Nothing," *New York Age*, May 15, 1913, 4; Rubio, *There's Always Work at the Post Office*, 29.

33. Kathleen Long Wolgemuth, "Woodrow Wilson's Appointment Policy and the Negro," *Journal of Southern History* 24, no. 4 (November 1958): 461; Morton Sosna, "The South in the Saddle: Racial Politics During the Wilson Years," *Wisconsin Magazine of History* 54, no. 1 (1970): 30–34.

34. Oswald Garrison Villard, "Scores Segregation," *The Appeal* (St. Paul, MN), January 31, 1914; Margaret C. Rung, *Servants of the State: Managing Diversity and Democracy in the Federal Workforce, 1933–1953* (Athens: University of Georgia Press, 2002), 43.

35. W. E. B. Du Bois, "Another Open Letter to Woodrow Wilson," *The Crisis* 6, no. 5, September 1913.

36. Rubio, *There's Always Work at the Post Office*, 29; "Woodrow Wilson: Federal Segregation," History and Experience of African Americans in America's Postal Service, Smithsonian National Postal Museum online, https://postalmuseum

.si.edu/research-articles/the-history-and-experience-of-african-americans-in
-america%E2%80%99s-postal-service-3, accessed May 15, 2022.

37. Kevin K. Gaines, *Uplifting the Race: Black Leadership, Politics, and Culture in the Twentieth Century* (Chapel Hill: University of North Carolina Press, 1996), 217; Sosna, "The South in the Saddle," 34.

38. Abhay Aneja and Guo Xu, "The Costs of Employment Segregation: Evidence from the Federal Government Under Woodrow Wilson," *Quarterly Journal of Economics* 137, no. 2 (2022): 911–58.

39. Hartford Boykin interviewed by Karen Ferguson; Albert Muzquiz, "The Evolution of US Postal Service Uniforms," Heddels, May 21, 2018, https://www.heddels.com/2018/05/the-evolution-of-us-post-office-uniforms/, accessed May 11, 2022.

40. US Census Bureau, Seventeenth Census of the United States, 1950, vol. 2, "Characteristics of the Population, Part 1: United States Summary" (Washington, DC: Government Printing Office, 1953).

41. John R. Larkins, *The Negro Population of North Carolina: Social and Economic* (Raleigh: North Carolina State Board of Charities and Public Welfare, 1944), 23; Rubio, *There's Always Work at the Post Office*, 144.

42. Rubio, *There's Always Work at the Post Office*, 58; "President's Order Prohibits Civil Service Discrimination," *Pittsburgh Courier*, November 23, 1940.

43. Rubio, *There's Always Work at the Post Office*, 49, 53, 54, 82.

44. Rubio, *There's Always Work at the Post Office*, 107.

45. Rubio, *There's Always Work at the Post Office*, 95.

46. Nadasen, *Household Workers Unite*, 28–31; Rubio, *There's Always Work at the Post Office*, 2.

47. Charles Payne, *I've Got the Light of Freedom: The Organizing Tradition and the Mississippi Freedom Struggle* (Oakland: University of California Press, 1995), 29–30.

48. Video interview with Amzie Moore, Blackside, Inc., Washington University in St. Louis, http://repository.wustl.edu/concern/videos/1544bq682.

49. Aaron E. Henry, "Voting Restrictions in Mississippi," Amzie Moore Papers, 1941–1970, Wisconsin Historical Society, https://content.wisconsinhistory.org/digital/collection/p15932coll2/id/22918; Payne, *I've Got the Light of Freedom*, 25–31; "Amzie Moore," Student Nonviolent Coordinating Committee, https://snccdigital.org/people/amzie-moore/, accessed May 19, 2022.

50. Payne, *I've Got the Light of Freedom*, 31.

51. Interview with Amzie Moore by Michael Garvey, March 29 and April 13, 1977, Center for Oral History and Cultural Heritage, University of Southern Mississippi.

52. Payne, *I've Got the Light of Freedom*, 33–35.

53. "Amzie Moore," Student Nonviolent Coordinating Committee.
54. Amzie Moore Memorandum for Administrator of Veterans Administration (April 12, 1961), Moore—Correspondence, 1960–1962, Amzie Moore Papers, 1941–1970 (551, Box 1 Folder 4), Wisconsin Historical Society; Payne, *I've Got the Light of Freedom*, 44; video interview with Amzie Moore.

CONCLUSION: BRUNELL

1. For an examination of African Americans and tuberculosis, see Samuel Kelton Roberts, Jr., *Infectious Fear: Politics, Disease, and the Health Effects of Segregation* (Chapel Hill: University of North Carolina Press, 2009).
2. Stephen A. Mein, "COVID–19 and Health Disparities: The Reality of 'the Great Equalizer,'" *Journal of General Internal Medicine* 35, no. 8 (2020): 2439–40.
3. Lindsey Norward, "An Oral History of Pandemic Life Told by Black Essential Workers," *Elemental*, on Medium, September 14, 2020, https://elemental.medium.com/an-oral-history-of-the-pandemic-told-by-black-essential-workers-d217a59cb5b8.

INDEX

Abbott, Robert, 151
abolitionism, 33, 43, 237
Accomack County, 161–68
  Black business owners, 169–71
  Black self-defense, 178–79
  education, 176–77, 310n36
  Great Migration from, 161–64, 167,
    179–80, 182–83
  racial deference, 177, 310n37
  sharecropping, 174–76, 177–78,
    310n33
  white racial violence, 171–73, 177,
    207–8, 309nn23–25
  See also Accomack County agriculture
Accomack County agriculture
  Black community and, 169–70
  Black labor organizing and, 167–68,
    171–73
  Black labor skills and, 166–67
  Eastern Shore Produce Exchange,
    165–66
  plantation economy and, 164–65
  Tasley Fair, 170, 171, 309nn19,22
Adams, Charlotte, 212

Adams, Rachel, 47
African Blood Brotherhood, 219
African Methodist Episcopal (AME)
  Church, 60, 143–44
Allgood, John C., 243, 244, 266
Alpha Suffrage Club, 146
American Federation of Labor (AFL),
  106, 153, 154, 220
American Revolution, 10
Anderson, Charles F., 128–29, 134
Anglican Church, 42–43, 289n41
Arnesen, Eric, 305n47
Atlanta Negro Voters League, 252
Atlanta Washerwomen's Strike (1881),
  101
Aunt Jemima stereotype, 208

Baker, Ella, 195, 196, 257
Baker, Frazier, 242–43, 266
Baker, Julia, 242–43
Ball, Charles, 22–24, 26, 38, 40, 46,
  286–87n19
Barbados, 42–43
Barber, J. Max, 144

washerwomen and, 74–75, 85, 92–93,
   100–107, 111, 113, 299n17, 301n53
white racial violence and, 171–73,
   309nn23–25
See also Brotherhood of Sleeping Car
   Porters
Black labor skills
   Emancipation and, 50
   farming, 29, 31–32, 33, 166–67
   postal workers, 230, 260
   postbellum dismissal of, 77–78
   sharecropping and, *176*
   urban South migration and, 4, 6, 81–82
   washerwomen, 72–73, 78–79, *78*,
      80–81, 296n32
   See also enslaved labor skills
Black literature, 13
Black male rape myth, 234–35, 243–44
Black middle class, 82, 231–32
   See also postal workers
Black military service
   Civil War, 236, 238–39, 247
   Second World War, 249, 255, 256
   segregation and, 156, 234, 256
   veterans, 234, 236, 247, 248–51,
      255–56
Black newspapers
   Accomack County, 170
   Brotherhood of Sleeping Car Porters
      and, 147, 149, 151, 152, 306n64
   Great Migration and, 121–22, 124
   March on Washington Movement and,
      157
   socialism and, 145
   white racial violence and, 173
Black political engagement
   business owners and, 117
   community and, 15
   current rates of, 272
   domestic service and, 204–5
   end of Reconstruction and, 58, 291n68

Great Migration and, 8
Harlem and, 219
Reconstruction era, 53–54, 56–57
white racial violence and, 54–55, 57–58
See also Black voting rights
Black Reconstruction (Du Bois), 285n11,
   288n28
Black resistance
   against segregation, 107–8, 111–12,
      252–55, 256–57, 300n46
   Black churches and, 143–44
   civil rights movement, 254–55,
      256–59
   desegregation and, 252–54
   domestic workers and, 215–16, 217,
      221–22
   enslaved people and, 27–28, 37,
      286nn16–17, 288n28
   Great Migration and, 158–59
   Harlem and, 219
   March on Washington Movement,
      156–57, 198
   McCarthyism and, 253
   postal workers and, 251–55
   Pullman porter unionization and, 146
   race men/women and, 313n34
   socialism and, 144–45, 153
   See also Black labor organizing; Black
      political engagement; civil rights
      movement
blacksmiths, 37, 38
Black and Tan Party, 255
Black voting rights
   civil rights movement and, 255,
      256–57
   disenfranchisement, 5, 244, 252, 256,
      261, 272
   Great Migration and, 204
   postal workers and, 252, 255, 256–57
   Reconstruction era, 48–49, 52–53,
      55–56, 57–58

voting and, 48–49, 52

white racial violence and, 51, 52

See also Reconstruction era

Emergency Transportation Act, 153–54

employment discrimination

antebellum free Black people, 32–33, 238

armed services, 156, 234

domestic service and, 186, 188

Executive Order 8802 and, 157–58

Great Migration and, 9, 186, 199–200, 311n2, 313n35

invisibility of Black working class and, 15–16

New Deal and, 153–54

postal workers and, 236–37, 241, 250–51

Pullman porters and, 133–34, *133*, 138

Reconstruction era, 239

urban South migration and, 6, 9, 81, 120

white-run labor unions and, 7

enfranchisement. *See* Black voting rights

enslaved labor skills

architecture, 29–30, 32, 35, 287n20

blacksmithing, 37, 38

Black women's employment and, 296–97n33

cotton cultivation and, 22, *23*

farming, 29, 31–32, 33

laundry work, 77, 78

postbellum dismissal of, 77–78

washerwomen, 78

enslaved people

Accomack County, 164–65

acts of resistance, 27–28, 37, 286nn16–17, 288n28

African faiths and, 28, 39–40, 41, 47, 287n19

archives and, 36, 287nn25–26

Christianity of, 39–41, 46–48

Civil War and, 37, 75, 228, 287n24, 288n28

collective activism, 17

commodification of, 27–28, 36–37, 286nn16–17, 288n27

community of, 28–29, 35, 36, 284–85n10, 286–87nn19,24

cotton cultivation and, 22–24, *23*

education and, 45–46, 49

enslaver imposition of Christianity on, 41–44, 45

ex-slave pension movement, 87–90

families of, 38–39, 45

freedom seekers, 27, 32, 120, 179, 238

laundry work and, 77, 78, 95

manumission, 32, 120

number of, 24, 284n8

as postal workers, 236

predicament of, 286n18

rival geographies of, 47

stereotypes of, 10, 16, 25, 30–31, 206

sugar cultivation and, 42–43

wage labor and, 38

work life of, 85

See also Emancipation; enslaved labor skills

enslavement

brutality of, 24–27, 31, 42, 206, 284n10

domestic slave trade and, 22, 24, 26–27

Indigenous land theft and, 21–22, 24, 284n2

as intergenerational bondage, 10, 41

overseer/patroller system and, 25–26

postal workers and, 236–37

Pullman porters' working conditions and, 132, 137, 304n27

racial health gap and, 268–69

racial hierarchy and, 10, 12, 25

reparations for, 34, 87–90, 289n41

See also enslaved people; enslavers; plantation economy

labor organizing. *See* Black labor organizing; white-run labor unions
La Guardia, Fiorello, 157
Lamar, Joseph Rucker, 35
Lange, Dorothea, *xiv, 1*
laundresses. *See* washerwomen
Leffler, Warren K., *226, 227n, 249*
Lincoln, Abraham, 130–31, 238
Lincoln, Robert Todd, 129
Linsin, Christopher E., 296–97n33
Lloyd–La Follette Act, 259
Louverture, Toussaint, 144, 238
lynching, 2, 170, 241, 270
   See also white racial violence
lynch law, 5

mammy stereotype, 206–11, *207*
March on Washington Movement, 156–57, 198
Marshall, Thurgood, 252
Marx, Karl, 144
May, Vanessa H., 312n8, 314n45
McAdoo, William Gibbs, 245
McCarthyism, 253–54
McDowell, Calvin, 170
McKay, T. L., 244
McLean, John, 237
McNeill, Robert H., *163*
Memphis Free Speech, 170
Messenger, 145, 147, 149, 151, 152
Military Reconstruction Acts, 53
minimum-wage laws, 197, 220
minstrelsy, 66, 93, 206, 208–9, 293n9
miscegenation, 209
Mitchell, Cleaster, 96
Mitchell, Margaret, 208
Moller, A. W., *86, 87n*
Montgomery bus boycott, 254
Moore, Amzie, 255–59
Moore, Ruth, 257

Morgan, Jennifer, 286n16, 286n18
Morrison, Cordie Mae Raeford, 267
Morrison, Willie, 267
Moses, Bob, 257
Moss, Thomas, 170, 242, 243
Murphy, John Jr. (Jude), 177
Murphy, John Sr., 177–78
Murphy, Leroy (author's father)
   childhood of, 181
Murphy, Sarah Jean, *180*
Murphy, Theodore Brooks (Bruce) (author's grandfather), 163–64, 166, 177–78, 179–82, *180*
mutual aid. *See* Black community

NAACP (National Association for the Advancement of Colored People)
   Black business owners and, 174
   college admissions discrimination and, 252
   Harlem and, 219
   postal workers and, 257
   washerwomen and, 195
   white racial violence and, 256
   Wilson administration and, 244–45, 246–47
National Alliance of Postal Employees, 230, 251–52, 253–54
National Association of Colored Women's Clubs, 110
National Democratic Fair Play Association, 244
National Ex-Slave Mutual Relief, Bounty and Pension Association, 87–88, 90, 91–92
National Industrial Recovery Act (1933), 153
National Recovery Administration (NRA), 196–97
New Deal
   Black political engagement and, 8

Pullman maids, 135–36, 140
Pullman porters, *114, 115n, 131, 133*
  community and, 137
  Dellums's employment, 119–20
  dissent suppression, 129, 138, 139–40
  duties of, 134–35, *135*
  employment discrimination and,
    133–34, *133*, 138
  federal government and, 138–39
  Great Migration and, 120–22, 123,
    137, 138
  housing discrimination and, 155
  March on Washington Movement and,
    157
  mobility of, 137
  position design, 131–32, 141, 143,
    304n27
  pride of, *142*
  racial deference and, 132, 141, 305n47
Pullman porters (*continued*)
  racialized anonymity of, 132
  tipping system and, 141, 305n47
  unionization of, 129, 137, 303n15
  white disrespect of, 124–26, 302–
    3nn13–17
  white-run labor unions and, 137, 139,
    140–41, 153
  working conditions, 128–29, 132, 137,
    138, 139, 143, 304n27
  See also Brotherhood of Sleeping Car
    Porters

racial categories, 36, 288n26
racial deference
  domestic service and, *184, 185n*, 187,
    187, 192–93, 202, 311n4
  Pullman porters and, 132, 141, 305n47
  segregation and, 71–72, 177, 294n18,
    295n21, 310n37
  white racial violence and, 177, 294n18
racial health gap, 268–70

racial hierarchy, 10, 12, 15, 50
  See also employment discrimination;
    segregation
Radical Republicans, 52–53
Raeford, Earnest, 266
Raeford, Julia Blair, 265, 266, 267
railroads
  Accomack County and, 165
  antebellum boom, 129–30
  Great Migration and, 121, 182
  passenger segregation on, 133, 136
  postal work on, 230
  See also Pullman porters
Railway Labor Act (1926), 152
Railway Labor Act (1934), 154
Railway Mail Association, 230
Randolph, A. Philip
  Brotherhood of Sleeping Car Porters
    and, 128, 145, 146–48, 151, 152–53
  childhood of, 143–44
  Coolidge meeting, 148
  Executive Order 8802 and, 158
  FDR meeting, 156
  March on Washington Movement and,
    156–57
Randolph, James W., 143–44
Randolph, Peter, 40, 47–48
rape. *See* Black male rape myth; white
    sexual violence
Ray, John R., 105, 106
Reconstruction era
  Black churches, 60–61
  Black Codes, 52
  Black community, 53–54, 61–62
  Black political engagement, 53–54,
    56–57
  Black voting rights, 48–49, 52–53,
    55–56, 57–58
  education, 88, 169
  employment discrimination, 239
  end of, 58, 296n68

Slave Compensation Act (1837), 43, 289n41

slaveholders. *See* enslavers

Slavery Abolition Act (1833), 43

Smallwood, Stephanie, 286n18

Smith, George Booth, 250–51

Smith, Hoke, 246

Smith v. Allwright, 252

Society for Promoting Christian Knowledge, 41

Society for the Propagation of the Gospel in Foreign Parts (SPG), 41–43, 289n41

Souls of Black Folk, The (Du Bois), 13–14

Speed, John Gilmer, 141

Stahl, John, 209

stereotypes
  Black churches, 60–61
  Black male rape myth, 136, 234–35, 243–44
  Black speech, 293n9
  Black women, 96, 206, *207*
  domestic service and, 202, 205–11, *207*
  enslaved people, 10, 16, 25, 30–31, 206
  Folklore Project and, 293n10
  Jezebel, 206
  mammy, 206–11, *207*
  minstrelsy and, 66, 93, 206, 208–9, 293n9
  Pullman porters and, 132, 136
  washerwomen, 66–68, *67*, 72, 93

Stevens, Alexander, 52

Stewart, Catherine, 293nn9–10

Stewart, Thomas W., 187

Stewart, Will, 170

Stigler, George, 201

streetcar segregation protests, 107–8, 111–12, 300n46

Student Nonviolent Coordinating Committee (SNCC), 257–58

subservience. *See* racial deference

sugar cultivation, 42–43

Summerfield, Arthur, 250–51

Sumner, Charles, 237, 239

sundown towns, 172

Swanson, Claude A., 173

"Sweat" (Hurston), 76

Sweatt, Herman Marion, 252–53

Sweatt v. Painter, 253

Talbert, Frank, 55

Temple, Shirley, 209

Terrell, Mary Church, 148

Thornton, John, 286n18

Thurber, Cheryl, 207

Thurman, Howard, 40

Tillman, Ben, 245

To 'Joy My Freedom (Hunter), 101

Towne, Laura, 61

Trenchard, John A., 285n13

Trotter, James Monroe, 247

Trotter, Joe, 313n35

Trotter, William Monroe, 245, 247

Trump, Donald, 15, 271–72

tuberculosis, 243, 244, 266, 267, 268

Tubman, Harriet, 75

Tucker, Daniel, 43–44

Tulsa Race Massacre (1921), 115–17, 118, 158, 301nn4–5

Turman, Phoebe, 47

Turner, Henry McNeal, 56–57, 60

Turner, Nat, 144

Tuskegee Airmen, 255

unions. *See* labor unions

United Daughters of the Confederacy, 208

Universal Negro Improvement Association, 219

University of Virginia, 29–30, 32, 287n20

urban South migration
  author's family and, 1–6, 265–67
  Black churches and, 83

Black labor skills and, 4, 6, 81–82
community and, 82–83
education and, 5–6, 266–67
employment discrimination and, 6, 9,
    81, 120
postal workers and, 229–30
racial health gap and, 266, 267, 269
sharecropping and, 1–4
streetcar segregation and, 107–8
white racial violence and, 5, 82–83, 120
US Constitution, three-fifths clause, 24
Uzzle, James D., 169, 170, 171–72, 173,
    309n23

Valk, Anne, 296n32
Vanderhorst, Richard, 60
Vardaman, James, 245
Vaughan, Walter R., 89–90, 91
Veterans' Preference Act (1944), 249
Vietnam War, 260
Voice of the Negro, The, 144

wage of whiteness, 25, 133, 218, 271,
    285n11
Walcott, Marion Post, *176*
Walker, Maggie Lena, 108–10,
    300nn46,49
War of 1812, 22
Ward, Mrs. George, 95, 98–99
Warren, William, *114*, *115n*
washerwomen, *64*, 65–75, *65n*, 75–85,
    86, 87–113, *87n*
    Black freedom and, 73–74
    Black women as majority of, 77, 296n30
    child care and, 84
    collective work, 68–69, 109
    community and, 73, 74–75, 109–10,
        300n49
    earning difficulty, 69, 293–94nn12–13
    employer accusations against, 70,
        97–100, 293–94n13, 299n22

enslavement and, 95
entrepreneurship and, 298–99n16
ex-slave pension movement and, 87–88,
    90, 91
Federal Writers' Project interviews
    with, 65–66, 70–71, 292nn1-4,
    293–95nn9,11–15,19–21
Great Depression and, 69, 293n12
historical/cultural importance of, 75–76
independence of, 79, 92–93, 95–97,
    297n34, 298–99n16
labor organizing and, 74–75, 85,
    92–93, 100–107, 111, 113, 299n17,
    301n53
labor skills of, 72–73, 78–79, *78*,
    80–81, 296n32
long-term work of, 83–84
mobility of, *96*, *97*, 107
resistance against segregation and,
    107–8, 111, 300n46
resistance to domestic service, 95–96,
    100, 298n15
segregation and, 85
stereotypes of, 66–68, *67*, 72, 93
white femininity and, 93–94
white racial violence against, 100
white sexual violence and, 106
Washerwomen of Jackson, 101
Washington, Booker T., 75
Washington, Fredi, 209
Wells, Arthur A., 140
Wells-Barnett, Ida B., 146–47, 170,
    234–35, 242
White, Walter, 156, 157
White, William J., 53–55
white femininity
    Black washerwomen and, 93–94
    domestic service and, 211, 315n53
white immigrants, 200–201, 313n36
white indentured servants, 10
white privilege, 25